Power in struggle

Feminism, sexuality and
the state

Davina Cooper

Open University Press
Buckingham

Open University Press
Celtic Court
22 Ballmoor
Buckingham
MK18 1XW

First Published 1995

A catalogue record of this book is available from the British Library

ISBN   0 335 19211 4 (pb)   0 335 19212 2 (hb)

Typeset by Dorwyn Ltd, Rowlands Castle, Hants
Printed by Biddles Ltd, Guildford and King's Lynn

To my parents, Kitty and Charles Cooper

Contents

Acknowledgements

Earlier versions of certain chapter sections have been published elsewhere.

Earlier versions of parts of Chapter 2 have appeared in 'Productive, relational and everywhere? Conceptualising power and resistance within Foucauldian feminism', *Sociology*, 28 (1994), 435.

Earlier versions of parts of Chapter 4 have appeared in 'An engaged state: Sexuality, governance and the potential for change', *Journal of Law and Society*, 20 (1993), 257.

Earlier versions of parts of Chapter 5, co-authored with Didi Herman, have appeared in 'Getting the family "right": Legislating heterosexuality in Britain, 1986–91', *Canadian Journal of Family Law*, 10 (1991), 41.

Earlier versions of parts of Chapter 6 have appeared in *Sexing the City: Lesbian and Gay Politics within the Activist State.* (1994) London: Rivers Oram.

I would like to thank the following people for their help and encouragement. Joel Bakan, Lynda Birke, Susan Boyd, Jean Carabine, Bob Fine, Susan Halford, Colin Hay, Niki Lacey, Terry Lovell, Judith Masson, Helen Reece, Joe Sim, and Carl Stychin provided challenging and helpful feedback on draft chapters. Janet Macharia and Adele Tomlin carried out library and field research that strengthened the book's framework and argument. My thanks to Jacinta Evans and Joan Malherbe of Open University Press for their support and assistance. I would also like to thank Warwick University Law School for the range of ways in which they facilitated the writing of this book. Finally, my appreciation goes to Didi Herman who read more drafts than she cares to remember. Her exacting comments, ongoing textual assistance, and emotional/intellectual support allowed me to live out, but also contain, my drive to get this book finished. Thank you.

Introduction

From their apparently dichotomized locations within the public and private, the state–sexuality nexus has emerged as a key aspect of modern policy-making, activism, and theory. Age of consent legislation, AIDS education, lesbian litigation, funded gay centres, all in different ways link state policy with sexual identity and practice. While many writers have explored state control or regulation of sexuality and the resistance of sexual minorities, fewer have focused on the other side of the story. This concerns the ways in which sexuality as a disciplinary structure, identity and culture shapes state form and practice. There is also a third story: entry onto the state's terrain by social forces with sexual agendas. Together, these narratives comprise the substance of this book.

To explore the implications for social change strategies of relations between sexuality and the state, I draw principally on three bodies of theory: neo-Marxism, radical feminism, and poststructuralism.[1] My aim is not to arrive at a synthesis, but rather to draw on the tensions and common ground between these disparate approaches to generate a framework for political and normative theorizing. Such theorizing centres around four key concepts: power, sexuality, the state and struggle.

In considering the relationship between these concepts, power provides the linchpin. It offers a way of understanding the means by which people struggle as well as the form and character of state authority and control. Thus it also generates a basis for normative theory which, rooted in a political ethics, targets dominant forms of power to produce social change. The notion of 'power in struggle' is intended to capture these different dimensions. It also draws attention to the conceptual struggle over what power does (and should) mean. Although my starting point is a Foucauldian feminist framework, I deviate from some of its assumptions, in particular the notion that if power is inevitable, then so too is domination or inequality.

Foucauldian feminism tends to identify power in two ways. The first focuses on power as a social relationship of inequality, asymmetry and dominance, the second, on power as the matrix of forces structuring social life. The approach I adopt centres this second formulation in order to conceive of power productively as *the generation of effects*. While these effects may entail inequality or oppression, they also need not. Thus within this framework, discourses of power's ubiquity lose their inherent pessimism. Outcomes will always be generated, but the processes or technologies through which this occurs, hence the character of effects, are perpetually open to change.

In exploring the relationship between power and sexuality, I adopt a social constructionist perspective to argue that sexual desires and practices are socially generated. In various, often contradictory ways, they 'reflect' the society out of which they arise. Thus if we possess a critique of current society, sexuality also offers a site of interrogation, including those sexualities defined as subversive, transgressive or downright 'queer'. I therefore question a sex radical or radical pluralist politics which seeks to affirm consensual, minority sexual practices irrespective of their content. Instead I argue that sexual desires and activities are problematic when they reflect asymmetrical and violent aspects of society; but this is not necessarily an argument for their prohibition – often a counter-productive strategy. Rather, it suggests the need for other approaches – interventions in the *production* of sexual desires and practices to disrupt or transform current hegemonies.[2]

The ethics of such an interventionist strategy are discussed later in the book. However, whether it would even work depends on a number of factors, including the relationship between strategy and effects. As I discuss, people synthesize or live their sexualities through drawing upon dominant tenets in different ways. A productive politics also raises the question: is sexuality being re-formed to 'improve' interpersonal (sexual) relations or because of the impact sexual changes might have on wider society? Although questions of sexual satisfaction are important, my focus in this book is on the second possibility. In considering sexuality as a disciplinary system (or systems), I argue that sexuality is not, as some theorists have implied, epiphenomenal – circulating on the outer non-deterministic reaches of the supersphere. Instead, sexuality shapes, or impacts upon, a range of social, cultural and economic practices and relations. This capacity of sexuality to affect different terrains is a central theme of this book. In particular, I am interested in the ways in which sexuality impacts upon the state, becoming embedded within its technologies of power.

What is the state, however? Working with neo-Marxist, poststructuralist and radical feminist frameworks generates a range of possible responses. Is it a coherent entity as some structuralists and instrumentalists suggest or a fractured, uneven terrain? Rather than choosing between these competing interpretations, I adopt an approach which conceives the state as irreducible to a single core, conceptualizing it instead as a historically contingent articulation of different identities. Thus the state is both unified and fragmented, a complex of apparatuses as well as a social relationship. Multifaceted and fluid, its character varies according to context as one or other of its identities emerges as foremost – while still linked to and informed by wider articulations. For instance, as I discuss in Chapter 6, the capacity of local government to adopt a counter-hegemonic identity during the 1980s was limited by central government's depiction (and active production) of the state as a hierarchy of apparatuses, with local government a subordinate agent of government policy.

The final, key theoretical area explored in this book concerns the relationship between social struggle, power and resistance. Many writers, influenced by Foucault, have tended to conceptualize resistance as the antithesis of power. Within this framework, subjugated forces resist state power; they do not deploy it. Linked to this trend is another which embraces all political struggles under the umbrella of resistance. In Chapters 2 and 7 in particular, I challenge this approach. First I argue that resistance provides a motive or style for exercising power rather than its antithesis. Second, power can be engaged with, or deployed, in a range of ways that are not helpfully reduced to resistance. However, while different forces *can* exercise power, they neither own nor fully control the power they deploy. For not only is the terrain on which they struggle already skewed, but as well their interests, subjectivities and agendas are formed and re-formed as a result of power practices.

Exploring the ways in which social forces have challenged, resisted or re-formed state practice in order to defend and affirm their sexual politics raises important normative questions. Are all forms of resistance valid? Is diversity inherently good? On what basis should value judgements about political activism be made? While I argue for a pluralist and diversified approach to strategy, I nevertheless suggest this needs to be embedded within a political project that evaluates change, struggle and resistance according to their substance, not simply their form. In other words, I dispute the validity of change for change's sake.

In making this argument the normative standpoint I deploy is based on an ethics of 'sustainable equality of empowerment', the belief that people should have an equal ability to impact upon society and achieve their preferences. From this basis, I consider the character of strategic interventions that aim to deploy, constrain or transform particular sites or technologies of power. To what extent do they facilitate or undermine systemic equality? At the same time, I do not take preferences as given. Instead, I critically interrogate those choices that appear to frustrate greater equality of empowerment by sustaining particular forms of collective disadvantage.

Evaluating political strategies or interventions according to their capacity to generate specific effects raises questions of certainty and predictability. To what extent can we know whether changing particular forms of power will lead to the production of different outcomes? Yet lack of certainty does not make political action pointless. Rather, it implies the need for a nuanced, reflexive approach which recognizes both the possibility for guessing (and planning) as well as the sometimes haphazard character of this affair.

Power in Struggle offers a series of linked essays that together provide a theorization of relations between power, sexuality, the state, and social struggle. Chapter 2 begins by setting out a productive framework of power which draws on Foucauldian feminism. The first part of the chapter explores the two directions Foucauldian feminism has taken: the focus on power as relational, and as productive. My argument is that the ways in which these two strands have been synthesized constructs power as both omnipresent and oppressive. This, I argue, is problematic, in part because it undermines the possibilities for radical social change strategies. In the second half of the chapter, I therefore develop an alternative formulation of power which links together productive and relational approaches in a way that centres inequality, while not assuming its inevitability.

Chapter 3 continues this discussion of power and asymmetry by focusing on the specific terrain of sexuality. Through an exploration of cultural and political strategies to liberate sexuality, as well as sexual strategies to undermine social inequality, I examine a range of sexual politics from radical lesbianism, through to sex radicalism, queer politics, sado-masochism and transgressive/phallic performances. In considering the contribution and limitations of each, I focus on questions of sexual difference, the transformation of desire, and the impact of sexual culture on disciplinary relations. I conclude by arguing for a politics that recognizes the sexualization of everyday life, that does not treat sex as a private affair, and that rejects sexual politics as the exclusive concern of a young, educated élite.

In Chapter 4, I consider the notion of institutional embeddedness by exploring the sexualization of state practices and relations. Drawing on poststructuralist, feminist and neo-Marxist analyses, the chapter begins by developing an anti-essentialist state paradigm in order to explore the multiple and contradictory relationships between the state and sexual forces. In examining the different ways in which lesbian and gay organizations and activists have engaged with the state, I argue that their effectiveness is constrained by the sexual structuring of state power. The final section of the chapter therefore examines the ways in which different facets of the state's identity are sexualized and the effects this has on lesbian and gay struggle.

Chapters 5 and 6 move away from the broad theoretical questions of the first part of the book to explore two specific sexual engagements with the British state. The first examines the 'virgin birth' scandal in the spring of 1991 that followed the enactment of a new framework for regulating donor insemination services. My interest here concerns the way in which the Right attempted to use the legislation – the Human Embryology and Fertilisation Act 1990 – and the subsequent discursive panic to limit single heterosexual and lesbian women's access to donor insemination. In examining the extent of their success in reaffirming and entrenching a conservative reproductive economy, I also raise more general issues about the efficacy of regulatory legislation, and the extent to which social groups can exempt themselves from its net.

Chapter 6 considers the state in a different light. Here I focus on the development of a counter-hegemonic municipal politics, in the form of lesbian and gay local government activism in Britain. Paralleling the previous chapter, I explore the extent to which lesbian and gay municipal actors were able to utilize state power to convey their sexual politics, and examine the constraints they faced. The chapter explores how bureaucratic processes, political pressure and state discourse combined with policy-makers' antipathy to limit lesbian and gay equality initiatives and to hegemonize a liberal sexual politics. At the same time, I argue, lesbian and gay municipal actors were able, albeit only in part, to contest the disciplinary character of the local state.

In Chapter 7 I draw together my discussion of strategy by exploring the character and normative possibilities of political struggle. Beginning with an argument for the decentring of resistance, I go on to consider different ways of interacting with dominant power relations. My argument proposes a pluralist approach to political strategy, while clearly distinguishing this from pluralist methodologies, analyses or normative frameworks. Based on an acknowledgement of overdetermination, an unwillingness to privilege particular relations a priori, and the need for contextualization, I advocate a situated, nuanced, reflexive and *generous* approach to activism. In the final section I consider the extent to which diverse strategies should be drawn together by exploring both the benefits and disadvantages of counter-hegemonic and anti-hegemonic approaches.

I conclude with an afterword. In it I explore the political values that might be inscribed within a counter or anti-hegemonic project. My starting point is an ethical principle of sustainable equality of empowerment. In briefly setting out what it might entail, I emphasize the need to problematize desires and identities, to repeatedly consider the impact of seemingly progressive discourses on other forms of inequality, and to recognize the ways in which inequality of empowerment is not a historic given but a continually reproduced practice.

Notes

1 The distinctions between postmodernism and poststructuralism have been extensively discussed elsewhere. While some writers have tried to separate the two terms according to subject area, others have adopted a more conceptual approach. In this book, I use poststructuralism to refer to the work of Foucauldians, and postmodernism to identify the literature emanating principally from Derrideans, although clearly both have been shaped by other writers. However, in a number of instances the work overlaps, for instance, in the writing of Judith Butler. I therefore in such cases use the terms interchangeably.
2 Although my focus is on sexuality as a disciplinary framework, to restrict sexuality to a particular form of power would be to miss the different inflections sexuality possesses. For instance, what sexuality might mean in the situated frame of a rape trial is linked but different to its meaning within lesbian feminist erotica, a sex education class, or gay theory.

2

Beyond domination?: Productive, and relational power

> The best way of putting an end to the theory and practice of masculinist power is to bring into being the theory and practice of feminist power.
>
> (Flammang 1983:74)

Introduction

In understanding the relationship between sexuality and the state, power offers a key conceptual tool. While earlier feminist and gay writing tended to use power to explore how the state repressed minority sexual communities and women, more recent theory, drawing on Foucault, has focused on power's productive capacity. Different writers, for instance, have analysed the creation or generation of sexual/gender identities as a result of state practice. Yet such work still tends to identify power in a principally negative way: power may produce subjectivities, but the subjectivities it creates are those of marginalized, oppressed, or administered peoples. As stated in the introduction, my aim in this book is to develop a framework of power which is more analytically and normatively polysemic. Conceptualizing power as the generation of effects does not imply any inherent articulation with inequality; state power may subjugate, but it also may empower (as Chapter 6 on lesbian and gay municipal politics explores).

Despite desiring a broader conceptualization, I have chosen to ground my approach to power within a Foucauldian feminist paradigm.[1] Work in this area has developed extensively in recent years, exploring the relationship between gender, sexuality, inequality and resistance (e.g. Diamond and Quinby 1988; Sawicki 1991; Bell 1993; Ramazanoglu 1993). In particular, the literature has developed in two interconnected directions: the first focuses on power as a relationship of domination or inequality; the second on power's productivity – the impact of its technologies in creating effects.

Theorizing the relationship between these two conceptual strands provides a central theme for this chapter. My argument is that the way they are often integrated within Foucauldian feminism is problematic, particularly for a paradigm of power which does not wish to treat domination or inequality as inevitable. While synthesis can take several forms, the one I find particularly unsettling adopts the following logic:

1 power concerns the generation of effects;
2 since effects will always be generated, power must therefore always be present;
3 but power also entails non-egalitarian, asymmetrical relations;
4 therefore if power is inevitable, inequality will always be with us.

This sequential logic can be escaped at several points. One might argue that although power generates effects, it is not the only way of doing so. That is, there may be other ways of producing outcomes which do not entail power.[2] Alternatively, one could suggest that inequality or domination at a different historical moment might not carry the same denigratory resonances they hold today. For instance, rather than identifying systemic asymmetries through class, race, gender or age, domination might simply refer to majority control through democratic decision-making processes.

However, despite these forms of escape, the sequence described above has become absorbed as a new pessimistic orthodoxy, played out amongst feminists in a range of terrains, most particularly around sexuality (see Chapter 4). While I wish to move away from this assumption of inevitable domination, at the same time it is important not to erase issues of domination and inequality from considerations of power. There is a danger of this occurring once power becomes conceptualized as simply the generation of effects since specific social relations can end up ignored or marginalized.

In order to maintain the analytic centrality of asymmetrical relations to any consideration of power, I wish to begin with the Foucauldian relational approach. This identifies power as the unequal relation between social classes and groupings. Through considering some of the problems this approach raises, I identify those aspects I wish to retain. I then move on to consider a productive framework of power. Again, my concern is to explore some of the tensions within current feminist literature in this area. The final section of the chapter brings together my earlier discussion to explore a paradigm of power which centres issues of inequality and domination, while also locating power within a trajectory of social transformation.

Relational power – Domination and resistance

> In reality power means relations, a more-or-less organized, hierarchical coordinated cluster of relations.
>
> (Foucault 1980:198)

A Foucauldian relational approach starts from the premise that people are unequal; power is thus concerned with domination and subjection – an above and below (Foucault 1980: 201). Relational paradigms reject a resource-based analysis which conceives of power as something particular classes or groups possess (Sawicki 1991:20; Bell 1993:39). Neither power nor subjectivity has meaning or existence outside of a particular relationship between social forces.[3] It does not make sense, therefore, to talk about men *holding* power as if this capacity exists independently of women,[4] or as if men can ontologically precede gender relations.

Conceptualizing power as relational raises several important questions. Who is the relation between? Does it have to entail identifiable individuals or social groups, or can it involve amorphous forces such as patriarchy or capitalism? What is the character of this 'relation'? Is it one of control – subjugating the body of another to one's own interests – winning in situations of conflict, or something else? In considering these questions, I wish to focus on two key issues: what is the relationship between power, domination and systemic inequality? Second, how do we conceptualize resistance if only dominant forces exercise power?

Agency and the benefits of power

A relational paradigm draws attention to the agency of dominant forces. While people can be controlled without anyone in particular doing the disciplining, a relationship requires forces at both ends of the polarity.[5] Feminist work highlights the identities constituted around these polarities. Whites, men, heterosexuals, the bourgeoisie: each (overlapping) group is located at the governing end of its respective, relational axis. Yet although it is often important to identify the class or individual exercising power or benefiting from its exercise,[6] eliding power, benefit and dominance as if they are inherently coterminous is problematic. What about the white man, for instance, who tries not to dominate women, or the woman who feels oppressed by anonymous social or cultural forces rather than by individual men? In exploring power, it is important to be able to differentiate these different kinds of relationships in ways that recognize agency while retaining power's irreducibility.

Instead of adopting a class relations analysis which implicates all men equally, I use gender to refer to men and women's relationship to

Patriarchy (handwritten)

patriarchy. By patriarchy I mean a specifically gendered organizing framework composed through a series of historically emergent articulations between gender and other social practices.[7] Thus patriarchy encompasses issues to do with cultural values, the public–private divide, and sexuality as well as more obvious gendered concerns. Constituted by, and in turn constituting, social interactions, processes, and relations, patriarchy benefits men.[8] It 'advantages' them (Dowding *et al.* 1993), enabling men to exercise power in ways not similarly open to women.

> [A]lthough men cannot be said to *possess* power, nor to *exclusively* exercise power, feminist analysis demonstrates the differential and hierarchical positions of men and women in relations which *repeatedly accord men the greater access to the exercise of power*.
>
> (Bell 1993:42; my emphasis)[9]

Some exercises of power involve *dominating* women, that is using women specifically as a resource in the furtherance of men's own objectives. However, male dominance is wider than the specific domination of women. It also includes a gendered ability to exercise agency and achieve desired outcomes in ways not available to women, although women may not necessarily be subjugated or exploited in the process. While not all men choose to exploit this advantage – to exercise power – an individual's abstention does not make the advantage disappear. Neither men nor women can simply 'opt out' of gender's organizing framework, although both can find ways of disrupting or transforming it.

Recognizing that gender relations are not reducible to male domination is important, yet this analysis is itself limited in its suggestion that social relations of gender can be analysed separately from those of race, class, geography and so on. If we want a framework that incorporates various social relations, recognizing the ways in which they transform and condense each other, we need to go beyond any single organizing framework to explore how different frameworks merge and intersect.

Feminists have conceptualized the multiple dimensions of inequality in various ways. One approach has been to argue that an élite exists of white, heterosexual men who exercise power over everybody else (Hartsock 1990:171). Another is to treat relations of power as crisscrossing, with each individual located at different points along different axes (Fraser 1989:165; de Lauretis 1990:131) or classes (Ferguson 1991:32).[10] While these approaches are useful, they also have drawbacks. The first's trouble is it creates two camps: the powerless and powerful, with people occupying an often unchanging site at one station or the other.[11] The second approach is less static. However, it still tends to treat relations of inequality as operating in analytically discrete, ontologically identifiable ways. Thus one is supposed to be able to pinpoint someone's range of locations according to different axes, for example, 'she is a white (powerful), disabled (powerless) woman (powerless)'. The problem with this method is twofold. First, it suggests there are only two positions on each axis. Second, it implies these two positions exist only in relation to each other. Thus their meaning and effects are not inevitably shaped by other axes of power.

An alternative way of conceptualizing these multiple relationships is to complicate the conception of patriarchy outlined above.[12] Rather than basing analysis on *axes of oppression*, gender, class and race can be conceived as 'organizing frameworks' or, less systematically, as 'principles' that overdetermine each other in their operation and effects.[13] Thus in exploring the impact of race, we not only need to consider how it is articulated to, and shaped by, other structuring systems such as gender and class, but also to take into account that race itself provides a complex, often contradictory framework which produces more than two subject positions. This is apparent if we consider the different, situated experiences of British Asians, European Jews and Afro-Americans. To argue that they are all simply subjugated by racism or white people is to miss the diversity and complexity in the way race shapes experiences of oppression and resistance (see Mason-John and Khambatta 1993:32–37).

Resistance

Within a relational Foucauldian paradigm, resistance occupies a central location. '[W]herever there is a relation of power it is possible to modify its hold' (Sawicki 1991:25, see also Foucault 1980:142, 1981:95, 1988:123).[14] According to Foucault (1981:95), resistance plays 'the role of adversary, target, support, or handle in power relations'. In the following section on power's 'productivity', I explore some of the ways in which resistance is 'organized out', in particular through the construction of docile or consenting subjects. However, since people do resist relations of inequality, I wish to explore briefly the process through which this occurs. I have suggested that resistance implies domination, it also, I would argue, problematizes the notion of powerlessness since resistance requires if not power then at least a certain ability to *impact*. Theorists such as Chantal Mouffe claim that resistance emerges from a contradictory positioning as both powerful and powerless, for instance, as a middle-class woman. Not only does such a condensed location provide the wherewithal to resist, it also generates the motivation (Mouffe 1988:95). Laclau and Mouffe (1985:153) argue that such motivation is crucial in turning relations of subordination, which are accepted, into relations of oppression, which are not.

Yet it is not only middle-class women who struggle. Women who lack power according to all formal indexes of race, geography, and age often possess the will and capacity to fight back. Laclau and Mouffe (1985:154) suggest this is due to an exterior discourse which both calls forth and legitimizes the contestation of relations of subordination. For instance, hegemonic discursive elements such as citizenship, equality and rights provide a basis for interrogating and undermining the validity of inherited status and formal inequality (Mouffe 1988:95). Thus even for people consistently positioned as subjugated, dominant discourses can be drawn upon to enable social protest and opposition. Can it make sense to equate power with particular, dominant, subject positions when even those with no apparent social power, for example, poor, black women, not only protest but do so using dominant forms of knowledge and other resources?

The notion of subjugated people deploying power is (intellectually) resisted by many Foucauldian-influenced writers. They argue that since power is exercised by those who rule, subordinates are only left with power's antithesis – resistance. The deployment of the notion counter-discourse – invested forms of knowledge that oppose dominant truths – exemplifies this approach. If discourse is power, subjugated peoples can not meaningfully utilize it. Their agency comes through its mirror reflection – reverse knowledge.[15]

Some theorists have tried to find a middle route, one that recognizes the power-like practices of subordinated communities without using the same language reserved to describe the activities of the powerful. Fiske (1993:11–12), for instance, distinguishes between localizing and imperializing power; the former he equates with resistance (1993:18), while the latter is what dominant forces deploy. The difficulty with this approach, however, is first that it raises definitional ambiguities for groupings at the borderline: can middle-class women deploy power, for instance?[16] Second, it becomes problematic when the resources deployed by subordinate communities or identities are the same as those utilized by dominant groupings, for example, money, legal rights, and dominant discourses.[17]

If, however, we take a different approach and argue that oppressed people *can* exercise power, power cannot be simply conceived as a relation of domination. Instead, it provides us with a way of conceptualizing the practices and mechanisms forces deploy in the hope of producing desired effects. Yet to argue that subjugated forces *deploy* power does not presume an ontological hierarchy of origins. Communities do not predate discrete forms of power whose exercise leaves them intact. In diverse ways, power shapes the interests, desires, agendas and subjectivities of subjugated (and dominant) forces. Yet, this does not mean we should reify power. As I go on to discuss, forms and relations of power are also constantly reshaped, reformulated by the activities of different social groupings.

Productive power and oppressive effects

Maintaining the centrality of domination and inequality is important in an exploration of power. Without an analysis and appreciation of systemic subordination and advantage, a progressive[18] politics can become directionless. At the same time, as I have argued, power cannot simply be equated with the control exercised by a particular group. First, this ignores the ways in which even dominant forces are subjected to power (by this I do not mean the control exercised upon them by superior bodies or classes, but the ways in which their ideas, behaviour and choices are also disciplined or socialized). Second, in a society where, for many, our identities are complex amalgams of advantage, marginalization and repression, identifying a dominant class becomes less clear-cut. Third, conceptualizing oppositional struggle and resistance is difficult when only one class is perceived to have access to power.

Identifying power as productive moves away from a focus on the relationship between social forces, to an exploration of the ways in which practices and subjectivities are generated. Foucault's conception of power as productive emerged as a critical response to what he saw as the repeated elision made between power and repression.

> That hypothesis assume[d] that power functions essentially negatively, through such operations as interdiction, censorship and denial. Power, in this view, just says no. It says no to what are defined as illicit desires, needs, acts and speech.
>
> (Fraser 1989:27)

Power, Foucault (1980:119) argued, was more effective when it said 'yes' than when it said 'no', that is, when it created particular needs, pleasures and discourses rather than generating their prohibition or suppression. According to Foucault (1980:59), power would be a fragile thing if it only repressed. Its strength comes from producing effects at the level of desire and knowledge. Foucault linked his critique of repressive power to a rejection of the notion that power originated at the pinnacle of the social hierarchy and then filtered down (Foucault 1980:60). Instead he argued that power originated in many places including micro-interactions and relations. Thus it circulated through a range of terrains and social relationships producing effects on the bodies, desires and knowledge of social subjects.

In this section, I want to explore some of the difficulties, tensions and issues raised by this formulation of power, particularly in the way it has been developed by feminists. My focus is on the following:

1 How does power discipline, and to what extent do invisibility and silence provide a means of escape?

2 What is the relationship between productive and repressive power?
3 Is productive power necessarily 'positive' power?

Discipline, scrutiny and invisibility

Despite the equation by some Foucauldian feminists of productive and positive power (which I discuss below), in the main, most feminist writing in this area has tended to focus on the oppressive character and effects of power's disciplining processes (e.g. Bartky 1988). In discussing power's structuring of women's lives, two Foucauldian concepts have been treated as key: the metaphorical 'panopticon' and the 'confessional'. Both operate by making visible and open to scrutiny women's desires, choices and behaviour. However, in the panopticon, scrutiny is exercised by the woman herself, while in the confessional, by others.

Applied to women, the panopticon is a metaphor for women's internalization of the male gaze to produce self-monitoring subjects (Bartky 1988).[19] External coercion is generally unnecessary, for women ensure their own conformity to feminine norms. Counterfactuals reveal this process more clearly, for instance, the hostility shown to women who spurn bodily discipline, who sprawl when they sit, retain visible body hair, or are unashamedly fat. Often when women do not monitor themselves other forces step in, for instance, the violence that confronts visibly 'out' lesbians and gay men on the streets, or the disciplinary treatment afforded to women within the mental health system.

The disciplinary power of the panopticon attaches to behaviour without necessarily being internalized at the level of norms or values. In this way it differs from an ideological process of inculcation which relies on people's understanding and perception changing. Just as prisoners tend not to believe in or desire the guards' rules and scrutiny but internalize them anyway, so many women may be disciplined by the 'patriarchal gaze', irrespective of their own ideological frameworks. The number of feminists who find themselves removing 'unwanted' body hair or dieting is, perhaps, an example of this process.

Alongside the panopticon is the 'confessional': 'one of the main rituals we rely on for the production of truth' (Foucault 1981:58). The confessional is a practice of power that generates the social urge to explain, justify and seek forgiveness for intimate feelings, decisions and actions. Sawicki (1991) describes this process of confession and self-improvement as generating the disciplinary subjection of the modern individual. Played out in women's magazines, daytime television shows, doctors' surgeries, and counselling sessions – with its requirement for both speaking and witnessing (listening) subjects – the confessional presents itself as a means of liberation. It offers an apparent escape from repressive power rather than being seen as power's vehicle (see Phelan 1990:436; cf. McNay 1992:45–46).

[I]t seems to us that truth, lodged in our most secret nature, 'demands' only to surface; that if it fails to do so, this is because a constraint holds it in place, the violence of a power weighs it down.

(Foucault 1981:60)

A number of feminist and gay writers have worked with this idea of the confessional to argue that sexual movements, such as lesbians and gays, are problematic in that they emerge from a 'confessional' need to identify and classify, to explain and justify who we are to the world around us.[20] This urge to explain has been denounced by the 'in your face' approach of current queer politics which (while constructing its own categories) explicitly rejects society's labelling and classification of sexual identities (Seidman 1993).

Yet this critique of the confessional as applied to lesbian and gay politics has several problems. First, it is based on a particular paradigm of power. Thus it relies on the assumption that if power generates the confessing subject this must be problematic since power is inherently involved with domination. This neglects the role lesbians and gay men have played in the social construction and labelling of their own identity; it also oversimplifies the range of processes that more generally take place in the formation of identity.[21]

There is as well a danger in denying the possible benefits specific forms of identification, visibility, and knowledge can generate. This is particularly evident in areas where a 'will not to know' among status quo forces exists. For instance, Jan Mohamed (1992) discusses the silencing that enclosed the racialized sexuality expressed by white men towards black women. Similarly, Weeks (1980:17–18), in an early article, discusses the ways in which certain definitions make resistance and transformation possible. Judith Butler (1991), while treating lesbian and gay identity as a construct of dominant discourse, nevertheless argues that such identities provide a space for oppositional activity.

If it is already true that 'lesbians' and 'gay men' have been traditionally designated as impossible identities, errors of classification, unnatural disasters . . . then perhaps these sites of disruption, error, confusion, and trouble can be rallying points for a certain *resistance* to classification and to identity as such.

(Butler 1991:16)

The danger of identifying power as both productive and oppressive is that it can result in arguing for an *absence* of production: that is, for invisibility, ignorance, silence.[22] In some instances, these may prove useful, offering the possibility of tolerance that is lost in a climate of greater scrutiny. However, in an attempt to reveal the problems of production, some theorists have gone overboard in advocating its antithesis without always considering what the implications might be in a given context.

A more nuanced account of the emerging (confessional) imperative to be 'out', visible and proud is provided by Roy Cain (1993). Although he argues that disclosure has often taken place on the basis of essentialist notions of orientation, and privileges the experiences of affluent gay men, at the same time he states:

> The new views of disclosure and secrecy . . . pose new challenges and political dangers. However, to identify their dangers is not to deny their utility for the gay movement or for gay individuals . . . The challenge lies in grabbing hold of the benefits, while being wary of the costs.
>
> (Cain 1993:309)

From repressive to positive power?

Both the internalized gaze and the will to confess reveal the ways in which power can generate oppressive effects. Indeed, one might define such effects as *repressive*, since they limit and contain the possibilities for action. But does such a merging of productivity and repression contradict those Foucauldian analyses that stress the differences between the two on the basis that the *production* of consenting or acquiescent subjects is fundamentally different from the old forms of repressive power? Are repression and production two sides of the same coin?

There are two points here. First, what seems important is less the direction of power – whether it says yes or no – than its style. By this I mean proscriptions and prescriptions as *injunctions* may be more entwined with each other than with less directive forms of power such as discouragement and persuasion. In addition both of these are different from forms of power that more anonymously structure and produce particular effects, for instance capitalist economic practices. Second, these different forms do not operate in isolation. If some choices, desires or forms of knowledge are facilitated, encouraged or produced, others are likely to be forbidden, discouraged and repressed. For instance, prohibiting homosexuality is the other side of producing heterosexual subjects. Or, to give another example, the teacher's ability to issue instructions, to force children's bodies into particular arrangements, is as central to the disciplinary power of the school as is the arrangement of desks, classrooms or timetables. Both practices reinforce each other. It is important therefore when focusing on power's productivity, not to marginalize rules, orders and violence (physical and psychological). Doing so underestimates the extent to which the experiences of oppressed communities are shaped by violence, prohibitions and mandates (Jan Mohamed 1992).

Is productive power positive?

The analytical emphasis on productive rather than repressive power within feminist Foucauldian writing also needs to be seen in the light of another opposition: 'positive' rather than negative power (Woodhull 1988:168; Phelan 1990:424). This may seem a surprising emphasis given power's articulation with regulation and domination. Is positive simply a semantic substitute for productive, a reference to the benefits generated by (and for) a dominant class? Or does it refer to the ways in which even the exercise of control or discipline can lead to positive outcomes for those subject to power's force?

Equating power's positivity with the benefits subordinated forces can receive has been explained in several ways. Fraser argues that power produces 'liberationist discourse . . . to mask the actual functioning of domination' (1989:27). Another approach links 'positive' power to the unintended and contradictory effects even domination may produce.[23] While power's potential positivity may seem unsurprising,[24] linked to inequality it nevertheless emerges as a mistake: the inevitable but unwished for effect of dominant forces' activity. If power, however, is not equated with domination, control or asymmetrical discipline, positive power (from the perspective of subordinated forces) is a constant, open possibility. While it may emerge unexpectedly – the contradictory effect of hegemonic practices – it may also be the anticipated outcome of progressive deployments.

A post-Foucauldian framework?

Conceptualizing power as polysemic centres attention on the character of strategic power engagements. How do we reallocate access? How do we transform the character dominant power forms take? These questions though beg a prior one: what indeed is power? Despite prolific discussion and theorization of power in Foucauldian-inspired work, little guidance is actually given as to what power means. The effect of this omission is to give power a physical reality or presence – we do not need definition since the meaning of power is self-evident – an approach many of the writers themselves would undoubtedly reject. This reification is reinforced by Foucauldian assertions such as force is not power (Phelan 1990:425). Yet whether power includes force depends on whether we want it to; there is no original, ontological answer.

Power does not simply exist. It is an explanatory or normative device that highlights and articulates some social relations, decentring others; for instance, Foucault's (1981) framework downplays the 'power' of the modern sovereign or state. Where conceptual boundaries are therefore drawn is a political issue. Indeed, it is important to acknowledge the ways in which disciplinary and discursive contexts impact upon the development of conceptual frameworks. How we understand power is shaped by the 'sociophysical' (Cooper 1994b) environment within which we live. In turn, our perception of power affects the ways in which we engage with our environment at the level of interpretation and 'material' practice. We can reconceptualize power as part of a political strategy, however such a strategy is both responsive to, and rooted within, our own historical conditions.

The approach I wish to develop, as I have said, identifies power as the facilitation of particular outcomes, processes and practices. These may include the maintenance and reproduction of the status quo or, alternatively, its dismantling or transformation. Before setting out my approach in more detail, I wish to address a number of questions this formulation raises:

1 Is power just another word for causation?
2 Are omissions exercises of power?
3 How central is conflict to the operation of power?

Power as causation?

To some extent, my approach to power can be seen as an analytics of causation, that is, as an exploration of how causation occurs – concretizing the process of producing effects.[25] Yet power is not simply causation. To begin with, the impact of power on a terrain may not be sufficiently strong or direct to be defined as 'causing'. For instance, age of consent legislation may impact upon the cultural and social provision available to young gay men, without in any meaningful sense 'causing' it. Causation also tends to focus on the *relationship* between processes and outcomes in order to identify which act caused which effect. Although studies of causation may recognize that outcomes are overdetermined, it is the identification of a determining relationship that is centred. In criminal law, this often takes the form of deciding whether an act was a primary cause or an intervening incident: was it of sufficient impact to change the course of events?[26]

Exploring power, in contrast, is to centre the *differential ability to cause* and the characteristics of those phenomena which create an impact. It therefore raises other questions: what forms of power do different forces have access to? What qualities does such power possess? How does the exercise of power affect subsequent social relations and interactions? Exploring the exercise of power in this way also highlights questions of agency and intentionality. For instance, two lesbians kissing on a street may *cause* some passers-by to 'cross over'; however, to call the generation of possibly undesired effects an *exercise* of power is not necessarily helpful. A better approach is to conceptualize the kissing as a form of cultural power imbricated within a particular discursive and disciplinary field. Such power can operate without being 'exercised' by anyone, although if the two women *intended* to affront others passing by, they could be said to be exercising it. This question of intentionality becomes particularly important in my later discussion of an ethics of power. Arguing for an ethics of equal empowerment – that is, that people should have an equal capacity to impact upon their environment – becomes totally meaningless if the link between intentional agency and power is lost.

Omissions as power?

If power concerns the generation of effects, what about the *failure* to generate? Can this also be seen as an exercise of power? The question of omissions has been an important theme running through debates on power (e.g. Lukes 1974). Two dimensions need to be considered. The first concerns the omissions of subordinate forces (Bachrach and Baratz 1970). Defined as 'non-decision making', the processes by which dominant forces prevent the grievances of others from entering the political arena,[27] this suppression or 'mobilization of bias' (Schattschneider 1960:71) usually requires some individual, grouping or institution to act.[28]

The second scenario involves not only omissions by subordinate forces, but also a lack of obvious activity on the part of dominant forces. Can we still argue that power is being deployed? This is important in considering the relationship between the status quo and power since maintaining and even reproducing the former may often not require activity on the part of dominant forces. A British example of this can be seen in the implementing of Section 28, Local Government Act 1988, a legislative amendment that prohibited local authorities from 'promoting homosexuality'. Although the section did not apply to school governors, many council education officials were reluctant to tell governors of this fact, keeping back the information in order to minimize lesbian and gay educational developments. Can we see this silence as the deployment or exercise of power?

The political decision of officers can be analysed by considering what forms of power contributed to the demise of lesbian and gay education policies at a local level. Thus the disappearance of educational initiatives becomes an effect that can be analysed, even without explicit action on the part of dominant forces. In explaining the demise, one factor might then be the differential access to legal knowledge. Policies did not develop, or in some instances ceased, because governors were unaware of their legal position, an outcome generated by the disciplinary, bureaucratic structures within which they worked, and the messages conveyed (implicitly) by council officers.

Does it make a difference to understanding the exercise of power that officers *knew* school governors could have acted differently, that officers could have given governors different legal information? Arguably, officer knowledge did not affect the outcome, since if they had not known they would probably have behaved in the same way. We can identify the knowledge they *did* convey, as well as any attempt to stop people from finding out about alternative interpretations, as exercising power. However, the information about which they kept silent can be seen as *potential* power.[29] If they had informed governors of their legal exclusion from the section, outcomes may in some instances have been different; thus education officers possessed the *capacity* to generate different effects even though it was not utilized.

It is at this level of acknowledging potential power, that is the *capacity* (even if unutilized) to generate effects, that a relational approach becomes useful. Relations of power, as I argued earlier, do not just involve the domination of others, but also the extent to which some can take actions that others are denied on the grounds of race, class, age, disability and gender. For instance, the ability of most heterosexuals to get married constitutes an aspect of their power whether or not they choose to exercise it. While an absence may not seem to generate ascertainable effects, and therefore appears hard to define as the exercise of power, the ability or potential to produce specific outcomes is an important aspect in understanding the relative power of different social forces.[30]

Decentring conflict

Adopting a productive approach decentres conflict (cf. Sawicki 1991:25). In this way, my analysis differs from that of Foucault (1981:94), whose linkage of power with resistance suggests power always involves the potential for some form of contestation (see also Foucault 1980:142). Removing antagonism or conflict as a prerequisite of power may seem paradoxical within a radical framework; however, I have done so to avoid the series of problems that arise as soon as non-observable conflict is introduced into the analysis.

What do I mean by this? In *Power: A Radical View*, Lukes (1974), who adopts a conflict model, argues that power works most effectively in situations of latent conflict, when competing interests are not only stopped from being raised but even, at the furthest extreme, rendered unthought (1974:25). Yet how can this latter be demonstrated? How can one show that decisions are being made contrary to people's interests when even they themselves are unaware that this is the case? Luke's response is to construct a counterfactual situation to reveal what people *would* want if their material conditions were less oppressive, or in what he defines as an 'abnormal situation'. Yet this is to assume that interests precede power, that is people have certain, definable interests which power can repress but not truly eradicate.

Employing a paradigm in which power constructs certain interests and 'organizes out' others, pointing to a conflict of 'objective' interests as evidence of the workings of power is problematic. First, how do we define such real interests when people's needs and wants will always be shaped by the society within which they live? How helpful is it to create an ahistorical interest that transcends the productivity of specific social relationships? Second, even if in a different situation (the counterfactual), overt conflict might actually exist, how much does this tell us about the present situation? The requirement to uncover underlying conflict deflects attention from power's capacity to *minimize* or *remove* conflict through the construction of shared knowledge, desires, interests and values.[31]

A paradigm of power

In developing a framework which decentres conflict, which differentiates the *intentional* exercise of power from anonymously generated effects and from a *capacity* to exercise, four 'modes' of power are key. Foucauldian feminists have tended to focus on two: the production of knowledge and discipline. I would like to extend their analysis to embrace ideology, force, discipline, and resources (cf. Brown 1992). Although I discuss them separately, these modes, and the processes and relations through which they work, are closely entwined, overdetermined by each other and the social context of modern life. Resources, force and discipline, for instance, cannot be understood except through ideology, that is, through frameworks of social meanings. Similarly, ideology and discipline can act as resources to be deployed in social struggles. My objective, however, in separating them – to construct what might seem an artificial schema – is to explore and differentiate the *range* of ways in which effects are generated. For example, whilst resources, such as money, only have meaning through ideology, exploring changes in the meaning of money (ideology) may raise different issues to changes in its distribution (resources).

So what are these four modes? First, ideology refers to the range of interpretive frameworks and meanings through which social relations, practices and society generally are constituted and understood (Cooper 1994a).[32] Dominant ideologies are generated by, and help to produce and sustain, certain social relations as hegemonic, natural and inevitable.[33] Oppositional ideologies express counterposing value systems and provide contestatory explanations. Since the world can only be known through ideology, the term itself carries no pejorative connotations. It is not in opposition to truth, science or materialism, nor is it entirely free-floating. Sociophysical entities, although understood only through ideology, at the same time impact upon and shape meanings in a mutually determining process within a long, historical trajectory.

The second mode, force, refers to the subjugation of the will or the body of another by physical or psychological means that include coercion, threats and violence. Lukes (1974:18) describes this situation as one where somebody is stripped of choice between compliance and non-compliance. It is for this reason that Foucauldians exclude force (see Phelan 1990:425), since their approach to power centres on the structuring of another's actions in a way that requires the other to retain agency. However, I would argue force is an important means of shaping and determining outcomes. The notion of power acting on and through the voluntaristic actions of others (Phelan 1990:425) presents only a partial picture of the ways in which bodies and social processes are re-formed or subjected.

The third mode, discipline, is a complex and contested concept despite its current intellectual popularity. Dews (1987:161) describes discipline as a system of micro-power relations that are essentially non-egalitarian and asymmetrical. Discipline is also closely linked to organizational tactics and technologies such as management, surveillance and control (Fraser 1989:22), and to the production of normality and abnormality (Walzer 1986). My approach draws on these different perspectives to conceive of discipline as the spatial and temporal mechanisms (see Turkel 1990:184–5) through which social interactions, institutions and bodies are structured or ordered. These may be asymmetrical, in the sense of empowering certain forces at the expense of others. However, they need not be. This is an important point. As I argue in Chapter 3, discipline does not have to be conceptualized solely as a way of maintaining domination or oppression. This being the case, a key strategic issue becomes how we shift to more symmetrical forms of discipline rather than how (and whether) we can eradicate discipline altogether.

Finally, resources is a mode of power that works through its ability to create a material advantage that can be both acquired and deployed, for instance, legal rights, skills, time and wealth. Resources emphasize agency by focusing on the tools actors marshal together in order to act.[34] Like force, including resources as a component of power may appear to conflict with a Foucauldian approach. However, while Foucauldians reject the notion of power as a resource, in this framework, I am suggesting the converse: that resources are a form of power, for they are a way of impacting upon social processes, decisions, preferences and relationships.

Identifying resources as a mode of power posits a pluralist framework, in as much as a range of different resources can generate effects.[35] Thus power cannot be reduced to wealth or control over the means of (re)production. However, such pluralism is highly constrained as I discuss below. Including resources also helps us to distinguish between potential power and its exercise, since it makes it possible for actors in a particular situation to possess or have access to resources they choose not to deploy. Thus the deployment of resources is shaped not only by countervailing resources, but as well by the field of power within which they exist and are constituted.[36] For instance, heterosexual feminists may desire and have the social, economic and emotional resources to live with another woman; however, the wider ideological and disciplinary field would tend to discourage the exercise of such a 'choice'.

Within a framework which does not reduce power to social inequality, resources do not necessarily operate as zero–sum.[37] This distinction between zero and non-zero-sum power can constitute an important site of strategy. For instance, is the primary objective to increase the productive power of a community or to redistribute its resources? If the former, one might focus on non-zero-sum forms, such as training, and economic regeneration; if the latter, zero–sum forms might be more important, for instance through taxation and welfare policies. However, redistributive social policies may well have non-zero-sum effects: what the government gains through taxation may be greater than the financial loss to individuals; in addition, achieving an increase in a community's productive powers might well require (or produce) redistributive policies.

So far I have conceptualized the four modes of ideology, force, discipline and resources at a relatively abstract level. However, their actual operation takes a more concrete form. Modes of power operate through historically specific *technologies* (de Lauretis 1987:28). For instance, ideology functions through language, knowledge and culture; force through physical violence, military might and criminal sanctions; discipline, through surveillance, hierarchical structures and architecture; and resources through wealth, legal rights and time.[38]

In addition to modes and technologies of power, there are *sites* (geographical, institutional, systemic) across and through which power operates, such as the courts, armed forces, economy, welfare state and the body. These sites shape the specific form power technologies take; for instance, disciplinary power deployed within the military is of a different character to that within the home or school.

Finally, there are *effects*: the consequences of activity or non-activity within a particular terrain. Effects may be the product of repeated actions congealing and solidifying over time, or the unexpected result of a new interaction. In *The Politics of Truth* (1991:153), Michele Barrett explores the plural nature of effects and the role of chance in producing unintended outcomes. Jennifer Terry (1991:56) in her article, 'Theorising deviant historiography' makes a similar point.

> *Effects* are the most acute manifestations of events, often where and when they appear to be most in contradiction or resistance to rationalistic sequencing.

In conceptualizing power as modes, it might seem as if human agency is once more becoming marginalized (see Hoy 1986). Indeed, within this framework, the abstract *existence* of modes – the generation of effects – appears beyond human volition (see Walzer 1986). It is doubtful whether we can, for instance, stop outcomes or processes from being shaped by social meanings or resources (although in the long run the impact of different modes may change, so that some, such as force, become redundant or of limited effect). Similarly, although the ways in which power is actually exercised tends to be the result of human volition[39] – using money or legal rights, for instance, as a form of resource – these technologies reach us as the historical condensation of past actions.

> [T]here is no power that is exercised without a series of aims and objectives. But this does not mean that it results from the choice or decision of an individual subject . . . the logic is perfectly clear, the aims decipherable, and yet it is often the case that no one is there to have invented them, and few who can be said to have formulated them.
>
> (Foucault 1981:95)

Or, to paraphrase Marx, we rarely start from scratch in choosing or determining the forms or technologies through which we exercise power.[40]

Having said that, however, human and institutional actors have the capacity to recreate or transform the social forms through which power operates. There is a process of creativity involved in this, whereby people struggle to negotiate the condensations which shape us and the conditions within which we operate.[41] It is this ability to transform (or reproduce) particular power technologies which forms a central element of this book, since I am concerned with the ways in which social struggles are not only about gaining access to power but also about changing its character and relative efficacy.

Organizing principles and the exercise of power

In general, most modes of power are not deployed exclusively by one social force but are accessible, albeit unevenly, to different collectivities in ways that are shaped by organizing principles of class, race, age, disability, and gender. In saying this, I in no way wish to suggest that power is evenly distributed. Between forms of power, access operates to accentuate rather than diminish inequality since the ability to deploy one form of power often tends to facilitate access to others. For instance, within the home, women may initially have disciplinary and ideological power in relation to newborn children. However, men's economic and physical power may work to undercut this and, over a period of time, to invest them as fathers with greater ideological and disciplinary authority as well.[42]

Gender, race, class and other organizing principles are important in understanding not only who has access to power, but, as well, the quality or character of such power. For instance, in the case of discursive practices, not only is there unequal access to the production of knowledge, but the content of dominant forms of knowledge is also racialized, gendered and so on. Many feminists have explored the ways in which dominant narratives take the white male subject as central and articulate the world from his viewpoint. Accounts from the perspective of subjugated identities, in contrast, are likely to be underdeveloped and to hold at best a marginal position (see generally Weedon 1987:111; Phelan 1990:433; Sawicki 1991:26). Indeed, at an epistemological level the very notion of a subjugated, counter-basis for truth is conceptually problematic. From where do oppositional epistemologies receive their validation if they cannot be traced back at some point to dominant discursive forms?

Organizing principles thus tend to shape the exercise of power at all stages – from questions of access, to the nature and content of particular technologies, the terrains through which power operates and the sites of its effects. Although these principles will be condensed differently according to the form or site in question, they are not constantly recreated from scratch at each instance (Eisenstein 1988:19).

Conclusion: The implications of productive power

In discussing productive and relational paradigms of power, I have argued for an approach that accentuates fluidity and change. Unlike resource based frameworks which aim to identify the distribution of power at a fixed moment, I am interested in power as an ongoing process – the ways in which the generation of effects in one realm, such as sexuality or the state, impact upon the generation, or capacity to generate, effects in others.

Underlying my argument in this chapter is the notion that how power is conceptualized is a political decision. I thus began by setting out some of the problems that arise from certain Foucauldian feminist frameworks – in particular the elision between power as ubiquitous and timeless, and power as a manifestation of domination. But what about the dangers of no longer equating power with domination? Hartsock (1990:168–9), for instance, criticizes Foucault for losing the element of domination in his analysis of power (see Bell 1993:39–40).[43]

> Domination is not a part of this image; rather, the image of a network in which we all participate carries implications of equality and agency rather than the systematic domination of the many by the few.
>
> (Hartsock 1990:169)

Peter Dews (1987) also argues for the retention of some notion of domination when he argues that for power to have any import, there must be some
principle which power crushes.

Although, in this chapter, I argue that power involves inequality in terms
of access, deployment, and effects, my conception of power remains irreducible to such asymmetry. Progressive social forces continue to construct more
symmetrical disciplinary structures, struggling to achieve hegemony for socialist forms of knowledge. But does defining these oppositional technologies as power detract attention away from relations of domination and
inequality? Popular conversations on power largely (although not entirely)
focus on issues of control and subjugation, who is powerful and who is not.
If power is no longer a denigratory concept, does it marginalize such concerns? And if being 'powerful' is not necessarily negative, does this take
responsibility and condemnation away from those who are more privileged,
who exert control over or exploit others?

These are important questions which cannot be answered in the abstract.
Rather they depend on a close examination of the specific implications of
reconceptualizing power. In considering this, one parallel trend in the discursive deployment of power has been that of empowerment. Feminist,
black and disabled activists in particular have struggled to become empowered, identifying such a process not as one of becoming oppressor but
rather of becoming liberated. Thus there is already a tension in progressive
use of the concept of power between empowerment and domination.

Within the productive framework discussed above both uses can be incorporated. Power may be oppressive, entailing domination or the control
of another's actions. Alternatively, power can involve the creation and use
of new forms of knowledge and discipline, or the reallocation of resources.
The polysemic nature of power conceptualized in this way highlights the
importance of an ethics – a framework that helps us to explore both ways of
deploying, as well as of engaging with, power.

Notes

1 Although I take account of Foucault's writing, my focus in this chapter is on the
  body of work that has developed, integrating Foucault's approach to power with
  feminist concerns.
2 If power concerns only those effects generated through domination, effects generated as a result of other mechanisms, for example, technological developments
  or affective interactions, would not be considered power. Thanks to Didi Herman for this point.
3 I have suggested that 'relational' power refers to the relationship between social
  forces; however, there is some ambiguity on this point. Some writers appear to

suggest that it is the *mechanisms* of power that are relational. This implies the relation is either between the forms and subjects of power or an alternative way of thinking about the form of power itself. Let me give an example. If one of the mechanisms of male domination is gendered employment practices, for example, lower pay for women's work, then one could either see relational power as the relationship between low pay and women or as a way of understanding low pay itself. While these dynamics are important, I feel they are sufficiently covered within a productive paradigm which focuses on the mechanisms of power. I therefore retain the relational approach to identify relations of domination or inequality between (classes of) people. This may be on grounds of race, class and gender (Weeden 1987:110) or based on other dynamics such as occurs between pupils and teachers, prisoners and their guards, patients and medical professionals.

4 Some writers have taken Foucault as implying that women are partially responsible for the exercise of male power since they are as much implicated in its operation as men. However, Foucault need not be interpreted in this way. Power relations between men and women may *depend* on women's presence – it cannot exist without them and is shaped by their 'participation' – without implying that women as a category are in any way culpable.

5 This does not mean those forces at the dominant end of the polarity necessarily construct or create the situation, but rather that their domination emerges as a result of the wider social relations within which they are embedded.

6 Foucault has been criticized for decentring the agency of the powerful (Hartsock 1990).

7 For a still useful discussion and exploration of patriarchy, see Sargent (1986) *The Unhappy Marriage of Marxism and Feminism*. In particular, see the contribution by Ehrlich (1986).

8 This is not always the case. Organizing principles of gender can work in ways that arguably disadvantage men. For instance, many people argue that men do not benefit from their gendered role within the military as front-line soldiers. However, while there may be a disjunction between patriarchal practice and oppositional notions of the good life in this respect, according to conventional criteria of the good life, men's role in the army is both constituted by and reproduces a gendered (and economically classed) status as brave, honourable, dutiful, loyal citizens.

9 Bell (1993:41) argues that domination might be a name feminists give to a state of 'perpetual asymmetry . . . where a reversal in power relations appears to be almost impossible'. Yet even in the context of domination, Bell argues that contradictions exist; thus no domination possesses absolute closure. While Bell's argument is useful, in her desire to differentiate power from domination, she runs into the danger of suggesting currently asymmetrical relations cannot be fundamentally transformed.

10 Fiske (1993:10) takes an approach which merges these two. He argues for two separate groupings of 'power blocs' versus 'the people'. However, people shift between these two domains depending on the context. Thus in some instances, subordinate whites will identify with the 'power bloc' rather than the 'people'.

11 See Foucault (1980:142), where he argues that we should not assume a binary

structure with the dominant on one side and the dominated on the other, but rather explore the multiple relations of domination that exist, and can be integrated or articulated together into overall strategies.

12 Considerable work has been carried out in recent years on the relationship between sex, gender and class, see for example, Moraga and Anzaldua (1983); Bulkin *et al* (1984); hooks (1990); Vorst *et al.* (ed.) (1991); Anthias and Yuval-Davis (1992).

13 Other theorists have described such frameworks as 'modes' (Brown 1987) or 'vectors' (Rubin 1989). In Cooper (1994b), I also utilize the terminology of 'vectors', however, in retrospect it seems too reductive. The language of 'frameworks' and 'principles' in contrast emphasizes the range of effects gender, class and race can have, and the ways in which they organize different aspects of social life. This approach avoids essentialism at the level of the individual subject since what it is to be a woman, for example, will depend on the different ways in which these organizing frameworks are condensed, lived, negotiated, and reproduced at given junctures. Moreover, describing gender, race, and class as frameworks is to construct them without an essence, since frameworks operate as a matrix of connections without a core.

14 See Duffy (1986:23–24), where she argues that resistance plays a pivotal role in traditional sociology of power, since power there entails realizing one's will when pitched against the resistance of others. Duffy argues this creates the gendered 'problem' of ignoring the operation of power where no resistance is apparent. Foucauldians, in contrast, often assume resistance in situations, as I discuss in Chapter 7, where other processes may be taking place.

15 Foucault is also critical of counter-discourses which simply reverse the valuations of their opponents (see Phelan 1990:433).

16 To say that it depends on whether they are struggling around issues of class or gender underestimates the ways in which these are usually bound together, for instance, covert employment discrimination which makes it difficult for women to obtain senior management positions.

17 Fiske (1993:70) argues that these resources are often reinflected when deployed by subjugated forces. However, his focus is the reinflection by poor white men of dominant cultural texts rather than other kinds of resources.

18 I do not use 'progressive' in the teleological sense, but rather to identify a politics which aims to increase the egalitarian aspects of social life and to challenge asymmetrical relations and practices. For a fuller discussion of the framework I am using, see the afterword.

19 I would question what it means to say that the gaze is 'male'. Perhaps a better way of thinking about it is to say that the gaze is the internalization of norms produced by a complex amalgam of organizing frameworks. Thus it 'works' in (somewhat) different ways in relation to women of different classes, races etc. Yet despite such differentiation, certain norms dominate. For instance, a wheelchair mobile, white woman may internalize different gendered norms concerning her appearance and movement to a pedestrian mobile one. However, she is also likely to internalize an aesthetic which defines her own body, however well disciplined, as less attractive than that of a 'walker'.

20 Some theorists have linked this to a critique of essentialism, arguing that not only

do such movements presuppose a core identity, but an identity constituted as a result of oppression. However, if lesbian and gay identity is the negotiated effect of different condensed organizing frameworks at a particular juncture not only does it lack a core but it also cannot be seen simply as the effect of dominant social relations.

21 See, for example, Herman (1994a) for a discussion of the ways in which sociological and psychological knowledge have shaped the construction of lesbian and gay identities within legal discourse.

22 See generally for a discussion of Foucault on this point, Weedon (1987:111) and Phelan (1990:437). One might also question whether an 'absence' of production is possible, or whether these invisibilities and silences are also equally 'produced'.

23 The romance novel, for instance, might be analysed in this way as a risky patriarchal practice. Initially, feminists tended to treat it as exclusively oppressive, aiming to create subservient women whose sexual desires depended on acquiescence to male authority. However, later feminist writing questioned the extent of this closure (e.g. see Snitow 1983).

One might argue that romantic novels establish an ideal that largely mirrors hegemonic feminine notions of desire: loyalty, reciprocality, genitally decentred, sensual and undistracted. Thus it may be an ideal from which heteromasculinity currently falls far short. This is where the danger or contradiction lies, for romantic novels may 'produce' desires that cannot be met from within the limited boundaries of sexualities that they designate as acceptable. On the one hand, women may continually seek a man who meets their aspirations, alternatively they may look elsewhere for fulfilment.

24 Drawing on feminist although not particularly Foucauldian frameworks, Wartenberg (1990:184–93) argues that 'power over' can prove positive when it is used to communicate skills such as through mothering practices. Rather than inherently entailing domination, one aim of such hierarchical relations, he argues, is to engineer their own destruction by enabling the subordinate agent to become more autonomous.

25 See Isaac (1987) for a realist critique of a causational approach to power on the grounds that by focusing on particular exchanges, it neglects the structures and underlying social relationships that determine behavioural regularities.

The extent to which effects are generated by underlying structures or individual actions is a difficult question which I explore through the paradigm of power by examining the relationship between agency, social arenas and mechanisms of power in generating effects. However, while these are often condensed in particular knowable ways, I reject the notion of a fundamental, totalizing logic that can be known a priori.

26 How we identify causation also depends on our objectives in doing so. Thanks to Niki Lacey for this point.

27 See discussion in Lukes (1974:16–20).

28 Alternatively, we can explore a situation where dominant forces do not act but subjugated forces do as a result of the structural power of the former, for example, see Wartenberg (1990:144).

29 However, against this must be put those factors which limit education officers' ability to choose whether or not to release information. These include directives

from senior officers and politicians, the disciplinary and discursive impact of the wider political climate, electoral and financial constraints etc.

30 Yet the concept of capacity or 'assets' (Etzioni 1993:19) has its problems; see Hindess (1982:504).

31 Lukes (1974:23) recognizes that power is most effective when conflict is avoided. However, by conflict here he means observable conflict. Underlying conflict is fundamental to his notion of power which focuses on the ability of a particular individual, group or institution to achieve its goals.

32 Many Foucauldian-influenced theorists have shifted from ideology to discourse on the grounds that ideology is too strongly associated with a particular Marxist world-view (e.g. Barrett 1991; Fiske 1993: 14–15). I find the concept of ideology helpful in identifying different interpretive frameworks and value systems. In contrast I use discourse to refer to the production of knowledge. This is concerned with why certain tenets are granted truth-value, the practice of epistemology, inclusion and exclusion of particular voices, and the articulation of concepts to produce certain meanings, for example, 'the reasonable man' within legal discourse.

33 Identifying dominant ideologies is problematic since 1) oppositional ideologies may also emerge from hegemonic social relations, and 2) although dominant ideologies may be assumed to maintain the status quo, their actual effects may be more complex and contradictory.

34 For instance, the ability of a manager in the public sector to dismiss an employee can be identified as a resource that the manager possesses, in the sense of having a limited capacity to choose how and when to utilize it, and possibly to benefit from public knowledge of such power. However at a more general level, the existence of such a power can be seen as part of the asymmetrical disciplinary structure of the public body. The limit of seeing it just as disciplinary power, however, is that it marginalizes the agency and choices the manager possesses as to its utilization.

35 However, the (relative) power of resources is constantly changing; indeed, struggles take place as social groups or institutions attempt to define and fashion the resources they possess as key (Lipman-Blumen 1994:111–13). The extent to which different resources have value also depends on how they are understood by others (Wartenberg 1990:144–5).

36 Resources are also shaped and constrained by the criteria according to which they operate. Using resources in ways defined as socially illegitimate may therefore limit their efficacy.

37 Resources might also be seen as a variable sum form of power since they can also produce negative–sum outcomes, for instance, military or nuclear resources that destroy both sides in a war or cause radiation across the globe.

38 These processes are not discrete from each other. Technologies of power function as articulated strands of political code that cluster together to generate effects. They are not exclusive to specific modes. Discourse (the production of systematized knowledge), for instance, operates as a resource, conveys and reproduces particular ideologies, and provides a technique for establishing and affirming specific disciplinary apparatuses.

39 My analysis limits the exercise or deployment of power to human and institu-

tional actors. I do not treat ideology or discourse, for instance, as exercising power but rather as providing the means and terrain through which power is exercised.

40 Fiske (1993:70) argues this is particularly true for those with less power who have to try and utilize resources already inscribed with the power of dominant forces. The extent to which this is true is likely to vary according to the form of power in question. For instance, status quo interests may be harder to eliminate when subjugated forces gain legal rights or develop public policy, than when they construct oppositional forms of knowledge. Although even these are likely to be based on accepted epistemologies.

41 See however Hindess (1982) for a critique of creativity as introducing an inexplicable element into human conduct.

42 See Etzioni's discussion of the 'halo' effect (1993:20).

The relationship between forms of power is complicated by the fact that men can be economically dependent on women and still able to dominate them physically and sexually.

43 From my reading of Foucault, domination remains a central aspect of power.

3

The politics of sex: Metaphorical strategies and the (re)construction of desire

Introduction

Within western, liberal nation states, the discourses of sexual liberation and sexual power have radically changed. No longer is it simply a matter of freeing women's repressed sexuality, of offering tolerance to minority orientations. Instead, political lesbianism, sexual transgression, gender-fuck and sado-masochism have become the highly charged sites of an oppositional sexual politics. In this chapter, drawing on my analysis of power, I explore three kinds of political struggle which link together in different ways the sexual and the social:

1 transforming sexual expression and desire by means of cultural and social struggles;
2 creating change in wider social relations through (private, dyadic) sexual acts; and
3 transforming social relations as a result of the public enactment of 'oppositional' sexual identities.

Drawing on my earlier analysis, I explore how the relationship between power and sexuality is conceptualized. In particular, I focus on the role different resources – the body, labour power, cultural texts – are identified as playing in the affirmation and transformation of sexual possibility.

In general, my argument is that these projects are limited, albeit in different ways, by their understanding of the relationship between sexuality, social relations and power. To explore these limitations, I focus on several issues. The first concerns sexual ethics. How do the frameworks discussed in this chapter respond to the notion of sexual difference? By what means are judgements or distinctions made between beneficial, benign or problematic sexualities? Second, to what extent does the requisite (individual or collective) agency exist to allow desires to be recreated, and by what means can this best be achieved? Third, if sexuality impacts upon wider social relations, what form does this take? To what extent can sexual strategies transform relations of gender, class and race for a constituency wider than the sexual participants involved? Finally, who are the actors in these different sexual projects? Is participation opened up to a wide range of people or does inclusion depend on minority or élite criteria?

Transforming sexual expression and desire

Challenges to dominant sexual practices and desires have come from several quarters. In this section, I wish to focus on the politics of two conflicting approaches: sex radicalism and radical lesbianism.[1] While both aspire to be political struggles that 'free' the sexual, they differ in the ways such freedom is understood. For radical lesbianism, freedom has tended to mean the construction of an idealized sexual terrain based on either 'naturally' female desires or an ethical, prefigurative feminism.[2] For sex radicalism, it involves contesting sexual puritanism and repression, as well as challenging feminist hierarchies of sexual acceptability. Although sex radicalism proffers a project for change, it is also 'anti-political' in its demands that sex not be a basis for scrutiny and refiguring.[3] The emphasis of sex radicalism is on affirming people's deepest, most 'authentic' desires, not on critiquing, undermining or transforming them.

Sex radicalism, pluralism, and the affirmation of diversity

Sex radicalism, which came to prominence in the mid-1980s, is embedded in a longer history of contesting sexual repression. Its most recent roots, however, are in the sexual libertarianism of the 1960s and the 'sex positive' politics of gay sexual communities during the following decade. Situated within the lesbian and gay community, sex radicals have drawn on cultural, social and rhetorical practices in order to explore, validate and reconstitute a specific range of sexual possibilities. Although sex radicals such as Gayle Rubin, following Foucault, do not posit a natural sexuality that has been repressed (Rubin 1989:277), they nevertheless focus their criticisms on what they describe as the 'sex negativity' of dominant sexual attitudes. This, they argue, is epitomized in the quintessentially conservative puritanism of radical lesbianism (Hunt, M. 1990; Smyth 1992:26).

Sex radicalism advocates the expression of sexual desire as it is felt, rejecting any transformation into less 'threatening' forms. Its core principle is the notion of 'benign sexual variation' (Rubin 1989:283). Difference is healthy and 'natural' rather than pathological, evil or politically incorrect.[4] According to Rubin (1989:283), 'Variation is a fundamental property of all life, from the simplest biological organisms to the most complex social formations'.

The indigenous character of sexual diversity provides the basis for normative claims as to its desirability (Weir and Casey 1984:154), hence the need to encourage a proliferation of different sexual desires and practices.[5] But the drive for variety has not embraced all choices; those defined as boring and conventional – the 'vanilla' lesbian in particular – tend to be demeaned and discarded. This raises the question whether sex radicalism actually frees up the sexual, or simply leads to the entrenchment of new disciplinary forms (Whisman 1993:57). Richardson (1992:198) argues that 'in recent lesbian porn the anus and the vagina have been more privileged than either the clitoris or breasts'. She (1992:198) claims that this generates 'a pressure to accept as the norm for lesbian sex sexual values which have previously been associated with heterosexuality'.

In exploring sexual diversity as a normative project, the conditions of modern social life that negate or disrupt this process become central points for interrogation. A key theorist in this area is Jeffrey Weeks. His work on radical pluralism – a political project which centres humanist notions of agency and consent (1991, 1992, 1993) – has explored the conditions needed for substantial (sexual) pluralism to be attained (1992:406–7). These include recognizing 'that other people's ways of life are our concern' and must be protected and enhanced without violating the other's 'freedom from interference' (Weeks 1993:208).

> [T]he recognition of a plurality of truths is a starting point only. It in turn must be governed by what David Held has called the principle of democratic autonomy. This argues that citizens should be free and equal in the determination of the conditions of their own lives . . . so long as they do not use their freedoms to negate the rights and claims of others. Democratic autonomy implies a respect and tolerance for other people's needs as the guarantee of your own freedom to choose.
> (Weeks 1991:195)

In critically considering this project to free up the sexual, to generate and protect sexual difference, I wish to focus on two areas. The first concerns boundaries: are all choices and sexual practices equally acceptable? The second involves the production of sexual desire.

Among sex radicals and radical pluralists,[6] different approaches have been taken to the question of acceptable difference. At one end of the spectrum, the question itself is problematized as moralistic and judgemental, pretending an illusory transcendence. From this perspective, consent or pleasure are the only acceptable, evaluative principles.[7] According to Susie Bright, editor of the lesbian pornography magazine, *On Our Backs,* what counts is whether it's 'hot' (quoted in Stein 1993:21–22). At the other end of the continuum, certain radical pluralist writers acknowledge that concepts such as consent can be problematic, for instance in the context of incest and paedophilia, and argue for some (limited) conception of 'harm'.

In engaging with a discourse of harm, some sex radicals and radical pluralists have tended to focus on the damage caused by state censorship, regulation, and radical feminism (e.g. Smith 1993). Others, however, have considered the question of boundaries and limits to acceptable behaviour. Ferguson (1991:246), for instance, argues

> The transitional morality I advocate supports a cultural pluralism in sexual life-styles and personal life choices, as long as these life-styles don't substantially infringe on others' rights to respect and self determination.

Like other writers, Ferguson focuses on the relationship *between* groups; however, the danger of this approach is that harm *within* communities may be ignored. Raising the issue of intragroup harm is a controversial one (see afterword). Some writers have argued that discussion of such harm is patronizing since it suggests people do not know their own interests (Hunt, M. 1990). If certain practices or relations are desired and sought, these should not be interrogated from a paternalistic (or maternalistic) position of epistemological superiority. Yet given the problematic nature of constructing and identifying the inner space and boundaries of different sexual groups, to define such space as 'off limits' means that many issues cannot be explored. Heterosexuality, for instance, becomes a black box only explorable in its relationship to homosexuality and bisexuality. While the interrogation of dominant sexual relations does not raise quite the same difficulties as exploring more marginalized sexualities, it is, I would argue, important to be able to critically examine all sexual preferences and desires, albeit in ways that do not reproduce current forms of social disempowerment.

As well as demarcating intragroup harm as out of bounds, radical pluralists' focus on harm between groups also raises problems and uncertainties. For instance, how is harm and its correlative liberties or rights to be conceptualized? Even where the issues may *seem* clear cut, for instance, where one grouping stops another from entering a public building or destroys their material, the situation may be more complicated. For example the 'aggressors' might well claim that the expression of particular sexual identities in community spaces undermines their own rights or freedoms.

This tension has been most infamously played out between lesbian feminists and sex radicals over the presence of pornography and leather/sadomasochistic clothing in lesbian or feminist community spaces. Many lesbian feminists stressed the harm and distress caused by images of brutality to Jewish and black women for whom they held a special resonance (Sims *et al.* 1982; Star 1982; Reti 1993b). In response, sex radicals tended to reject the notion that harm or an infringement of rights had occurred. First, they argued lesbian feminists' perception of harm was simply the experience of personal affront and therefore did not constitute a recognizable invasion of their rights. Second, privileging a subjective interpretation of meaning, sex radicals argued that if harm had not been intended it had not been caused.

Condensed in this conflict are some of the bedrock tensions of political theory. How is harm to be conceptualized: narrowly to exclude lesbian feminist claims or more expansively to include discursive and cultural forms of power? The current inability of sex radicalism and radical pluralism to offer alternative paradigms to liberal approaches to freedom and rights raises the question of other more successful approaches. Can we find concepts other than harm by which to evaluate and bound difference? Here I wish to offer one strategy for dealing with 'troublesome' desires based on an engagement with the 'technologies of sexual production' (more general discussion of an ethical approach to difference is explored in the afterword).

Talk about troublesome desires immediately begs the question of values and norms. How do we define what desires and practices, if any, are problematic? My framework focuses on those desires, acts and interactions that reflect or (re)constitute the linking of violence and subjugation with the erotic, or that fetishize relations of domination and subordination.[8] This is a normative position which I develop at different points in this book. A more general critique of the eroticization of dominance, abuse and violence can be found elsewhere (see Linden *et al.* 1982; Reti 1993a; Herman 1994b).

Acknowledging certain desires and sexual practices as problematic raises the question of strategic change. How open is our sexuality to being transformed? Although we experience our desires as integral and true – and this needs respecting – at the same time, desires have constantly to be repeated and reproduced. Thus (borrowing from Butler), they are always open to the possibility of being constructed differently. This occurs 'naturally' as social relations change, as struggles in other areas of life impact upon the sexual domain. But it can also take a more intentional form through engaging with the multiple conditions – forms of power – through which sexual desires and practices are generated. While we cannot guarantee, nor know for certain a priori, what impact this might have, it seems possible that by re-forming the social practices through which sexual effects are generated different erotic articulations will be produced.

In saying this, however, we have to ask whether such changes are desired. One of the ironies of radical pluralism is that while it acknowledges the social constructionist nature of sexuality – that sexual desires are produced within and by an oppressive society – the desires themselves are affirmed.[9] The humanist emphasis on affirming minority sexualities means that the role culture and ideology play in shaping particular desires and identities is either discounted or ignored. Pluralist proponents argue that it is unnecessary and pathologizing to attempt to uncover the causes of particular sexual desires.[10] First, the 'truth' is too complex and uncertain (Cummings 1993:356–7); second, uncovering only happens to sexualities deemed deviant or in some way less 'natural' (see Phelan 1993).

While such fears are understandable, a radical repudiation of causation throws into doubt transformative projects which require some conception of a relationship between practice and effects. If we cannot identify political aspirations and then work backwards to the processes that might generate them, we are left with an expressive or deconstructive politics that lacks strategy and vision. This is a problem that runs throughout many postmodern approaches, constituting itself in the tension between counter-hegemonic and anti-hegemonic strategies (see Chapter 7). Before continuing with this discussion of sexual transformation, let me introduce radical lesbianism's approach to desire.

Radical lesbianism: Challenging oppressive desires

While the enemy for sex radicalism is bodily and psychic repression, radical lesbianism's target has been gender oppression (Radicalesbians 1973). Although its site – the terrain of the women's movement – contrasts with the lesbian and gay space of sex radicalism, radical lesbianism nevertheless draws on a similar range of technologies: rhetorical texts, cultural performances, oppositional forms of erotica, and lesbian centred discourse.[11]

Within revolutionary and radical feminist thought of the 1970s and 80s, sexuality functioned as the primary site of gender oppression. '[O]nly in the system of oppression that is male supremacy does the oppressor actually invade and colonize the interior of the body of the oppressed' (Leeds Revolutionary Feminist Group 1981:5). For radical lesbians, heterosexuality's political and sexual dominance, the subjugation of lesbianism, are key elements of sexual oppression (Rich 1981). Heterosexuality is identified as maintaining women's sexual subordination, ensuring male sexual access to women, and as providing a structural and ideological means of entrenching women's domestic, economic and emotional labour (Rich 1981; Durocher 1990). Women's sexual oppression is also formed through the cultural hegemony of particular desires: phallic, violent and unequal. Radical lesbians attack these as undesirable, both in terms of their own content and as products of a patriarchal society.[12]

Sexual withdrawal combined with the construction of a woman-centred, nurturing erotica have been central components of radical lesbian strategy.

> Giving up fucking for a feminist is about taking your politics seriously
> . . . But yes, it is better to be a lesbian. The advantages include the
> pleasure of knowing that you are not directly servicing men . . . loving
> and putting your energies into those you are fighting along side rather
> than those you are fighting against.
>
> (Leeds Revolutionary Feminist Group 1981:8–9)

From its arrival in the 1970s, however, radical lesbian politics encountered enormous criticism. Dismissed as romanticist and utopian (Weeks
1985:204; Seidman 1992:6), it was considered insulting to heterosexual
women, 'desexualizing' (Campbell 1987:36), reductionist (Hunt, M.
1990:37), as well as racist and classist in its assumptions that women both
could and should align themselves with women rather than with men of
their economic or racial community. Criticism of radical lesbianism has
been trenchant and thorough, and to varying degrees radical lesbians have
responded. I do not wish to focus on these debates here; my concern is
rather to continue to explore the possibility of constructing new forms of
sexuality and the difficulties this entails.

During the late 1970s and early 1980s in Britain, many feminists began
the process of redefining their sexuality and revising their sexual practices.
Some left men, began relationships with women, or simply ceased penetrative sex while remaining within heterosexuality. For many lesbian feminists,
these changes seemed the start of a sexual revolution. Yet by the mid-1980s
they had begun to die out. Lesbians 'went straight'; heterosexual feminists
asserted the pleasures of penetrative sex, and many feminist-identified lesbians publicly and vociferously denounced the 'vanilla' discourse of waves,
mountains and sandy beaches, choosing instead a language of danger: fuck-
ing, cumming, leather, and cunts (see Jeffreys 1990:305–8, 1994:30; Stein
1993:15).

In identifying this trend away from radical lesbianism, it is important not
to overstate the shift that occurred. Whilst the public, feminist, sexual imagery of the 1970s had all but disappeared a decade later, many lesbians
continued to *publicly* advocate the *eroticization* of nurturance, gentleness
and equality. Heterosexual women continued to leave male partners for
women and to refigure their sexual practices away from a penetrative,
phallocentric desire. Nevertheless, the revolution many lesbian feminists
wished for never arrived. Whilst there are many reasons and explanations for
this failure, one must be the perceived stubbornness of erotic desire,
epitomized in the comment of more than the odd heterosexual feminist,
who has 'often wished that [she] could love women erotically' (Kitzinger
and Wilkinson 1993:14).

Such failed aspirational statements can be interpreted in several ways:
with cynicism, questioning the commitment of the speaker – 'if she had

really tried . . '; as reflecting the biological or physical innateness of our sexual orientation – something beyond our choosing; or just simply as evidence that refiguring desire is a much harder project than many feminists ever imagined – 'as if a political critique could effectively undo the cultural construction of the feminist critic's sexuality' (Butler 1990:30, see also 1993b:94).

The belief that women could transform their sexual desires was in many ways a contradictory one, in tension with other radical lesbian tenets (Miriam 1993:41). On the one hand, radical lesbianism tended to identify sexual desires as socially and systemically constructed, as emerging within and constituted by the society of which they were part. At the same time, the possibility of sexual change was predicated on individual effort to 'unlearn' one's current libido and replace it with something more eth(n)ically feminist. Although such effort could take place collectively through consciousness raising and lesbian support groups, the assumption was that sexual desire could be changed through individual willpower alone. For some women this did prove possible. However, for heterosexuality and 'patriarchal' desires to be more emphatically repudiated, the social relations and practices that inform their construction also require attention (Rian 1982:46–47; Miriam 1993:40).

In exploring the roots of patriarchal desires, in particular eroticization of inequality and dominance, radical and revolutionary feminists have tended to focus on the pervasive influence of heterosexuality. Sexuality, they argue, is specifically constructed around a dominance/submission dichotomy, thus it is these things which are eroticized (Rich 1981:15; Wagner 1982; Jeffreys 1990:206). Yet this fails to explain why many lesbians can disentangle themselves from heterosexuality but not from erotic inequality (see Kitzinger and Wilkinson 1993:18; Kitzinger 1994). Why is the latter's grip sometimes so much more impervious than the former's? While the sexual desire for power differentials between lesbians can theoretically still be explained by patriarchal heterosexuality, the ubiquitous nature of this desire suggests the need for a broader explanation. If sexuality is shaped by organizing frameworks other than gender, the eroticization of dominance/ submission may similarly be produced through a range of different processes and relations.

Transforming sexual disciplinary power

I wish to explore the sexual problematic of eroticized inequality by means of the paradigm of disciplinary power. Disciplinary power, as I discussed in Chapter 2, describes institutional and social structures which organize the physical and temporal space of our bodies through a process of corporeal, rather than ideological, internalization. Disciplinary power is a useful concept because it decentres agency to focus instead on the impact of particular practices and spatial arrangements, for instance, the layout of the school, factory and prison, on the way people move, act and think. This notion of discipline can also be applied to the sexual – to conceive of it as a form of power which generates effects on our bodies, libido, and actions.

> [T]he normalizing social technologies of sex produce a material practice of heterosexuality in which women are produced as subjects who are encouraged to regulate our own behaviour in ways which comply with androcentric versions of sexuality . . . heterosexuality is assumed as a given and is 'compulsory' . . . women's sexual desire is relatively neglected . . . The practices, knowledges and strategies that reproduce this state of affairs can be thought of as 'technologies of heterosexual coercion'.
>
> (Gavey 1993:97)

Clearly, sexual disciplinary power does not take a unitary or static form, yet to the extent that we know (or know we ought to know) how to behave sexually within different orientations, our bodies, drives and behaviour are disciplined.

If the sexual is a form of disciplinary power, then it possibly takes its material and libidinal structures from other disciplinary forms. This is most apparent in the highly formalized activity of consensual sado-masochism and non-consensual ritual abuse where the eroticization of a range of disciplinary institutions and arrangements are explicitly enacted, as I discuss further below. However, even for those who do not stage their fantasies, the subject matter of the sexual draws on both the content and asymmetrical nature of disciplinings such as the prison, religious rite, or romance (itself predicated on various disciplinary, institutional frameworks, e.g. doctor/patient, manager/secretary).

Are we then stuck within existing erotic frameworks impassively awaiting the tide of history to move us forward? Do ways exist for moving towards a sexual culture that does not eroticize subordination, abuse and coercion, at the same time recognizing the complex, overdetermined character of sexual production? Let me consider three possible approaches. The first asks whether sexuality needs to retain its disciplinary character; the second interrogates the content of current disciplinary structures; while the third explores the possibilities for disrupting processes of cultural transmission and reproduction.

Arguing for a sexuality which is less regulated, controlled, and structured is not to argue for sexual pluralism. Such a pluralism may simply mean a bounded range of different disciplinary frameworks. Rather it expresses the demand for a free-flowing sexuality that constantly rejects categorization, one that uproots its basis in particular knowledges and truths.[13] According to Faith (1994:43), 'The uncategorizable is the inexplicable rebellion which cannot be normalized, routinized, classified, controlled or disciplined'.

In part, this constitutes the strategy of queer politics which contests labels and rigid identity divisions (Smyth 1992; McIntosh 1993; Seidman 1993). Although queer politics is in many ways antithetical to radical lesbianism, its attempt to free sexual politics from disciplinary rigidities may provide a means of pursuing an agenda to create less asymmetrical sexualities. Many queer activists no longer define themselves as lesbian, gay, bisexual, or even heterosexual but simply as queer (Watney 1994). Thus assumptions and expectations of what sexuality means are open to change. Given this, one might expect queer sexual practices to draw less on traditional disciplinary structures for their erotic content, finding instead more fluid, negotiable and, arguably, creative alternatives.

While queer politics has regenerated important debates about identity, as an anti-disciplinary strategy it is open to criticism (see Seidman 1993). To begin with, it is unclear whether queer politics reflects a less disciplinary politics or just the erasure of public identities based on specific, object-choice preferences. Lesbian, gay and bisexual may be out, but queer as an identity is definitely in. Helen (charles) (1993:102) explores the ways in which queer creates its own hierarchy – queer, queerer, queerest. Thus, as I discussed in relation to sex radicalism, new conventions and disciplinary practices become normalized.

Linked to the fetishization of queer as identity is the avowal of sexual pleasure from disciplinary scenarios. Queer has tended to encompass an acceptance (and in some cases affirmation) of sado-masochism and other role-playing practices, often defining these as anti-disciplinary in their trans-gression of sexual norms. Whether this is a reasonable analysis is something I return to below. However, the normative character of even queer politics suggests that discipline, rules and conventions are not as easy to avoid as is sometimes implied.

[O]ur queer spaces are precisely the same as all other socio-political spaces in that they depend on exclusions and normalizations. Our queer spaces only become bounded spaces because we, the excluded, exclude something else in turn.

(Smith 1993:25)

In her discussion, Smith then goes on to criticize 'pro-censorship' lesbian feminists for their exclusionary practices. Given her own words, however, as well as the experience of movements such as Queer, what is crucial seems less to be the existence of disciplinary norms – which may be inevitable – than their content and substance. To what extent can these latter be transformed?

Addressing this question takes us to a second possible strategy: challeng-ing the asymmetrical character of institutional structures – education, work, criminal justice, and political life – in order to transform sexual disciplinary power. If nurses/doctors, students/teachers, prisoners/guards interact according to more egalitarian norms, what effect will this have on the construction of erotica? Will desire simply shift ground to fetishize social relations that remain hierarchical or will it reconstitute itself in accordance with the newly democratized character of previously unequal relationships? In asking these questions it is important not to reduce discipline to a problem of asymmetry. Discipline highlights a range of ways in which our (sexual) behaviour is systematized and organized that go beyond issues of inequality. Many of these are learned in institutions such as the school, home and workplace. Fragmentation, disconnection, threats, competition, anxiety, all of these socially learned behaviours get played out (and sometimes eroticized) within the sexual frame.

The difficulty, however, with a strategy which focuses on transforming other disciplinary structures is that it assumes not only the political ability to achieve such change, but also that there is a direct link between the social and the sexual. While there are relationships and connections between sexuality and other disciplinary structures, these are more mediated and complex than the above analysis might suggest.

Desire and erotica also have their own historical trajectories organized in the West around principles such as risk-taking, secrecy, danger, visibility and boundaries. Likewise, certain scenarios – the school, dungeon/prison – have a history of imbrication within western erotica that cannot simply be transcribed from modern disciplinary relations. The content and inequality of organizing principles, such as gender, race, and class, also impact upon the structuring of sexual desire. This is not, however, necessarily in the straightforward way radical lesbian literature sometimes presumes. Creet (1991:31), for instance, describes how butch/butch lesbian sex is fed by images of gay male practices, while McClintock (1993b) describes the inversion that takes place in commercial heterosexual sado-masochism between upper middle-class male submissives and their predominantly working-class dominatrixes (see also McClintock 1993c).

Thus alongside the targeting of other disciplinary frameworks might go the disruption and rearticulation of current sexual knowledges. As well as highlighting unfamiliar histories predicated on oppositional sexual values (a strategy many lesbian feminists have tried to adopt), this can involve engaging with the processes by which young people's sexuality is learned – deconstructing, for instance, popular sexual imagery – and by making available other, more progressive, sexually explicit material.

In this section, I have discussed two projects for sexual change. The first argues for the release of sexual diversity from judgementalism and repression, the second for the exploration of non-phallic desires. While sexual pluralism relies on changes in civil society and the public sphere to enable diversity to flourish, radical lesbianism focuses on women's individual and collective efforts to refigure their desires. Both projects have much that is valid. However, the sex radical challenge to sexual repression fails adequately to deal with issues of unacceptable 'difference', implicitly retreating into a sexual essentialism in its unwillingness to interrogate the processes of sexual production. While radical lesbianism has been more ready to construct a direction for sexual progress, it has generally failed to develop an adequate theory of sexual transformation.

The impact of private sex on other social relations

Having discussed the impact of the social on the sexual, I now wish to turn to the political impact sexual practices can have on other social relations. My focus is sado-masochism and radical lesbianism. While both cover a range of different engagements and activities, I wish here to explore the impact dyadic sexual acts or encounters can make. Other sexual practices, such as pornography, flirting in the workplace, and public socializing, I discuss later below.

As will become apparent, the notion of sexual acts impacting on wider relations or practices is itself problematic. Indeed, few radical lesbians or sex radicals argue that dyadic sex acts alone provide a means of engineering social change. In some ways, the reductionism of this analysis functions principally as a caricature to be thrown at the other side rather than as a serious political position. However, I wish to consider the possible impact of sado-masochist and radical lesbian sex for two reasons. First, 'the sex act' operates as the paradigm of sexual practice. Second, its consideration reveals the importance of grounding sexual politics in a wider notion of sexuality.

Radical lesbianism and the power of withdrawal

> Every act of penetration for a woman is an invasion which undermines her confidence and saps her strength. For a man it is an act of power and mastery which makes him stronger, not just over one woman but over all women.
>
> (Leeds Revolutionary Feminist Group 1981:6)

Radical lesbianism, as I discussed above, embraces a number of political strategies: separatism, consciousness raising, the creation of culture and theory – all of which are intended to empower women to become autonomous of men (Frye 1983). Here, however, I wish briefly to consider that aspect of the political project which centres on transforming sexual practices on the grounds that 'private', penetrative, heterosexual intercourse supports the maintenance of current gender relations (Dworkin 1987; Jeffreys 1994:27). In intercourse, radical lesbians argue, the cultural and physical come together; it cannot therefore be experienced apart from the social meanings through which it is constituted (Kitzinger and Wilkinson 1993).

Radical lesbians utilize the imagery of manual labour, in which the body becomes both the instrument and site of physical work, to claim women should withdraw access, deploying the resources their bodies offer to empower other women instead.

> As members of the class of women . . . our sexual practice can there-
> fore have but two meanings politically: either it constitutes the con-
> scious or unconscious reproduction of the sex classes or of
> heterosexual ideology, or else it constitutes a break from heterosociety
> and its ideology.
>
> (Durocher 1990:14)

For some women, conscious sexual withdrawal from men has proven an empowering experience. Radical lesbianism's ability to politicize feelings of emotional/sexual unfulfilment or demeanment give a discursive legitimacy (albeit marginal) to such choices, as well as providing a context within which they can be made. However, as a wider political strategy, the sex reductionist approach – drawing 'on a vocabulary of visceral colonialism' (Campbell 1987:37) – has problems. First, its focus on withdrawal or strike action as the key sexual tactic replicates many of the difficulties experienced by other workers, particularly those in the position of sole employee. Despite a collective discourse of action, individuated workers tend to find it hard ideologically, emotionally and politically to rebel, while their isolated position renders their labour easy to replace.

Second, even if women's sexual activity is reduced to labour power – a description many would reject – identifying withdrawal as the only possible strategy misses a range of other 'industrial' possibilities: negotiation, 'profit-sharing', non-compliance, work-to-rule. While withdrawal may be appropriate for some women in certain contexts, for others, disruptive or transformative strategies may better take other forms. By dismissing the validity of these, radical lesbianism becomes a highly élitist strategy since participation depends on specific forms of action however locally inappropriate.

Yet there is a further problem from centring sex within women's oppression: the implication that sex or the body in turn provide women's main political resource. That is, if women wish to challenge patriarchal power, they must do so using their sexual labour power. Not only is such a reinforcement of traditional perceptions potentially disempowering, it also ignores the range of other resources deployed by women in struggles that do not originate within, or focus on, the 'private' sexual terrain.

Finally, the emphasis on private, dyadic sexual relations is in danger of neglecting sexuality's imbrication within wider social relations: for instance, the ways in which paid women workers are expected to interact heterosexually with employers and clients (Adkins 1992), whatever their 'private' sexuality. Thus choosing to avoid intercourse with a male partner, even leaving him for a woman, will not protect women from a wider heterosexuality. As I argue in the conclusion, these sexualized relations provide an important site for collective struggle, a site that is missed through too heightened a focus on who individuals are 'sleeping' with.

Having made these criticisms, however – criticisms which have been thrown repeatedly at radical lesbians by opponents – it is important to recognize that few proponents of radical lesbianism focus exclusively on the dyadic sexual act. As Durocher (1990) and others argue, male power and sexual identity cannot be reduced to private penetration. Not only is male power generated elsewhere, but heterosexuality is affirmed and organized in ways irreducible to intercourse (Rich 1981). While lesbianism may be threatening to men, the threat posed is at the level of social relations rather than sexual practices (Durocher 1990:16). Many men can quite happily observe lesbian sexual activity; what they are more likely to fear or distrust is the challenge to gender's wider organizing principles, of which male heterosexual access is only one part.

Sado-masochism as disciplinary challenge

Alongside pornography, sado-masochism, since the late 1970s, has found itself at the centre of lesbian sexual battles most particularly in Britain, northern Europe, Canada, and the USA (see Linden *et al.* 1982; Valverde 1989; Reti 1993a). Advocates of sado-masochism, who are not all (or mostly) practitioners, have sought to justify and rationalize sado-masochism in various ways. They have argued that it is cathartic, pleasurable, consensual, safe, therapeutic, shocking and transgressive (see discussions in France 1984; Weeks 1985:238; Modleski 1991). It has also been claimed that sado-masochism explores and reconceptualizes 'internal' power (McClintock 1993b:307); thus it can prove a liberating experience for participants – the opportunity to play with and confront power's limits within a safe environment.[14]

In exploring the impact of sexual practices on wider social relations, I wish here to focus on a different justification, one that explores the ability of private sado-masochism to transform power relations beyond the individuals involved. This relies on the notion of a symbolic realm that sado-masochism can impact upon through its challenge to disciplinary relations. Such a challenge is provided principally by the masochist whose resistance is identified as an active part of the fantasy. To what extent can the masochist's performance of 'no' be seen as subversive – identifying and enacting the ruptures in asymmetrical disciplinary power?

In *Feminism Without Women*, Tania Modleski (1991:155) argues that in lesbian sado-masochism what is being mocked and beaten out of women is the law of gender in its patriarchal form.[15] The masochist sees herself both as the subject of subordination and humiliation, but also as separate from it. Modleski (1991:157) discusses the tension she identifies within lesbian sado-masochism, where existing gender arrangements are simultaneously contested and preserved – preserved partly in order to be recontested.

In this chapter, I have argued against reducing disciplinary relations to those of gender. We might therefore see the tension performed within lesbian sado-masochism as not simply that of gender, but of obedience and disobedience to disciplinary relations more generally. At the level of the symbolic, the masochist's disobedience reveals the ruptures within regulatory regimes, the points of challenge within the domain of prison, school or rape. Through her resistance, scripts are re-enacted with the rules and injunctions externalized. The gaze of the disciplinary 'other', extricated from inside the body of the masochist, is placed back on the outside. There it forms a terrain of contestation and challenge.

This radical replay provides sado-masochism with a form of validation as a social change strategy. '[W]ith its exaggerated emphasis on costume and scene S/M performs social power as *scripted,* and hence as permanently subject to change' (McClintock 1993b:208). In this way, private sado-masochistic 'performances' can be identified as contesting status quo disciplinary relations. Yet how radical is such a strategy? As Modleski (1991:158) suggests, the *sexual* charge gained from sado-masochistic dynamics undermines any attempt to dissolve or fundamentally contest the relations symbolically enacted. In addition, although domination may be challenged, disobeyed and feared, in sado-masochist scenarios (at least as presented by sex radicals), the dominatrix rarely finishes by compromising. Thus the asymmetrical power of discipline is reinscribed.

This does not mean that sado-masochism is predictable. As Foucault (1988:299) suggests, both master and servant can lose if unable to meet the other's challenges. However, this defeat is more concerned with how far each party will go than with the content of the disciplinary narrative being staged.

Sado-masochism suffers from both being and not being a performance. As a private enactment, it is unclear what direct impact it can have on wider cultural meanings. Even if two individuals *do* disrupt disciplinary power in their bedroom, how do such meanings filter through to a wider public or cultural realm? At the same time, sado-masochist acts are more material and interactive than solo fantasy (Jonel 1982:19). Not only can roles seep beyond the dyadic act, but even private sexual interactions require forms of social and community support. Sado-masochism has generated an import-ant market in the commercialized production of sex aids as well as impact-ing upon the (re)structuring of lesbian and gay social space. It is questionable whether this public face challenges or even interrogates domi-nant disciplinary forms (except to the extent it brings into the public realm sexual practices that are supposed to remain socially invisible). Whatever disruptions may occur among those involved in individualized sexual prac-tices, the public face of sado-masochism is that of a disciplinary, sys-tematized, highly regulated sexual form.

Yet to criticize sado-masochism for failing to achieve the political ambi-tions bestowed upon it by certain advocates is to distort the meanings sado-masochism carries for most participants. As Gayle Rubin (1989:279), a sado-masochist proponent, states: sexual acts have become 'burdened with an excess of significance' (see also Cocks 1989:172–3). For many particip-ants, the purpose of sado-masochism is not social transformation but heightened sexual pleasure. Although it has been certain sex radicals who have sought to justify sado-masochism as a political strategy, Rubin (1989:212) blames radical lesbianism for this trend which suggests women's lust has to be ideologically justified.

In this section, I have explored two strategies for impacting upon wider social relations through (principally) domestic sexual practices. I have ar-gued that both radical lesbianism and sado-masochism, when reduced to specific sexual acts, do not have a substantial impact on other social prac-tices or relations. This is not to suggest that sexuality is epiphenomenal. 'Private', *dyadic* sexual engagements occur in a broad range of contexts, for example, the workplace, school, trade union and church.[16] Not only do they highlight other aspects of power within which they are embedded, such as relations of gender, class and race, but they also crucially affect the quality of life for participants as well as for other people within their ter-rains. Sexual practices within the home, for instance, help shape the charac-ter and meaning of homelife. Similarly, 'private' sex in the toilet cubicles, alley ways and parks plays a part in the complex constitution of these sites. The issue then is not to deny these meanings or the impact the changing character of sex might have, but rather to relinquish the temptation to validate sex acts such as lesbianism or sado-masochism through grand stra-tegic rationalizations they cannot carry.

Performing sexual identity in public

For many sexual strategies which aim to contest wider social relations, *public* expression has become the *sine qua non* of success.[17] In this section, I wish to focus on two such strategies: transgression and the refigured phallus. Both are closely aligned with sex radical and queer politics. Taking the body, publicly marked as different, as their principal form of power, these strategies centre on the enactment of 'perversity': butch–femme, drag, camp, leathermen, public sado-masochism and 'packing' (women strapping on dildoes). In this way, they differ from the strategies discussed above which target their 'own' community as the site of activism. Central to transgression is their situation within a wider realm, in particular that of the dominant 'other'.

The politics of transgression

Transgressive strategy is rooted in a framework which perceives the status quo as governed and protected by formal and informal laws. '[W]hat is implied is a flouting of the rules, or a rule, behaviour antagonistic to what is established, the opposite, a radical challenge to what is prescribed' (Wilson 1993:109). Breaking norms and rules is intended to undermine the status quo whose perpetuation is perceived as reliant on laws being upheld. Yet as well as aspiring to be disruptive, transgression is also erotic (Creet 1991:146). The desire of the sexual outlaw is constituted through being bad, through shocking people by the rejection or contestation of current social conventions.

Within modern lesbian politics, transgression has been given a further twist. It is not now the law of the father that is to be breached, but that of the mother – or sister (Miriam 1993:11, 66; Stein 1993:19). Faderman (1993:334) discusses the recent popularization of butch–femme, in the context of a lesbian, anti-feminist backlash, as a desire to contest hegemonic community norms. Creet makes a similar point in relation to lesbian sado-masochism:

> Perhaps the most striking feature of lesbian s/m writing, and of writing on lesbian s/m, is that it is less a conscious transgression of the law of the Father . . . than a transgression against the feminist Mother . . . it is the symbolic Mother vested in feminism that functions as the repressive force acting in the lesbian s/m fantasy.
>
> (Creet 1991:145)

While lesbian transgression frequently involves the breach of feminist conventions, few transgressive representations – lesbian pornography, for example – choose to deploy good feminist/bad feminist as sexual material. Thus the symbolic relation to the law of the mother does not itself provide the erotic material of transgression. This may be a more general point, that is, the norms transgressors wish to breach tend not themselves to be eroticized. Rather, erotic material is juxtaposed against the law. For instance, lesbian porn which depicts rape does not intend to validate rape but to challenge those 'rules' which define rape as unacceptable *erotic* material.

While transgression may seem to offer a means of denaturalizing and contesting social norms, its current fetishization within progressive lesbian and gay circles is problematic.[18] Its key limitation is an oversimplified understanding of society and of social change. To begin with it is unclear what the target of transgression actually is: specific norms or an 'uptight' society more generally? And what is supposed to occur as a result of transgression? Do people become liberated through transgressive shock? Or is the status quo simply unable to sustain itself once its norms are breached?[19]

Wilson (1993:109–110) discusses the way in which transgression becomes a 'spiral', since any successful disruption of norms simply sets up new norms to be transgressed. In this way it produces an incremental process of reform, constantly constructing new boundaries of acceptable behaviour. To identify this as progressive depends not only on the presumption that transgressions are successful, but also that the movement is in a particular direction, that it is repressive and reactionary norms which are being dismantled.

The question of success underscores the very logic of transgression – that breaching norms eventually undermines them. While this may be true in certain contexts, that of racial segregation perhaps, sexual transgressions underestimate the extent to which dominant forces can *enjoy* erotic, 'subversive' imagery (hooks 1993:71). Indeed, mainstream sexual discourse relies on the erotic appeal of the forbidden.

The incorporation of taboo sexual desires and practices also problematizes assumptions about what actually constitutes transgressive sexual acts. To argue that violent sexual depictions are transgressive suggests dominant sex entails gentleness and nurturance. While this may be a plausible representation of (dominant) feminist sexual norms, to equate such norms with those of the status quo more generally is to accept a highly romanticized version of heterosexual practices and relations. Indeed lesbian feminists have argued that it is *their* sexual practices and interactions which are truly transgressive, since they oppose gendered, dominant sexual norms.

Yet does the *existence* of non-conformity always identify radical activity? In their focus on transgression, radical theorists can neglect to consider the character of the values, principles and rules being contested. While norms may be the effects of power, that is, they are generated by particular power-technologies, deploying a polysemic paradigm of power means not all norms can be assumed to be inherently problematic. To consider all rules, conventions and injunctions as 'the enemy' is to identify current social relations as entirely constructed in the interests of dominant forces. If, however, one takes a more mediated view, and recognizes that gains have been made by subjugated communities, some norms may reflect these gains. There is an argument then for considering ways of supporting such norms – recognizing our own participation and investment in them – rather than simply engaging in a process of sabotage.

Most advocates of transgression do not propose the contestation of all norms. Nevertheless, it is often unclear on what basis decisions are made as to which norms should or should not be transgressed. Many norms are complex, giving out contradictory messages. For instance, public proscriptions of paedophilia go alongside the mainstream eroticization of childhood and of prepubescent female characteristics in adult women, as well as the social disempowerment of children. To focus therefore simply on transgressing anti-paedophile injunctions misses the sophisticated ways in which cultural discourses operate. Indeed, it might make as much – if not more – sense to transgress the eroticized infantalization of women. While some lesbian pornography does, in fact, challenge such representations, the notion of transgression is itself less comfortable in a project which aims to respond to productive rather than repressive forms of power. How do you transgress facilitative power-technologies?

A more complex version of transgression, which goes beyond the violation of particular norms, involves the inhabiting of a circumscribed terrain, such as the feminine, and then attempting to extend, explore and contest its space. Flannigan-Saint-Aubin (1993:400) advocates this approach (see also Champagne 1993:124–5). He argues that transgression begins not by rupturing but by inhabiting a racially and sexually fetishized realm, exploring one's relationship to it. Butler makes a similar point.

> Where the uniformity of the subject is expected, where the behavioral conformity of the subject is demanded, there might be produced the refusal of the law in the form of the parodic inhabiting of conformity that subtly calls into question the legitimacy of the command, a repetition of the law into hyperbole, a rearticulation of the law against the authority of the one who delivers it.
>
> (Butler 1993a:122)

This approach has been recently developed in what one might call 'phallic studies'. Writers in this field criticize lesbian feminist attempts to reject phallic signifiers, arguing its current impossibility since the phallus provides the central signifier – 'that which controls the field of signification' (Butler 1993a:136) – in relations of gender and sexuality. In this final section, I wish to explore the recirculating phallus as a sexual strategy for the displacement of current gender relations.

The recirculating phallus

> [A]ccording to proponents of drag . . . because sexuality, like gender, is organized around the phallus in our culture, there can be no escaping phallic effects, no 'authentic' non-phallic desires or identities which would originate beyond (or perhaps before) the phallus and its signifiers.
>
> (Tyler 1991:32–33)

Since, it is argued, signifying or representational systems are relatively closed, 'no radical repudiation of a culturally constructed sexuality' is possible (Butler 1990:31). As a result, using their bodies and texts to disrupt conventional discursive and disciplinary relations, lesbian and gay writers and performers have explored the possibilities for doing 'the construction one is . . . in' (Butler 1990:31).

> [T]o operate within the matrix of power is not the same as to replicate uncritically relations of domination. It offers the possibility of a replacement of the law which is not its consolidation, but its displacement . . . we might develop a notion of sexuality constructed in terms of phallic relations of power that replay and redistribute the possibilities of that phallicism.
>
> (Butler 1990:30)

What does it mean to 'replay and redistribute the possibilities of the phallus'? Butler (1990) focuses on the potentiality of butch, femme and drag as ways of displacing the present law's assumptions of a unitary relationship between sex, gender and orientation (see also Faderman 1993; Morgan 1993). Similarly, Bensinger (1992:83–84) argues that lesbian porn is effective in generating the appropriation, displacement and reordering of the phallic economy of desire in ways that denaturalize the 'illusion' of an inherent heterosexuality. Biddy Martin spells out the issue:

> Lesbians' ongoing sexual, textual and theoretical explorations suggest that there might be something to gain again from prying 'the phallic' loose from its identification with men.
>
> (Martin 1992:101)

Within western culture, the phallus has traditionally represented masculinity, authority, presence and inclusion.[20] Against this woman is equated with absence and lack. Thus reclaiming the phallus, prying it from its penile anchors, is perceived as a way of empowering women. Faderman (1993) describes, for instance, how the 'butch' lesbian – the one with the phallus – challenges male authority by adopting a space not similarly available to her femme partner. If the phallus can only take shape as a penis, then only men can ever possess it. But if the penis is simply one phallus among many (Reich (1992:125), women's attempts to appropriate it cannot be rejected as parody or copy, for there is no original (Butler 1993a:89).

The notion of the phallus does not just symbolize masculine authority, it also signifies desire.[21] Thus lesbian desire involves the phallus too, whether materially as dildo or abstractly as the gazer rather than the gazed. Since it is argued that lesbian dildoes are not second-rate penises but phallic signifiers in their own right, enjoying dildoes as sexual accessories does not represent the perpetuation of male or heterosexual power

(Butler 1993a:Ch.2). Women have as much right to possess them as men. In addition, their appropriation by women not only denaturalizes the equation of penis and phallus but as well makes available physical and psychological sexual pleasures through women's capacity to act rather than simply be acted upon.

Yet to what extent can the phallus be disentangled from the penis's construction as the icon of (masculine) power and desire? It is not by chance that the phallus looks like a penis; indeed, I would argue the phallus operates metonymically, essentializing the penis's signification of masculinity and male power. While hegemonic ideology may operate through the 'naturalization of an exclusionary heterosexual morphology' (Butler 1993a:91), I remain unconvinced that lesbian phalluses will disrupt the male monopoly. For not only does hegemony operate through exclusion, but also by making visible failed attempts to attain the status of the real.

However, leaving that to one side, if we *can* disarticulate the penis–phallus nexus, the strategy of phallic recirculation becomes a means of separating out gender, sex and orientation. A woman can wield a phallus and she can wield it in relation to both men and women. But how radical is this project? Does it just create greater fluidity between gender roles whilst still maintaining the roles themselves? That is, anyone can be a woman, i.e. lack a phallus. As Reich (1992:125) argues, once woman as symbol and construction no longer equals female, the economy of desire for the 'other' does not have to follow a heterosexist matrix. While it is possible that such fluidity between gender, sex and orientation may impact radically upon the roles themselves, it is not clear that this is the aim of the writers. Rather, they tend to emphasize the erotic nature of rescrambling conventional sex-gender-orientation relations (see Creet 1991:33; Faderman 1993), of playing the game: guess who's got Phallus.

What are the implications for relations of race and class within this politics? If there is only a single phallus, how can it be redistributed in ways that contest differing forms of inequality? The tension can be seen in gay and lesbian pornography. While some simply replicates traditional racialized and class-based images (hooks 1993:78), other work has tried to provide new articulations. However, so long as there remains only a single signifier of authority, race and class positions may just get reallocated rather than transformed.

Yet the notion that anyone can be socially positioned as black, just as anyone can be 'woman' reveals some of the limitations of a cultural politics of phallic performance. This metaphor of performance, deployed by a number of writers in lesbian and gay studies, creates the danger of false possibilities and boundaries. It suggests that within the limited roles available, we have the necessary agency to choose which to adopt – all of us can play King Lear or, for that matter, Othello.[22] However, there is only the one play, since the stage is too small to perform a different coterminous script, thus, we cannot go outside existing roles and discourses.

Just as revolutionary feminism is limited by its metaphor of colonization which essentializes women's experience to that of a third world country, so notions of performance, while they highlight the socially constructed, repetitive imperative of social life, at the same time distort other practices and relations. Switching roles, even if desirable, is not that easily achievable. A butch lesbian will still be treated in many contexts as a woman, and the racial refiguring of some erotica does not of itself rearticulate race relations in other domains. While few queer theorists make such grand transformative claims,[23] the privileging of cultural texts and performance metaphors create a context within which the specific relationship between cultural and other political practices remains undeveloped.

One exception to this omission is the deployment of cultural performances within political activism (Watney 1990). The activity of the British organization, Outrage, and the work of ACT UP and Queer Nation with their kiss-ins, wed-ins, and direct actions in unlikely places, have utilized public transgressions and recirculating phallic positions within a context of making political and social demands (Butler 1990:233; Smyth 1992:17; Smith 1993). In doing so they have constructed an arena within which different people can participate, for taking part does not depend on adopting a narrow range of sexual desires, practices or identities. In particular, they are open to heterosexual men and women, which may in part explain their current popularity within mainstream, alternative culture.[24]

However, the potential radicalism of method may not be reflected in the substantive politics of these strategies. Organizations such as Outrage, for instance, despite their innovative and extrovert tactics have tended to focus on reform-based demands, the right to marriage, age of consent, etc. Similarly, activism around lesbian pornography has affirmed rather than contested the sexualization of power differentials (Smith 1993). As with socially transgressive strategies, these political challenges to wider society have tended to be grounded in its characterization as puritan, anti-sex and uptight. This has then provided the main target for attack rather than other more subtle or complex features.

Conclusion

In this chapter I have explored a range of strategies that draw on the social to change the sexual, and vice versa. In examining these different approaches, I have used the paradigm of power developed in Chapter 2 to show how resources such as the body and oppositional cultural discourses can be deployed to contest dominant sex/gender ideologies and disciplinary relations in arenas that range from the bedroom to community and public spaces.

In exploring different sexual projects, my analysis has focused on the overdetermined character of social and sexual relationships and the implications this has for change. The ways in which social life shapes sexual desires, identity and practices has often been underestimated, or given too voluntaristic an interpretation; this latter is evident in radical lesbian formulations which tend to assume women can change their sexuality through the power of individual or collective will. In contrast, the social structuralism of certain radical pluralist interventions reduces sexuality to a non-normative effect. Struggle thus becomes limited to validating socially despised sexualities in ways that distance sexuality from political critique.

In terms of the reverse relationship – the impact of the sexual on society – radical pluralists and sex radicals have taken a range of positions. Many have rejected what they see as the overwhelming determinism of radical lesbianism and the Christian Right, to argue that sexuality is principally epiphenomenal. Others claim that while dyadic sex acts may make little difference, public transgressive practices – butch–femme, drag, sado-masochism – rupture or challenge broader social relations. Yet the focus tends to be on sexuality as a discrete social practice or relationship rather than on the ways in which institutionalized terrains such as the criminal justice process, welfare provision and education are themselves sexualized.

Yet focusing on the ways in which public terrains are sexualized provides a means of involving people who see prefigurative, private sexual transformations or the proliferation of sexual alternatives as irrelevant. Most of the strategies described in this chapter engage a narrow range of people, principally, young, middle-class, white lesbians and gay men within a limited range of sociopolitical and cultural arenas. They are strategies which focus on the power of sex and bodies as a means of engineering change, whether the change is the freeing of the sexual or disturbing conventional gender relations. Despite the apparent availability of such bodily resources, however, in practice accessibility is skewed. The apparent democracy of a bodily politics ignores the range of factors which make it difficult or impossible for many people to participate.

This is not an argument for rejecting such political strategies. They are crucial in offering different narratives, other ways of living; however, alone they only provide a partial picture of an oppositional sexual project. The focus on what people do in bed and with whom reinforces the notion of sexuality as private, distanced from institutional civil and social relations. Public enactments of drag, sado-masochism, leather and dildoes can also separate sexual issues from wider social relations, maintaining the notion that sexuality is a minority issue.

In the chapter that follows, I explore the institutionalization of sexual politics by examining the relationship between sexuality and the state. Conceptualizing the state as the articulation of overlapping identity discourses, I examine the ways in which it provides both an opposing agency and structured terrain of power for sexual struggles. I also consider how the state's engagement with sexual demands and agendas is itself shaped by the sexualization of state identity.

Notes

1 I incorporate in my discussion of radical lesbianism a range of different positions: revolutionary lesbianism, political lesbianism, revolutionary feminism and radical feminism. Different women define themselves in different ways. However, since there are no systematically applied categories, and since some women specifically reject the label of feminist (e.g. Durocher 1990), I have chosen radical lesbianism as an umbrella term. This does not mean that all the work discussed here is carried out by self-identified lesbians.

2 By prefigurative, I mean developing a sexuality which both aims to reflect the sexuality of a more egalitarian society, and which, by aspiring to it, helps to constitute such a society. For some of the problems with prefiguration as a concept and political project, see Chapter 7.

3 This is not to suggest that such a project is non-political, but rather to highlight some of the hostility expressed towards what is seen as a normative sexual politics.

4 Whether there are boundaries or limits to 'benign sexual variation' is treated by different writers in different ways.

5 See the interest by queer theorists and writers in the performances of Madonna and Annie Sprinkle (Bright 1993; Champagne 1993; Henderson 1993; Straayer 1993), also the discussion generated by the photographic exhibition, 'drawing the line' held in Vancouver, 1990.

6 Sex radicalism and radical pluralism overlap and many writers and activists define their work under both labels. However, radical pluralism is more concerned with the affirmation and protection of difference, while sex radicalism focuses on the validation of 'transgressive' sexualities. The question of transgression is explored in more depth later in this chapter.

7 The emphasis on pleasure, initiation and the notion of techniques handed down from experienced sex practitioner to newcomer within the sado-masochist community parallels the historic conception of *ars erotica* explored by Foucault (1981:57; see also Dreyfus and Rabinow 1982:176), although there are also some interesting differences.

8 This does not mean that active/passive distinctions are necessarily problematic; rather, my concern is with sexual interactions and practices that require control, abuse, violence or domination for their eroticization.

9 Sex radicals and radical pluralists might well argue that minority sexualities do not simply reflect dominant social relations but contest or reinflect them. Thus

just because sexuality is socially constructed does not mean it is necessarily reactionary. Acknowledging this, however, concedes the political role sexuality plays. It therefore provides a space for questions about the kinds of sexuality that contest the status quo and how they might be generated.

10 For a more philosophical rejection, see Golding (1993).

11 Though see Jeffreys (1994:Ch. 7), where she argues that modern lesbian practice is based on the emulation of gay male sexual and cultural paradigms. It is also possible that radical lesbianism places greater emphasis on collective forms of action. However, although sex radicalism at an ideological level seems more concerned with individual self-discovery, its practices also involve collective change, for example, sado-masochist workshops and groups, meetings on sexual practice, sexual performances, etc.

12 Critiques of radical lesbianism tend to reduce the latter's opposition to violent, unequal sex to its opposition to patriarchy. However, while many radical lesbians identify patriarchy as the origin of such sexual ideologies, their objections go also to the values perceived as inherent within eroticized domination.

13 Some have conceptualized bisexuality in this way. Clausen describes it as an anti-identity, 'a refusal . . . to be limited to one object of desire' (Clausen 1990, quoted in Seidman 1993:122).

14 For critiques of sado-masochism, see Linden *et al.* (1982) and Reti (1993a).

15 See also McClintock (1993b:224) who argues that sado-masochism is less a violation of the flesh than of selfhood.

16 By 'private', I mean those interactions which do not aim to involve other people.

17 By public, in this context, I refer to practices intended to be noticed by others or zones where others are expected to be present. However, this does not necessarily mean realms or practices open to all. For instance, it may include lesbian pornography magazines, film shows, a gay bar or community centre, a queer demonstration on a city street, as well as enactments or simply a presence within more general public spaces such as shopping centres and public transport. Thanks to Carl Stychin for raising this point.

18 Wilson (1993) provides a very useful analysis of some of the limitations of a transgressive politics.

19 Wilson (1993:109) argues that in fact transgression re-establishes the norms it sets out to breach. '[J]ust as the only true blasphemer is the individual who really believes in God, so transgression depends on, and may even reinforce conventional understandings of what it is that is to be transgressed'.

20 One difficulty with many of these arguments is that phallic discourse has shifted from its term of art usage within French psychoanalytical theory. Thus, specific 'phallogocentric' terms of art are given everyday usages which may distort some of their meanings. However, because such terms are now used within this wider context, I wish to consider the implications of feminist phallic discourse severed, if not freed, from its Lacanian roots. For a useful explanation of the phallic signifier within Lacanian theory, see McClintock (1993a:9–12). See also Butler (1993a:Ch. 2).

21 See critique of this perspective by McClintock (1993a).

22 Zita (1992) explores an interesting variant in the notion of a male lesbian – a man who thinks and feels that he is a lesbian. But is this an example of sex-

gender fluidity or the replaying of essentialist sex-gender constructs: that is, a lesbian trapped within a man's body?

23 Butler however makes clear that she is not suggesting this degree of fluidity in her conceptualization of performativity which she distinguishes from the notion of performance (1993b:21–22, 24).

24 For example, see coverage in the predominantly heterosexual, progressive magazine, *Body Politics?* However Maggenti *et al.* (1991) in the magazine *Outlook* question the inclusivity of queer politics. The group Outrage in Britain has also come under attack for its lack of sensitivity to minority ethnic communities in the form some of its actions have taken.

4

Multiple identities: Sexuality and the state in struggle

Introduction

Sexual struggles have taken shape both against and within western and other states. Yet the ability to successfully challenge the state and to deploy it oppositionally, have been constrained by the ways in which the state itself is sexualized. Sexuality as a technology of power shapes state form and practice, and lies embedded within its structures.

In Chapter 3, I discussed the relationship between sexuality and social struggle. I explored the different sites and forms of power deployed by activists within a politics ranging from radical lesbianism through to sex radicalism. I argued that one of the limitations of many of these struggles was their emphasis on dyadic sexual relations and practices rather than engaging with the sexualization of social life more generally. Since the late 1970s, feminist and gay writers in particular have begun to explore sexuality's constitutive role in other social relationships, and in the structuring of other sites and institutions (Enloe 1988; Pringle 1988; Moran 1991; Adkins 1992).

In relation to the state, however, sexual disciplinary power does not operate as a coherent, organizing force shaping social structures according to its own immanent principles. Rather, its impact is mediated by the struggles of social forces attempting to redefine and negotiate its effects. The character of state power is also a determining factor. The state does not simply respond to discourses, it also re-forms them, as I discuss later in the context of lesbian and gay municipal activism (see Chapter 6).

In exploring the interaction between sexuality and the state, I also examine sexual communities' deployment of political and state power. Here too, it is important to consider the intersection of community resources and state power. While communities may deploy resources in order to win access to or re-form state power, state concerns are often different. Thus the state's engagement with community resources may reflect a desire to keep such forces at a distance, to distract or, alternatively, to co-opt them.

Yet, this kind of state talk raises complex ontological questions. Does the state have particular interests or agendas? Does it possess agency? More fundamentally, what do we even mean by the state? I begin with a discussion of these questions, then go on to explore attempts by lesbian and gay forces to resist, deploy and refigure state power. The final part of the chapter examines the sexualization of the state and the implications this has for progressive sexual struggles.

State identity

Competing conceptualizations

For many lesbian and gay political communities, the state's identity is two-fold. On the one hand, it resembles a coherent actor purposefully carrying out objectives and policies; at the same time, it appears a schismatic terrain across which forces struggle for hegemony and control. Can the state be both things at once? In addressing this question, I begin by considering some of the different ways in which the state has been conceptualized.

In their identification of the state, writers have focused on questions of space, function, role, effects, and control, articulating these together in different ways.[1] For instance, Weber (1946:83) brings together spatial, institutional and role-based characteristics in describing the state as a comprehensive organization which seeks to monopolize the legitimate use of physical force within a territory. Burstyn (1983:46), on the other hand, constructs a different articulation when she claims that the state schematizes a system of relations, structures, institutions and forces which are vast, complex, differentiated, and at times contradictory.

Some writers in this field have contested the conceptual value of the state altogether. In her contribution to *Playing the State*, Judith Allen (1990) questions whether feminists need a theory of the state. Her argument is that the state provides too totalizing a framework which ignores the specificity of particular state practices. She (1990:30–34) argues instead for 'nuanced, historical and sexually specified theoretical categories' such as the police, misogyny and legal culture.

Yet while it might often be useful to explore specific governmental practices, the concept of the state still has a role to play. In *The Female Body and the Law*, Zillah Eisenstein (1988:18) argues that emphasizing fragmentation privileges diversity, discontent and difference, silencing unity, continuity and similarity. In contrast, utilizing a state paradigm draws attention to linkages and connections – for instance, the specific inscription of race, class and gender principles – that can be missed with a more dispersed model. Through the state, public bodies are articulated together in ways that may lead to an intensification of power or, alternatively, generate conflict and the subversion of particular state practices. Rayside (1992:138), for instance, discusses how police and judicial homophobia is assisted and strengthened as a result of their institutional links with legislative, penal and military power.

While the military, police force and courts may appear quintessential state bodies, how far do the boundaries of the state stretch? By what means do we decide whether particular institutions are included or excluded? To what extent is it useful to define the state primarily as a set of institutions? How does this link with other conceptualizations which take a wider or more abstract approach, for instance, defining the state as a condensation of power, contradictions and struggle; as a social relation or process; or as inclusive of civil society?

For many feminists identifying what is meant by the state has become a key theoretical problem and source of slippage. As one feminist academic said at a day's workshop on 'the state and development',[2]

> First thing in the morning, with my women and law group, I define the state one way, then differently in the afternoon when I'm teaching law and development. Sometimes I want students to see the state as a contradictory, fluid terrain, sometimes as a coercive, authoritarian apparatus.

Rather than dismissing this approach as inconsistent and, hence, as lacking rigour, I want to argue that it highlights the possibilities of a more contingent, anti-essentialist perspective on the state.

Few progressive state writers define the state in any simple way. Usually their definitions or conceptualizations articulate together a range of different dimensions. Nevertheless most focus on, or start with, a particular aspect – whether spatial, functional, or form-oriented – and then theorize outwards to encompass other elements. Yet this approach can create problems. First, it grants the state an essence – a core identity. While this may be heuristically useful, it marginalizes the complex character of different states' development which often lack a conceptual epicentre. Second, it produces a static definition that fails to embrace adequately the diverse and changing contexts within which the state has meaning.

Without essence: The state's multiple and contested identities

The framework I wish instead to utilize is based on conceiving the state as a contingently articulated, multifaceted phenomena with no fixed form, essence or core.[3] Different facets or dimensions slide over each other, linked together in ways the character of which is ever-changing. In any given context, one or more state identities will be at the fore, while the others remain in the background, still articulated to and informing state identity and practice.[4]

Connections between different state identities therefore depend on the conjunctural moment; they also depend on the discursive frame through which the state is constructed and 'read'. The condensed relationship between these two can be seen if we consider the character of the state within international relations. As Greenaway *et al.* state,

> The study of international relations or diplomacy is traditionally one which has placed great emphasis upon the interaction of sovereign states. Individual states tend to be seen as sovereign rational actors . . . At its crudest, international relations may be pictured as if states were controlled by individuals playing a board game.
>
> (Greenaway *et al.* 1992:29)

Within dominant discourse, the state that participates in international relations is a more expansive, formally coherent entity than the state of domestic politics. Government representatives and statespeople claim to act on behalf of the (nation) state, that is on behalf of a geographically bounded political realm of citizenship. This matrix of identities can be contrasted with that which predominates in circumstances of domestic disruption – when the state's riot police confront trade unionists or local communities. At the fore then, within dominant discourse, is the state's identity as an agent deploying legitimate coercion and violence on behalf of the nation. However, a more oppositional reading might dispute the notion of legitimacy, emphasizing instead the nexus of class power and violence. Unions on a picket line, for instance, might be more likely to highlight the state's functional identity as representative of capitalism, while tabloid press narratives focus on democratic processes and majoritarian interests.

Does this lead, however, to an entirely 'subjective' notion of the state, that it is whatever different forces say it is? Once we move away from essentialist or fixed conceptions, questions of subjectivity and relativism raise their heads. However, I do not wish to argue that the state is simply a product of different discourses with no existence independent of the various ways in which it is ideologically conceptualized. In focusing on state identity my intention is to chart a middle course between an approach which argues that the state is a materially fixed, definable phenomenon and one advocating discursive relativism.

My starting point is the particular histories of different states. The socio-physical presence of state institutions – the discourses by which they are shaped and understood – impacts upon the possible identities a state can possess. For instance, if we identify the emergence of western, liberal capitalist states as a history of coercion, social and economic regulation and reproduction, and the organization of separate public and private spheres, it might seem absurd to describe the state as village architecture since this has no obvious connection with other state meanings or trajectories.[5]

In contrast, the state as 'democratic' resonates. This does not mean we cannot contest *whether* the state is representative, *when* it is representative (such an identity may be more at the fore at some times than others), and *who* it actually represents. Alternatively, we might argue that representation is an effect of mystificatory processes. Thus one aspect of the state's identity is its illusory *appearance* of democratic representation. This last claim highlights a key element within oppositional analysis (and far-left mobilizations) which aim to draw attention to those state identities that have been occluded by the status quo: for instance, the state's relationship to dominant class forces and the mode of production.

Describing and demarcating the state's identities becomes a highly contested process. Disputes arise over the meanings and extent of any one given identity – if the state condenses relations of power, does this include gender and race as well as class? – whether a particular description is correct – is the state the sole exerciser of legitimate coercion?[6] – and the ways in which different identities are articulated together. Through such struggles, certain definitions come to be rejected, while new ones emerge.[7]

Yet these new definitions and discourses are not simply epiphenomenal effects of changing state and societal relations. As well as providing a frame through which we can 'know' the state, they also help constitute the form and practices of the state itself, as well as its trajectory of development. This ability to proactively shape the state's identity was deployed in Britain during the late 1980s and early 1990s by the New Right who conceptualized the state as an enabler of market processes. Their success in impacting upon the state's character demonstrates the ways in which identity fuses both material and ideological elements. Conservative policies to change the nature and remit of state practice, especially at a local level, were constituted within normative discourses which stressed the state's subservience to the market. In turn, such policies helped to validate neo-conservative discourse – at least at a descriptive level – as the identity of the (local) state became transformed.

In this and the next two chapters, I focus on the following aspects of state identity, recognizing that the ways in which they are linked together is discursively and socially contingent:

1 as a set of specific, public arenas that include the courts, local and central government, military, police force, regulatory quangos and welfare providers/organizers;[8]

2 as the criteria of articulation/linkage and commonality between these arenas – constitutional, disciplinary, cultural, and resource based;
3 as a corporate entity – the nation state;
4 as a variously condensed manifestation of economic, racial and gendered power; and
5 as the key agent of 'legitimate' public coercion and violence.

These state identities are not intended as comprehensive. As with identifying the social subjectivity of people, naming a few identities, for example race, class and gender does not deny the existence of others.[9] Similarly, the existence of other identities does not invalidate the utility of exploring a few. Not only is it a matter of being selective; naming the identities of people or states reflects the concerns and knowledge at a particular juncture. We can see this in the process of 'commatization', the adding of new identities – gay, disabled, old, third world – to a growing list. New identities always arise, while those considered important change, as identities gain or lose their value.

Community engagement with the state

Boundaries and agency

Lesbian and gay engagements with the state have both been based upon and, in turn, generated particular perceptions of state agency, power,[10] and boundaries. Two types of strategy in particular stand out. The first attempts to contest state power, the second to use it. Although, as I explore below, these are not as distinct as might first appear.

In discussing the power exercised by both state and social forces, I am particularly concerned with issues of boundary and agency. If the state is a terrain of multiple identities, it will also have multiple boundaries, since each identity will have its own contested parameters.[11] State boundaries, however proliferative, fluid and contingent, are important in this discussion for two primary reasons.[12] First, where people understand the borders of the state to lie will affect the character of their own state engagement, that is, whether they perceive their location and the focus of their interest to be inside or outside of the state. Second, notions of legitimate state practice differ from conceptions of legitimate community activism. Therefore whether a site, practice or relationship is considered within or beyond the state will impact upon its discursive character and content. For instance, more radical practices may be possible if they are *considered* to be taking place outside of the state (see Chapter 6).

In relation to agency, I argue that the state both does and does not possess it. Feminist poststructuralist state theory has been concerned to stress that the state is *not* an actor, that any intentionality is to do with a group's (temporary) success in hegemonizing its claims within state arenas (Pringle and Watson 1990:229; 1992:63). However, while this appears to be the case from an 'internal' perspective (see Cooper 1993b), for many social communities, the state does seem to act according to its own particular agenda, a process facilitated by relations and linkages between public bodies.

Confusion over agency reflects once again the multiple identities at stake when the state is discussed. If the state is seen as a corporate body, then it can act through its subjecthood – the 'We' for instance of international relations (although this will be internally fractured to reflect competing needs, agendas and interests). On the other hand, as a set of arenas, the state constitutes a terrain through which other forces act, facilitating and structuring their agency in the way Pringle and Watson (1992) describe.

Contesting state power

Challenges to the authority of law, military power, government sovereignty, and ministerial policy can, theoretically, take place both from within and outside of the state. For instance, the power and legitimacy of local government policy-making can be interrogated and opposed at municipal committees as well as on marches or pickets. However, in the main, challenges to the *form* of state power or to the *character* of the state take place from what is discursively identified by forces involved as the 'outside'. Indeed activists engaged in this strategy often question the possibility of ever being anywhere else; that is, even if they attend a government meeting they are still outside the state, because the state is something by its very nature to which they cannot obtain access.

This position of external challenge to the form of state power has been modified by those forces who wish to positively *influence* its exercise. Unlike the position taken by those described above, these forces see themselves as able, albeit from 'beyond' the state, to impact on at least the content of state processes and practices. Hart (1992:122), for instance, describes the adoption of this approach by the Australian Gay and Lesbian Taskforce who placed pressure on the government to enable gay nationals to obtain immigration status for their foreign partners.

Adopting a strategy of influence is based on the implicit premise that the state is not a closed entity, motivated solely by its own agenda. The state is instead identified as a corporate body (relatively) open to a range of concerns. Reasons for such lack of closure vary. Some activists suggest it emerges out of a genuine democratic imperative; others identify in it the state's wish to maintain its hegemonic position through the incorporation of community demands and interests (e.g. see Kinsman 1992).

Struggling on the state's terrain

A belief that it is possible to influence the exercise of state power has motivated social forces to go beyond an 'external' perspective to try and enter what they perceive as the apparatus of the state itself (see Thomas 1986; Cooper 1994a). Indeed, movements which began with strategies that entailed pressurizing a coherent, voluntaristic state, for example, homosexual law reform organizations, often found what seemed a solid entity to be porous and penetrable.

Their entry in turn helped generate a new 'internal' perspective which conceived of the state not only as open to a range of 'external' agendas, but also as lacking unity and agency. Rather than being seen as an actor, the state became conceptualized as a series of sites through which different forces struggle for dominance. Thus in Canada, for example, lesbian and gay politicians, professionals and bureaucrats became involved in struggles to change government practice in the pursuit of lesbian and gay equality; statutory and constitutional enactments were also proactively utilized to challenge discrimination through the courts (Herman 1994a). While few activists considered the outcomes of governmental and litigious struggles as entirely open, effects were nevertheless perceived as contingent rather than predetermined by state agency or the instrumentalism of dominant forces.

Although some social forces have identified access to the state's terrain as a means of access to state power, the two are not necessarily equivalents. For lesbian and gay municipal actors in Britain, many felt they lacked state power despite their apparent presence within formal state structures (Cooper 1994a). Alternately, other actors have found themselves wielding state power, without considering themselves located within the state's terrain. For instance, in the development of lesbian and gay immigration procedures in Australia, the Gay and Lesbian Taskforce became the processing arm of the government's immigration department, exercising the power to make initial decisions on applicants' requests for immigration status, whilst remaining a voluntary organization (Hart 1992:125).

This relation between state power and terrain is more than an arcane concern. In a range of circumstances, social forces have been wary of gaining access to state power on the grounds that it would inevitably lead to incorporation within the state. As Femi Otitoju (1988) describes in the 'Should we, shouldn't we? debate', many London lesbian and gay groups in the early 1980s were troubled by the implications of receiving local government funds. Their anxiety reflected the tension of wishing to deploy or benefit from state power without becoming caught up in the maze of state practice. Entering the terrain of the state has tended to be identified by progressive groups as carrying with it a cost in terms of co-option, deradicalization, bureaucratism and political diversion.[13]

Gary Kinsman (1992) considers the problematic of incorporation in relation to AIDS policy development in Canada.[14] In an interesting account, he explores how the discourse of 'partnership' became the frame through which the state subcontracted work to the voluntary sector. As a result, the agendas of community based groups became reformulated (Kinsman 1992:222). Groups initially set up to empower people with AIDS (PWAs) became part of the state regulatory process, and activists who lacked appropriate credentials became marginalized as professional discourses took on increasing authority within the voluntary sector (Kinsman 1992:224–5).[15]

At the same time, as Kinsman indicates, it is important not to overstate the degree of incorporation. In the case of Canadian AIDS policy development, voluntary groups retained some autonomy, while at the same time extracting concessions from the state. Thus to the extent that the state does co-opt community groups onto its terrain, the character of the terrain may change in the process.[16] In addition, as the experience of municipally funded groups in Britain during the 1980s demonstrates, community projects found ways of avoiding incorporation and of maintaining their autonomy. Often this was by formally complying with state requirements, whilst surreptitiously maintaining their own agendas. On certain occasions this led to tensions and conflicts (as I witnessed when chairing Haringey Council's community development panel) between the uses to which groups covertly put their funds and the demands/constraints imposed by the local authority.

In this section, I have explored some of the ways in which sexual forces have engaged with the state – from external challenges through to attempts to deploy state power. As I have argued, community perceptions of state identity impacted upon the nature of political strategy: whether the state was an actor to be resisted or a terrain on which to enter. Yet as I have tried to outline, relationships between state identity, power and community activism proved too fluid to be conclusively defined. While many groups perceived themselves as remaining separate from the state, their nexus to state power and control became an intimate one. Does it make sense in such a context to say these groups existed beyond the state's boundaries?

Utilizing the paradigm developed above, one approach is to suggest that while such organizations tried to maintain a distance or separation from certain aspects of state identity – representative of élite interests, legitimizer of the status quo, reproducer of social/sexual inequality – they linked themselves to others – democratic, public funder, policymaking power. The tensions between these competing representations offered a site for progressive activism. First, how could the state be made to perform and hegemonize those identities which appeared most facilitative of a progressive politics – in other words, those identities to which organizations tried to align themselves? Second, to the extent this latter proved impossible, how could groups ensure *their* construction/interpretation of the points of alignment and distancing prevailed, so that they would not be seen as becoming co-opted or legitimizing the status quo? In Chapters 5 and 6, I explore this complexity in more detail through two case studies. Now, however, I wish to turn to another aspect of the state/sexuality nexus: the ways in which sexuality impacts upon state form. My argument is that the specific sexualization of state form, practice and culture constrained the capacity of lesbian and gay forces to deploy state power in progressive, oppositional ways.

Sexualizing the state

Sexuality as disciplinary power

In this discussion, I am concerned with two particular phenomena: first, the ways in which different aspects of state identity are shaped by sexuality; and second, the particular sexual characteristics embedded within the state. These two processes are connected but different, for the impact of sexuality on the state may not lead to an ostensible sexualizing of the state, while the state's sexual character may not be the product of sexual forms of power. This distinction will become clearer in the following discussion.

In considering what is meant by sexuality, I wish to draw on my discussion of disciplinary power in the previous chapter. There I explored the ways in which sexuality organizes desires and behaviour within a particular matrix, drawing upon asymmetrical forms of disciplinary power for erotic content. Here I wish to develop analysis of sexuality as disciplinary power further. In doing so, I am not suggesting that this is the only or even the best way in which sexuality should be understood, but rather that it provides a useful paradigm for thinking about the sexualized state.

As a form of disciplinary power, sexuality organizes identity, knowledge, behaviour, manners, dress, and social interactions around particular desires, libidinal practices and social relations. At the same time, it constructs and articulates desires, libidinal practices, and social (racialized, gendered and classed) relations in specific ways. Patriarchal heterosexuality provides the dominant form of sexual organization, but as I discussed in Chapter 3, it can also operate according to other matrices.[17]

The impact and imbrication of sexual disciplinary power within state form and practice raises issues that parallel those concerning the gendered state. A number of writers have explored the ways in which the form, organization and practice of the state reflects and is constituted by asymmetrical gender relations. These are apparent in legal (Smart 1989) and educational (Jones and Mahony 1989) discourses; in bureaucratic and welfare relations (Morgan 1981; Ferguson 1984; Piven 1984); in the regulation and maintenance of a 'private' sphere (McIntosh 1978; Eisenstein 1984;

Franzway *et al*. 1989:19–23);[18] and in the state's exercise of coercion (Franzway *et al*. 1989:9).

However, as Witz and Savage (1992:54) explore in a useful account of the current state of gendered organizational theory and research, the relationship between sexuality and gender in state organizations is a complex one that has received insufficient theorization. Although my focus is on the sexualization of the state, I do not wish to demote gender but rather to highlight the relationship between the two.[19] In particular, I focus on the following aspects of sexual disciplinary power: patriarchal heterosexual culture and relations; lesbian and gay discourse and activism; and the eroticization of violence. In exploring the ways in which these issues have shaped, or constituted themselves within different aspects of state identity, I examine:

1 state form and the division between public and private;
2 the exercise of power and the boundaries of state institutions;
3 the nation state, and 'state as a relation' and
4 the use of public force.

Within each identity, I consider the implications of its sexualization for progressive social activism and struggle.

The contradictory (a)sexualization of state form

Many feminist writers have explored the relationship between the state and the public/private dichotomy (O'Donovan 1985; Pateman 1989; Lacey 1993), focusing on women's location in and identification with the latter. Although writers dispute the extent of, particularly black and working-class, women's meaningful access to a private realm (Hurtado 1989), they nevertheless recognize the powerful ideological role the notion of separate spheres plays. Genders, activities and cultural values are allocated to one or other realm. The state's own apparent identity within the 'public' leads to its articulation with public qualities and values: due process, impartiality, citizenship and reason. These contrast, as many feminists have pointed out, with the qualities of 'private' or domestic life: nature, partiality, the body and emotion.

As well as being gendered however (O'Donovan 1985: Ch. 1), these spheres are also sexualized. The articulation of sexuality with nature, passion, irrationality and the body places it in opposition to an asexual state (Cooper 1993b). Thus in considering the ways state identity is sexualized, I want to begin with the paradox of its 'asexuality', since this has important implications for progressive, sexual struggles.[20]

The state's discursive construction as asexual is refracted through its identity as a coherent actor operating by means of a series of aligned public institutions. These focus on maintaining a 'healthy', productive sexuality within the private, while at the same time ostensibly protecting the boundaries of the public from sexual penetration.[21] While the Right have tended to rationalize their political interventions on the basis that they aim to remove homosexuality from the public,[22] progressive forces have been less hegemonically positioned. The 'organizing out' of sexuality from public bodies makes it difficult for lesbian and gay social forces to demand the state tackle anti-gay discrimination for in so doing they have to justify homosexuality as a legitimate public topic. The approach lesbian and gay rights groups have adopted has been to focus on advocating a safe private space of sexual freedom alongside citizenship rights which decentre homosexuality for a homosocioidentity.[23] Yet even these strategies cannot pre-empt questions about the location and parameters of the homosexual private, especially where children are involved (see Cooper and Herman 1991; Robson 1992:175), nor the specific *nature* of citizenship rights to which homosexuality grants (or does not withdraw) entitlement.

The limitations of a discursive framework which identifies homosexuality as a matter of private sexuality articulated to public (asexual) citizenship rights becomes particularly apparent where state bodies are requested *positively* to support gay lifestyles, for instance, through education policies, adoption and fostering provision and community funding. Because proactive heterosexual strategies are naturalized into invisibility, it is lesbian and gay forces who remain vulnerable to claims that they are trying to push into the public realm unacceptable sexual practices.[24]

Sexuality and penetrative state apparatus

Woven into the state's identity as an articulated (asexual) apparatus is its penetrative role/capacity. This is seen by activists and commentators in a range of ways. While feminists focus on intervention as a means of maintaining patriarchal social relations,[25] others have explored its racialized and class dimensions. In relation to sexuality, the state is identified as penetrating civil society in order to proscribe, penalize and disorganize 'unacceptable' activities. In exploring this process, my focus is on the ways in which the changing character of sexual discourses and identity structures the state's penetrative identity. However, in considering this relationship, it is important to recognize the extent to which sexual developments themselves can be discursively constructed or manipulated by social forces and state actors to *justify* particular interventions. Thus the impact of sexual change on state practice is both produced by, and located within, a network of wider political struggles.[26]

While escalating state intervention may constitute a conservative reaction to, and be legitimized by, (discourses of) sexual diversity, it can also assist social forces wishing to use state power in more progressive ways. The emergence of AIDS in Britain and the West generally has been used by the state to intensify its regulation and scrutiny of sexual practices and identities, particularly among people known or defined as possible 'carriers'. However, the effects of such interventions have, as Altman (1989:42) describes, proven contradictory:

> AIDS has made the previously unmentionable the subject of official discourse and helped legitimize (and, let it be acknowledged, control) gay sex as well as the gay movement.

Gay forces' ability, to make use of state channels into civil society as a result of governmental policy and discourse on AIDS has been a site of ardent and complex struggle. While right-wing organizations criticized governments for incorporating gay community organizations allowing AIDS activists to shape public discourse, many gay activists have, in turn, perceived their own impact on state policymaking as limited (Gamson 1993). Adam (1989) argues that AIDS was forced into a sign for 'no sex'; made to speak the language of monogamy and celibacy, no space was left within state channels for the deployment of gay discourse.

While gay discourse had to fight for space within state channels, its relative success in shaping the character of state interventions and presentations is apparent when we consider the absence of both lesbian speaking and subject positions. From government advertisements which advised 'don't go anywhere without a condom' to public funded AIDS education, the implications of AIDS for lesbians, as well as the more general possibilities for non-penile erotic practices remained marginalized.[27] In the concern of progressive and gay activists to disrupt perceived right-wing control of state communicative mechanisms, the discursive and ideological space from which to explore an oppositional, non-penetrative sexual politics became 'organized out'.

The marginalization of feminist discourse and its consequent implications for attempts to shape state practice have been particularly apparent in feminist strategies to expand state boundaries or to increase the penetrative power and remit of the state. The dangers of feminists engaging in campaigns for greater state control – demanding more restrictive legislation – has been well explored, particularly in the areas of pornography and prostitution (see Walkowitz 1980; Hunt 1990; Segal and McIntosh 1992).[28] Part of the problem concerns the power of existing principles for state intervention: public harm, corruption, undermining the family, sexualized in ways that affirm a patriarchal heterosexuality. The ability to contest such principles from within the state is limited, for although (re)produced there, they also take shape within other domains. A sexual culture which emphasizes the private, the privileging of male sexuality, heterosexuality and the nuclear family, structures state responses in ways that make feminist principles for state intervention difficult to envisage.

However, having said that, the hegemony or discursive authority of such principles across western liberal states is neither static nor homogenous. The Canadian anti-pornography judgment, *Butler*,[29] has been hailed by some as 'feminist' (Mahoney 1992; Busby 1994) because of the way in which harm to women as a basis for intervention has been both conceptualized and prioritized. At the same time, others have criticized advocates of the decision. Opponents argue that not only do supporters of the *Butler* judgment ignore the positive potential of certain pornography but they are also naïve. Irrespective of the judgment's wording, implementation of *Butler*, they argue, will impact most heavily on non-conventional, namely lesbian and gay, pornographic texts (Eamon 1992–93; Bearchell 1993; Smith 1993).[30] Thus the incorporation of apparently feminist discursive elements by one state body may be undermined by the practices of others, for instance, Customs and Excise, the police and lower court bodies.

Criticism of state intervention highlights the importance of not separating the sexualized aspects of the state's identity as penetrator and regulator of civil society from other organizing principles. While the state may not *function* to maintain the interests of a particular class or grouping, gender, race and economic principles inform the state's reaction to changing sexual discourses and practices. Feminists often highlight the links between sexuality and gender, but the ways in which race and economic class impact upon the sexualization of state interventions is more frequently marginalized.[31] This does not mean that intervention should be rejected or bracketed as a political strategy, but rather that strategies attempting to reformulate the sex/state nexus do so in ways that disrupt and transform its racialized and classed character as well.

Sexual metaphors: The nation state and state-as-a-relation

State form is sexualized not only in the activity of interlinked public bodies but also through its corporate identity. Here, sexuality operates as a metaphor; in other words, the identity and relations of the state can be *read* through the symbolic frame of patriarchal heterosexuality. Gendered, sexualized symbolism offers 'a device through which an idea of the nation [state] is realised' (Moran 1991:160).

As a nation state, viewed in relation to other states and entities, the state resembles a coherent actor. Internal disunity and contradiction, when externally apparent, are consequently seen as a failure to achieve full statehood rather than as (re)presenting the inevitable, inherent nature of state identity itself. The *sexualized* nature of the corporate state becomes particularly apparent in international settings where the western state seems more 'at home', in part, perhaps, because it can here appear as a unified, hence charismatic, body. But what kind of sexuality does the nation state possess?

In an article on the relationship between national security and homosexuality, Moran (1991) explores the ways in which homosexuality, as practice, metaphor and identity, became constituted after World War II as a danger. The code it generated of instability, weakness and exhaustion framed the manly state as antithesis (see also Mosse 1985). At the same time, homosexuality is more than the 'other' against which the manly state defines itself; it is also present within the iconography of interstate relations. Even with more aggressive or authoritarian states, the western, liberal state maintains a distance that is more apparent than real, for homosocial exchanges prevail. At the same time, states deemed wild, irrational, and out of control are feminized, or rather *ef*feminized, disliked and feared for their capacity to reveal the ruptures within the contingent coherence of the masculine state's corporate identity.

The sexualized character of the western, liberal nation state contrasts with its domestic identity. Wendy Brown (1992) argues that the late modern state bears an uncanny resemblance to the 'new man', ostensibly sympathetic to social movement demands and the needs of the subjugated but seemingly able to do little. One might go further and argue that this relationship is, metaphorically, a heterosexual one of difference where the community – those subject to state power – become the feminized 'other'.[32] While this approach treats the state as the dominant party in a power relationship, a slight shifting produces a paradigm in which the state comes to characterize the relationship itself. While this has become a fashionable way of understanding the state, the danger in equating the state with a particular kind of relationship is that those state relations which operate differently are either squeezed artificially into the dominant paradigm or else ignored.

The welfare–client relationship, for instance, could be presented as the typical 'state-as-relation', constituted by professional authority, dependency and asymmetrical power. One might argue that although sexual desire may not specifically be present, other constituent aspects of patriarchal heterosexuality exist.[33] This is evident in the ways in which the client's behaviour is constructed and disciplined as submissive, compliant and out of control.[34] However, in other instances the relationship is different. For instance, Pringle and Watson (1992:60–61) argue that the relationship in Australia between the state, commerce and the unions offers a fraternal paradigm quite different from the character of the state's engagement with women. Thus rather than equating the state with a particular *kind* of relationship, we might explore the *range* of relations that constitute the state's identity at particular historical and social junctures.

To the extent that the new, heterosexual man identifies the dominant character of state relationships, what implications does this have for sexual activists? The first may be to treat with scepticism promises and commitments not yet actualized. This may seem an obvious point. However, the emphasis placed by many activists on symbolic change sometimes deflects attention from whether new possibilities are actually being realized, or whether the only change is at the level of prefigurative signifiers, the discursive 'as ifs' of a brave new world (Cooper 1994a). The heterosexual corporate state also raises the possibility of a state differently characterized. What might a queer or lesbian state look like? To what extent is it possible fundamentally to transform the relational nature of the state so that it does not represent a heterosexual metaphor of inequality or asymmetry? These remain key questions for radical state theory.

Sex at the heart of coercion

According to Weber (1946), the exclusive deployment of legitimate force offered the central defining aspect of the state. In this final section, I wish to discuss the ways in which this identity is sexualized, that is, how does sexuality inform the state's deployment of violence?

The state's hegemonic monopoly of public custodial power – its right to coerce its populace – is inextricably linked to a sexual imaginary or culture formulated around the eroticization of domination. While many communities centre violence within their erotic imagination (see Chapter 3), the state deploys desire in its production of force. Soldiers read pornography before military engagements (Enloe 1988:18) and rape enemy women in an 'eroticized' expression of hatred, strategic humiliation and control (Enloe 1993:121).[35] At the same time, state disciplinary power is deployed in *opposition* to 'uncontrollable' sexual desires, particularly in prisons, schools and the military, institutions that epitomize coercive regulation, where bodies are tightly disciplined. Newburn (1992:59), for instance, describes how the British Sexual Offences Bill 1956, proposed by Leo Abse in response to the Wolfenden Committee's Report, while accepting liberalization in the private realm, explicitly raised the penalties for homosexual acts in the armed forces.

The process is further complicated, however, by the fact that the rigid bodily discipline effected by state coercion often generates sexual expression as both an aspect of its discipline – the highly structured, ritualized nature of sex in men's prisons, for instance – and as a form of release. While this may seem to undermine state attempts to enforce an asexual regime, one might argue that not only does asymmetrical, disciplined sex maintain an organized social hierarchy, but that the equation of sex with irrationality and uncontrollable animal desires makes subjects emotionally – if not physically – easier to control.

The apparently contradictory nature of using sex to improve coercive efficacy, and force to keep sex private reveals itself in the police force's treatment of women working as prostitutes. Arrested, held and often imprisoned for sexual offences, prostitutes are also treated sexually by the state forces that regulate them (McClintock 1992).

The sex–violence nexus has a range of implications for progressive state engagements. First, the intense disciplinary regulation and proscription of sexuality within certain state institutions makes progressive sexual policies hard to develop. Lesbian and gay initiatives in the military or prison service, for instance, are well behind comparable 'advancements' elsewhere. Developments are also set back by the machismo that prevails. The dominant discourse and practices of homosexual sex in prison seem to offer a different articulation to that of gay sociopolitical identities, although connections could perhaps be usefully drawn.

Second, the sexual nature of coercive and violent state practices makes challenging the latter much harder. How do progressive sexual forces engage with the coercive practices of a soldier, prison warden, schoolteacher, when they are also eroticized? The latter gives violence and coercion an intensity in inverse relation to its propriety. By acknowledging and exploiting the sexual nature of coercion, the state thus not only improves the quality of its violent acts but also helps protect them from challenge.

Conclusion

In this chapter, I have explored some aspects of state identity and its relationship to sexuality. My focus has been on the state as a multifaceted phenomenon, an entity with many overlapping identities, a concept always in discursive flux. Yet it is not only the state that lacks fixity; sexuality too can be, indeed has been, conceptualized and identified in a range of ways. The approach I have adopted in this chapter focuses on the processes through which sexuality impacts upon the state. Although my framework centres sexuality as a form of disciplinary power, this cannot be separated from the ways in which it functions as culture, desire, activity, identity and metaphor. Thus the relationships between the state and sexuality are conceptually and empirically multiple, varied and in motion.

As I stated at the beginning of this chapter, my focus in exploring this sexuality–state matrix concerns the implications for sexually progressive struggles. A range of sexual forces have looked to the state as a way of ending discrimination, prejudice, harassment and inequality. Other sexual forces have attempted to avoid the state either on the basis that it cannot achieve such goals or because other goals are sought: new norms, imaginations, and the proliferation of cultural and civic variety. However, while critics of the state are right to be sceptical, their certainty overstates the case. Moreover, it ignores the extent to which they too are caught up with state practice, not only because they may receive public funding or utilize public buildings, but because their struggles, however ostensibly 'outside', may impact upon state form and practice. It is this latter aspect which advocates of state intervention need to bear in mind when they dismiss those who struggle in other arenas. The capacity and potential of the state depends on those conflicts and contestations which shape the ways in which the state is constructed.

While my focus in this chapter has been on sexuality, it cannot be understood in isolation from other struggles, nor can the agendas, power technologies and projects of the state be conceptualized without regard to the impact of organizing principles such as race, gender and class, the power of influential social forces and individuals (whether from industry, the church or the trade unions) and the impact of other, intersecting terrains (such as the cultural domain and international economy).

While extensive work has been done in the field of political economy and state theory, with feminist and race state analysis growing areas, very little theoretical work integrates these issues with those of sexuality. Arguably, this is an effect of dominant sexual discourses which marginalize sexuality as an issue of the private or domestic domain, far removed from questions of state. Working within a framework that emphasizes connections rather than separations, overdetermination rather than underdetermination, and which rejects a priori hierarchies of effect, sexuality becomes just one among a number of social determinations that shape state form and practice. Butler (1993a:240) makes a similar point.

[I]nquiry into both homosexuality and gender will need to cede the priority of *both* terms in the service of a more complex mapping of power that interrogates the formation of each in specified racial regimes and geopolitical spatializations. And the task, of course, does not stop here, for no one term can serve as foundational, and the success of any given analysis that centres on any one term may well be the marking of its own limitations as an exclusive point of departure.

In the following chapters, I provide two situated accounts of the relationship between sexuality and the state, highlighting the ways in which this is shaped by the particular political and institutional context. The focus of Chapter 5 is the deployment by right-wing forces of discursive and disciplinary state power to regulate and constrain donor insemination by women outside of nuclear family structures. Chapter 6, in contrast, explores what happened when lesbian and gay social forces gained entry to the policymaking domain of local government. It analyses the extent to which they were able to utilize state power to convey an oppositional sexual politics, the processes by which their discourses became reshaped, and the struggles that occurred over local government's role and legitimacy.

Notes

1 For different conceptualizations of the state by Marxists, poststructuralists and feminists, see in particular Miliband (1977:67); Poulantzas (1978); Clark and Dear (1984); Franzway et al. (1989:33, 37–8, 52); Jessop (1990:149, 225, 233–4); Pringle and Watson (1990, 1992); Brown (1992:12).
2 Workshop held at University of Warwick, December 1993.
3 Indeed, the notion that the state has an essence can be seen as one of its identities – produced through specific state discourses.
4 For instance, Hay (1994:243) explores how, during moments of crisis, the state may be discursively reconstituted as unified. Thus its dominant identity becomes that of a single, sutured entity with any sign of fragmentation or contradiction regarded as problematic.
5 Although see Mitchell (1991) where he argues that the architecture of public buildings represents the state at the level of cultural form.
6 Feminist and gay theorists have disputed the state's monopoly of legitimate violence, arguing that individual (i.e. non-state) violence towards women and gay men is considered acceptable, see Franzway et al. (1989:37); Connell (1990:148). Redner (1990) also disputes the current validity of equating the state with the use of force. He argues that since the state now possesses the possibility for total destruction its ability to use force is limited.
7 For instance, see Althusser's (1971) functionalist conception of the state as inclusive of ideological apparatuses such as trade unions and the family (see also Hirst 1979). Whilst controversial, this conceptualization resonates through its linkage with other conceptions of the state as, for example, producer of knowledge, values, norms and subjectivities. Considering Althusser's expansive definition also raises the question of usefulness: what more do we learn by using the concept of state in this particular way, that is, to denote the reproduction of dominant social meanings? Does it help our understanding of what is taking place?

    While many have criticized and rejected Althusser's approach (e.g. Miliband 1977:54–7; Therborn 1980:85), at the same time his work usefully draws attention to the shared ideological elements and links between a range of public and civic bodies. In doing so, he highlights the question why such very different bodies should communicate certain common precepts.
8 This is not to argue that institutions can be identified unproblematically or precede other aspects of state practice. Mitchell (1991:94) helpfully argues that state institutions are an effect of modern technologies that make them appear physically separate from the practices they frame.
9 Identity politics among people may seem a problematic analogy since people possess an essential physical presence, thus allowing identities to be grounded in a coherent, corporeal reality arguably not open to the state. However, if we treat

the physical as one identity that people possess, others such as disability, race, gender, class and sexuality can be compared to the different identities of the state. In different social situations, these different human identities come to the fore; however, those at the rear still exert a determining presence.

Human identity politics also provides a useful analogy in that race, class and gender are not fully homologous; similarly the different identities of the state exist at different levels of abstraction and as different conceptual dimensions.

10 The notion of state power meshes together several ideas: the power actors within the terrain of the state can deploy; the effects generated by state processes and structures; the impact of the state as a single entity engaged in interstate activity.

11 The concept of state boundaries has been problematized by Mitchell (1991), who argues that such boundaries never mark a real exterior but simply a line drawn internally within a network of institutional mechanisms. Smart (1991:160) makes a similar point arguing that the state tries to establish where such boundaries should lie in order to determine what is inside and outside the state.

While these arguments are helpful in interrogating the concept of the state as an objectively bounded entity, their (implicit) functional approach underestimates the extent to which both the marking of such boundaries is produced by political struggle, and the importance of demarcating boundaries to the strategizing of oppositional forces.

12 Identifying the boundaries of the state is also important in considering whether activities come within the parameters of particular formal, regulatory frameworks. In Canada, a similar issue arose over whether certain institutions could be defined as part of 'government', see *McKinney* v. *University of Guelph* (1990) 91 CLLC 17,004; *Vancouver General Hospital* v. *Stoffman* (1990) 91 CLLC 17,003; *Douglas College* v. *Douglas/Kwantlen Faculty Association* (1990) 91 CLLC 17,002. In these three related cases, the Supreme Court of Canada majority judgment took a restrictive approach to government status. They focused their decision on whether the bodies were carrying out the quintessential tasks of government and directly subject to government control.

The minority decision argued that a wider test should be adopted that recognized the evolving nature of the modern Canadian state and the political importance of facilitating state regulation of public bodies. It based its test on whether the legislative, executive or administrative branch of government exercised general control; did the entity perform a function recognized as the state's responsibility and third, whether the body acted according to statutory authority to further a government objective.

13 In the case of funded voluntary groups, while at one level they were able to remain at a distance from the state, retaining their community status, at another level, the very receipt of government funds bound them to the state in complex ways. Groupings receiving municipal resources became obliged to set up formal structures that mirrored state ones: regular meetings, AGMs, officer positions, annual accounts. They had to open up their financial accounts and practices to state scrutiny, and abide by state policies (see also Ng 1990; Schreader 1990). For instance, after the passage in Britain of Local Government Act 1988, S. 28, all groups wishing to receive local authority funds had to promise they would not promote homosexuality. Thus by gaining access to state funds voluntary groups

became partially integrated into the state machinery, obliged to exercise their financial resources in ways the state permitted.

14 According to Greenaway *et al.* (1992) incorporation was less apparent in Britain where medical professional rather than gay communities were the source of expertise and information. Their argument is that the British government used the main AIDS organization, the Terrence Higgens Trust, for implementation rather than policy-making, and as a route into the gay community.

15 For discussion of similar developments in the USA, see Patton (1990).

16 As 'boundary actors' (Prottas 1978) negotiating relations between public bodies and lesbian and gay communities, many of the issues relating to 'street level' workers might apply (see Chapter 6; also Lipsky 1980; Maynard-Moody *et al.* 1990). If this is the case, community activists involved with state provision may have more control than is sometimes suggested.

17 I argued earlier that it is important not to reduce sexuality to a form of disciplinary power that is simply *imposed* on people. While dominant disciplinary systems help to constitute subjectivity according to heterosexual alignments, collectively and individually people struggle to adapt the forms sexual disciplinary power takes. An illustration is the personal, social and media challenges feminists issued to the subordinate 'missionary' posture women were supposed to adopt during heterosexual penetration, and the advocacy instead of a greater range of sexual position(ing)s.

18 However, as many feminist writers have explored, the relation between the state and women is a contradictory one. Despite the ways in which the state condenses gender inequality, the state has also played a role in limiting men's domestic power and in redistributing wealth to women through welfare benefits. Feminists overall have been divided on whether these effects have been generally empowering or disempowering.

19 Witz and Savage (1992:54) express the concern that sexuality paradigms are being substituted for those of gender in the analysis of organization. This criticism can be made of the interesting article by Moran (1991) discussed on pp. 71–72, which in exploring the use of homosexuality in constructions of nation and national security nowhere links this analysis to questions of gender.

20 At the same time, we might also consider the discursive role of the state within sexual practice, where the state becomes the 'other' or surplus against which sexual identities and activities are constructed. For instance, conceiving the state as repressive makes certain sexual practices appear liberatory. Even within conventional sexual relations, the public, regulatory and impersonal identity of the state accentuates the private, consensual, natural, and personal character of the sexual.

21 Conflicts also arise over whether particular arenas are public or private. Mc-Caskell (1988) describes how gay baths are seen as private spaces by gay men and as public by the police and legal system.

Thus as I go on to discuss, although dominant discourses identify the state as asexual, and the state works to maintain this ideological image, from the perspective of oppositional discourse, the sexual surplus possessed by the state pervades state practices.

22 The far Right however are explicit that homosexuality is required to be rooted

out of the private and banished/contained within public, penal institutions. Eisenstein (1994: Ch. 5) discusses this ideological trajectory in the context of AIDS detention policies.

23 Butler (1993a:233), in contrast, argues for strategies that sexualize public space by parodying heterosexuality or reproducing homosexuality in oppositional ways. She argues that since the discursive production of the public excludes sex, it is therefore disruptive to re-enter as the excess (1993a:188).

24 Gay identities are discursively constructed as so sexually saturated that the two cannot be disentangled. The struggle between forces trying to reconstitute their needs as claims for government provision and the attempts by countervailing groupings to redomesticate them is explored by Fraser (1989). She describes needs that have broken out into the public realm as 'leaky' or 'runaway' needs.

25 Feminists have also explored non-interventionism by the state as a way of maintaining patriarchal forms within the domestic.

26 Faderman (1992) describes the escalating state intervention in the USA during the 1950s. The penetration and surveillance of homosexual employees, clubs and literary texts was a product of the right-wing panic of this period in a context of increasingly visible sexual diversity, particularly for women who, after World War II, began increasingly to lead independent city lives (see also D'Emilio 1983; and Enloe 1988:140–6 on the increased regulation and surveillance of women in the American and British military during the 1980s, ostensibly to root out lesbians).

27 However, as Cummings (1993) describes, sado-masochist activists were able to carve a space by arguing for the incorporation of sado-masochist fantasies within 'safe' sex.

28 Gittins (1985:136) makes a similar point in relation to feminist demands for more intervention within the family. She argues that the nature of state processes mean these changes may have a different form and effect to those that feminists intended. Legislation, for instance, achieved as a concession to feminist demands may generate principally oppressive effects.

29 *R* v. *Butler* (1992), 89 (4th) DLR 449.

30 Herman (1994b), however, argues that both sides have overestimated the impact of the *Butler* decision.

31 This encompasses two dimensions: 1) the ways in which changing sexual discourses and practices are shaped by principles of class and race, and 2) how these principles affect the state's response.

32 Defining the state's relationship as heterosexual in a context of heterosexual hegemony does not detract from the state's discursive construction as asexual, since, as I have argued above, heterosexuality's naturalized status renders it invisible.

33 For a more optimistic view of the welfare state and its empowering potential, see Piven (1984).

34 Other state relations may be more explicitly eroticized, for instance, between teachers and pupils, and doctors and patients.

35 Enloe (1988: Ch. 2) explores the tension between sex making soldiers 'real men' and the need for moral control which ensures that military sex is regulated along class and racial lines. See also Connell (1990:529) where he argues that it is important to differentiate between the different kinds of masculinization within the military according to rank and function.

5

Penetration on the defensive: Regulating lesbian reproduction[1]

> A virgin who claims that she will probably never make love with a man is about to conceive and bear a child not, this time, in Bethlehem, but in a clinic in Birmingham.
>
> (Armstrong, *The Times*, 12 March 1991)

Introduction

> It is becoming fashionable to remain a virgin.
> (Dr Bromwich quoted by Duce, *The Times*, 11 March 1991)

In the spring of 1991, a panic arose in the British press. It concerned women who wished to use the services of donor insemination clinics, not because their husbands were infertile, but simply because they did not wish to engage in penetrative, heterosexual sex. The media dubbed the issue, the demand for 'virgin births'.

The panic over 'virgin births' constructed a problem in need of a solution: how to ensure procreation did not become the latest fashion accessory of the independent woman.[2] It emerged only months after the passage of the Human Fertilisation and Embryology Act (HFEA) 1990, which regulated but did not exclude single women's access to insemination. In their depiction of a reproductive economy out of control, right-wing forces argued for stricter provisions, either in the form of new legislation that would prohibit reproductive assistance for certain women, or, failing that, a tightening of the draft Code of Practice about to be issued for consultation.

The targeting of reproduction as a site for the promotion of a neo-conservative familial politics provoked considerable opposition. Unlike other reproductive controversies, where feminists worried about the implications of women's *inclusion* within the new technologies (Spallone 1987), here the issue became the discriminatory nature of *exclusion*. Paralleling similar developments in Canada, the USA and other western countries, British activists identified the legislative amendments to the HFE bill, and the ensuing panic over 'virgin mothers', as an attempt by right-wing government forces to hamper the parenting possibilities open to lesbians, gay men and other non-married adults.

In this chapter I focus on the British Right's utilization of state resources to promote their reproductive politics. More specifically, I am interested in the impact their legislative amendments and the subsequent panic had on treatment clinics and on lesbians' access to assisted insemination. The relative efficacy of the Right in deploying state power provides a contrast for my discussion of lesbian and gay municipal activism in the following chapter. It also generates more general, international questions regarding the strategic implications and competence of legal regulation. The first part of this chapter sets out the legislative constraints and panic over 'virgin' mothers. I then go on to explore the discourses deployed by conservative politicians, and the common ground between themselves and medical professionals. In particular, I focus on the ambivalent state location of professionals and the way in which this was deployed and reordered by central government. Exploring the changing boundaries of the state, and the character of state agency, leads on to a discussion of regulation as a means of implementing a conservative reproductive politics. I then consider the effects this had on both clinics, and lesbian and gay communities engaged in reproductive decisions. The final part of this chapter examines the relative success of conservative forces in communicating a particular reproductive discourse.

Coherence and state boundaries

Panic and legislation

The origins of the 'virgin births' exposé lie in two 'incidents'. The first concerned a letter published in the British medical journal, *The Lancet*, in March 1991. A hospital psychotherapist wrote in requesting colleagues' advice regarding a client of the hospital's fertility unit referred to her for counselling. According to the psychotherapist, the woman was angry that obstacles were being placed in the way of her obtaining assisted conception.

> The patient saw nothing unusual in her request . . . She believed she would be a good parent and this would be jeopardised if she married the wrong man . . . Are such women genuinely reluctant to enter into a sexual relationship, yet truly want a child? In some cases I doubt whether having a child is the primary motivation.[3]

This letter and the issues it raised found their way into the national press at a time when regulating reproductive technology formed a prominent component of the government's legislative agenda.[4] Although it was initially unclear whether the woman in question was heterosexual or lesbian, the scandal of 'virgin births' raised a general spectre of women not only having children outside of conventional heterosexual relationships, but in addition of *using* men to create a domestic scenario in which they might be permanently absent.[5] Women, it was feared, wanted men's sperm without any of the reciprocal obligations that accompanied a traditional, nuclear family structure.

Outcry over the letter's revelation led to further interest in the existence of other possible 'virgin births'. As a result, the British Pregnancy Advisory Service (BPAS) also found themselves under the media spotlight when it became known that the organization had three 'virgins' undergoing or being counselled for donor insemination (DI).[6] Alarm spread; with it went calls for new statutory measures that would prohibit such 'unnatural' acts. Rejecting legislative demands, Virginia Bottomley, Minister for Health, pointed to the introduction of recent restrictions in the form of HFEA. In particular, she emphasized the role of the new Regulatory Authority whose job it was to license clinics according to the statutory framework laid down (Sherman, *The Times*, 12 March 1991). Thus not only did Bottomley indicate that the Licensing Authority's consultative document offered an appropriate site for struggles to restrict insemination, but, as well, that HFEA created the preconditions for satisfying conservative critics' demands.

Legislative attempts to restrict donor insemination for lesbian couples and single women did not originate in 1991. From HFEA's genesis in the Warnock Committee, questions of access formed a central terrain of debate. The Committee heard arguments from those wishing to restrict treatment to married couples and those, including lesbians and gay men, who believed access should be wider. Their conclusions, however, prefigured the position subsequently adopted by Parliament (Spallone 1987): '[W]e believe that as a general rule it is better for children to be born into a two-parent family, with both father and mother.'[7] During early parliamentary debates, however, access considerations took a back seat as conservative attentions focused on more general issues concerning the morality and ethics of reproductive technology. Although Ann Winterton raised the matter in a Commons debate on the Warnock Report in 1984, her anxiety that 'lesbian and homosexual couples can acquire a baby'[8] remained unaddressed.

Almost six years later, eligibility became formally raised and explored in the House of Lords. There, conservative peers argued intensively for restricted donor insemination, their views reflecting concerns about blood, heredity and nationhood.[9] Yet even among them a range of opinions were expressed, reflecting not only different perceptions of who deserved reproductive assistance but also diverse understandings of the relationship between legal regulation and morality.[10] Lord Ashborne, for instance, wanted services restricted to 'the eggs of that woman and the sperm of her husband'. Lady Saltoun of Abernethy was prepared to broaden the parameters of donation, while still withholding access from 'unmarried women, lesbian couples or unmarried couples'.[11] Other conservative speakers expressed a willingness to include, or at least not to rule out, unmarried couples.[12] Nevertheless, despite a range of opinions, conservative peers were clear on one thing: children should not be raised without fathers. Introduced into the Commons by the then Health Minister, Kenneth Clarke, this position became formally enacted as Section 13(5) of HFEA:

> A woman shall not be provided with treatment services unless account has been taken of the welfare of any child who may be born as a result of the treatment (*including the need of that child for a father*) [my emphasis], and of any child that may be affected by the birth.[13]

Responsibility for ensuring such needs were met lay with centres providing insemination (see Human Fertilisation and Embryology Authority Code of Practice). However, the vagueness of the clause enabled centres to maintain a range of interpretations. Indeed, despite the pressure for more intensive restrictions, the Authority too, after consultation, acted to mitigate the Section's potential narrowness by acknowledging the possibility of other adults fulfilling a paternal role. This was institutionalized in the final version of their Code of Practice:

> and where appropriate, whether there is anyone else within the prospective mother's family and social circle who is willing and able to share the responsibility for meeting those needs and for bringing up, maintaining and caring for the child.
>
> (S.3.16(b))

Right-wing discourse and professional legitimacy

> To deliberately make a woman pregnant who obviously has none of the natural feelings about the matter, I think is irresponsible.
>
> (Jill Knight, *The Guardian*, 11 March 1991)

Neo-conservative attacks on single women and lesbian couples seeking donor insemination found backing and support in dominant professional discourse.[14] While the Right condemned 'virgin' women as selfish and irresponsible, doctors and psychologists pathologized them, seeking to uncover the hidden fears which led women to seal off their orifices from male access.[15] Other professionals argued that children growing up in single-sex households would lack proper gender role models, experiencing, as a result, confusion regarding their own sexuality (Whitfield 1991).

Clearly not all professionals adopted an anti-lesbian position or assumed children's need for a father figure. Dr Dancey, a psychologist at East London Polytechnic[16] (quoted by Sherman, *The Times*, 12 March 1991), emphasized that the biological need to mother was shared by heterosexual and lesbian women alike 'independent of the urge for sexual relationships'. However, for the most part, the defensive tone of much 'sympathetic' professional discourse reinforced lesbian 'otherness'. Lesbians' status as parents depended on their ability to demonstrate that their children were as likely to be heterosexual and to fulfil assigned gender roles as the children of heterosexual parents (Golombok *et al.* 1983; Falk 1989:943, 946). Thus with few exceptions – primarily of lesbian feminist professionals who identified with the campaign against the government's policy – a common 'heterocentric' theme ran through the various policy positions on the family and reproductive assistance (Cooper and Herman 1991).

The shared ground between conservative politicians and child welfare experts on this issue made it possible for politicians to exploit the professional backing that existed for a pro-father position (see generally Smart 1991:157, 166). In the production of truth, conservative forces benefited from the perception of professionals as separate from, and beyond, the state sphere. Rather than deriving their position from political ideology or the imperatives of public policy, experts were discursively constructed as seekers of non-partisan knowledge based on positivist, scientific methodologies (King and Pattison 1991).

In as much as the professionals concerned were NHS doctors, social workers, academics and 'psy'-workers employed in state funded institutions, the suggestion they were outside the state appears a tenuous claim, however. At the same time, to see them simply as state agents ignores the complex and contradictory relationships that exist. In Chapter 4, I conceptualized the state as a multifaceted identity; using that framework we can identify professionals as both within and outside the state, caught by a range of different, historically emergent relationships (Johnson 1993).[17] While professionals have struggled to maintain, transform or renegotiate aspects of their relationship (McCormack 1991:109; Johnson 1993:150), so too has the state (Lewis with Cannell 1986:325).

HFEA can thus be seen as one mechanism for redrawing professional–state interactions. On the one hand, right-wing government actors drew on the credibility of professional, apparently non-partisan discourse, to legitimate their neo-conservative morality. At the same time, distrust of professional 'autonomy' motivated their attempt to increase state regulation of medically organized provision. Not only did HFEA intensify the web of state scrutiny as clinics became incorporated within a new regulatory structure, but in addition the legislation increased state control over the decision-making processes of women seeking assisted reproduction. As a result of

HFEA, their motivations and lifestyles became more closely screened. Yet despite the combined effect of discursive state alliances and reproductive regulation, to what extent can we conclude that the constraints on women seeking DI without male partners, and in particular on lesbians, formed an integral, coherent strand of a wider state project?

Considering this issue highlights the uncertain nature of state agency and intentionality (see Chapter 4). If we recognize the contingent character of the state, as well as the chance, last-minute way in which S. 13(5) HFEA was added, it is not self-evident that restricting DI comprised an essential element of some broader scheme. In part, however, questions of intentionality and agency depend on the location of the observer. As I discussed in Chapter 4, what might appear to be division and contradiction from an 'internal' perspective appears considerably more coherent from the 'outside'. To many feminists, HFEA, and in particular S. 13(5), represented an extension of the state's reach over civil society in order to reimpose a sexual hierarchy that left lesbian mothers near the bottom. While poststructuralists may query the state's capacity to act as an agent, the fact it *appears* to possess agency requires us to examine the ways in which state structures and processes achieve this effect. Legislation is important in this regard, because it appears as *the* voice of government or state (see Cotterrell 1992:45). It works to (re)present a state that can act and operationalize its objectives.[18] To this extent, the Right's success in amending HFEA proved important, for the concessions they won helped constitute the state's voice. In this way, they also facilitated the marginalization of competing voices – the surplus outside the state's project.

Regulating reproductive access

Discourse and discipline

Regulation has become a key theoretical buzz word, used in contexts that include autopoesis, regulation theory, sociology of law, and poststructuralism (e.g. see Donzelot 1979; Jessop 1990; Cotterrell 1992). For many feminist and gay theorists, the concept of regulation offers a way of complicating the character of government intervention, moving away from a linear conception of control, without having to accept the functionalist logic of some regulation-based frameworks. Within this paradigm, regulation is not an inevitable effect of a prior systemic requirement. Rather it is a strategy that articulates power. According to Franzway *et al.* (1989:18) regulation 'has overtones both of "domination" and of "reducing things to rules", making things orderly'. Dominant discourse, it is argued, is central to achieving these 'regulatory' effects.

While discourse plays an important part in constituting practices and subjectivities, the approach I wish to adopt decentres discourse to emphasize instead the construction of new disciplinary forms, that is, the reallocation of rights, responsibilities and powers between different bodies. In contrast to simple legislative prohibitions, regulation entails the creation of a bounded area of *permitted* activity organized around specific norms. For instance, age of consent legislation allows certain sexual activities within designated geographical arenas according to specified principles (e.g. for homosexual acts no more than two adults over 21 years to be present). Thus the scrutiny of practices by identified overseers, as well as subjects' own internalization of their gaze, become crucial aspects in the introduction of new regulatory mechanisms.

Although I wish to decentre discourse on the basis that regulatory law remains irreducible to it, discourse does, as I have said, play an important role. Not only does it offer justification for regulatory changes, but, in addition, discourses are generated through the emergence of new disciplinary systems. The intensified scrutiny of potential fathering, for instance, functions as an effect of discourses which claim children need male parental role models and mothers who are involved in intimate, heterosocial (if not heterosexual) relations. In turn, such scrutiny may generate or reinforce the naturalistic status of paternalistic, familial discourses. Yet the need for discourse to provide an a priori rationale requires that its constitution as a disciplinary effect be obscured. Knowledge must appear always already given.

Allocation and dispersal of control

The enactment through HFEA of a new regulatory structure (Montgomery 1991), rooted in the medical profession's history of self-regulation (Brazier *et al.* 1993), enabled the government to place responsibility for operationalizing its criteria, norms and procedures on the Licensing Authority and ultimately on centres themselves. Thus at the same time as regulation led to the centralizing of control over reproductive provision, a countervailing process of decentralization and self-monitoring was also taking place. Under the Authority's Code of Conduct (para. 1.3), each licensed clinic was obliged to create a 'person responsible' to ensure that centres complied with their licence requirements (para. 1.4). In addition, an annual inspection was to be carried out by the Authority to ascertain whether the terms of the licence were being upheld.[19] The Authority made it clear, however, that their job was not to second-guess clinical judgements but to examine the criteria clinics themselves utilized in the light of government legislation and the Authority's own interpretive framework.[20]

Legal regulation, with its emphasis on reallocating responsibility within a framework of altered resources and powers, proved a key political mechanism during the years of the Thatcher administration. Rather than simply rely on coercion and prohibitions emanating from the centre, central government preferred to devolve visible decision making within a framework of constraints so that other bodies became responsible for policy choices. Yet while regulation – the creation of new disciplinary systems – may diffuse power more than direct coercion, the Foucauldian suggestion that regulation is part of a wider process towards anonymous forms of power seems misconceived.

For example, in discussing Foucault, Bartky (1988:79) argues that in older authoritarian systems power was embodied in the person of a monarch and exercised upon subjects in haphazard and discontinuous fashion. Now, however, the power exercised by new apparatuses seeks to transform bodies, minds and actions:

> Whether the new modes of control have charge of correction, production, education, or the provision of welfare, they resemble one another; they exercise power in a bureaucratic mode – faceless, centralized, and pervasive. A reversal has occurred: power has now become anonymous.
>
> (Bartky 1988:79)

In her discussion, Bartky links control of the mind with the disciplining of the body. However, legal regulation is in many ways a response to a breakdown of ideological 'control' and more anonymous forms of discipline. The need to restrict donor insemination eligibility, for instance, would probably not have arisen had it not been for the willingness and social capacity of unmarried and single women increasingly to bear and to rear children outside of traditional family structures.[21]

Ideology is perhaps the most anonymous form of power. Although dominant ideas are articulated and deployed by identifiable actors, their naturalized status undermines the agency of their utilization. Similarly, the implications of changing economic and social relations also tend to appear as nameless processes. Law, on the other hand, thanks to its enactment procedures, does not acquire the same degree of anonymity despite the unintentionality of certain of its effects. While regulation may be more impersonal than directly proscriptive, legislative forms, the construction and deployment of new disciplinary technologies and discourses identifies state actors and agendas in ways that may limit their effectiveness. Consequently, legal regulation may not be an ideal form of power. The creation of new monitoring regimes, the reallocation of resources, and entrenchment of defensive discourses through legal regulation generates opposition and exclusion.

Although protest may undermine the construction of hegemony, this does not necessarily mean the effectiveness of regulatory legislation is lessened.

The introduction of regulation to a highly contentious area of civil society, previously governed by unexplicit professional norms, provokes politically important public debate over criteria of acceptability.[22] For right-, and even left-wing forces, this can prove intensely beneficial. Before HFEA, lesbians could obtain donor insemination from certain limited clinics, but since this was beyond the 'public eye', such access was neither a mark of legitimacy or illegitimacy. Legal regulation, in contrast, as an act of state intervention, raised the stakes. By making public what had previously remained civil, the state bestowed recognition and legitimacy on that which it permitted.[23] From the perspective of neo-conservatives, the terrain of eligibility provided a context within which their moral framework could be both advocated and affirmed.[24]

In this section, I have explored the practice of legal regulation as a disciplinary response to changing social attitudes and practices. Yet notions of regulation imply that it is possible to reshape behaviour and practices. In the case of access to donor insemination, to what extent was this true? Was the British government able to restrict the availability of male gametes? What effects more generally did the legislation have?

The implications of regulation on lesbian mothering and donor insemination

Clinical practice

The era of Conservative government in Britain witnessed attempts to regulate sexuality and reproduction in various ways. In the main, such attempts proved unsuccessful.[25] Regulation suggests people change their behaviour in logical, predictable ways.[26] Either they internalize new rules and norms or else, weighing up the advantages and disadvantages, they decide compliance is preferable. In the case of donor access, politicians and activists anticipated that clinics would change their procedures, base provision on new paternalistic paradigms of welfare, and consequently refuse access to 'unsuitable' women, who might previously have been considered eligible.

In January 1994, I carried out a simple survey to get some indication of the legislation's impact on donor access for lesbians.[27] What became particularly apparent was how few clinics had changed their practice towards lesbians as a result of HFEA. Most of the centres that refused provision had also refused before the Act,[28] while of the two best known for making semen available – British Pregnancy Advisory Service (BPAS) and Pregnancy Advisory Service (PAS) – BPAS ceased all donor insemination shortly before HFEA came into force. PAS, however, continued to provide DI for lesbians on terms similar to those previously in operation.

If most clinics did not provide DI for single women or lesbian couples before HFEA, however, why were the Right so anxious to enact further restrictions? Several possible reasons emerge. To begin with, the enactment not only symbolized the Right's political authority, but also offered a means of reinforcing and hegemonizing patriarchal familial discourse in ways that placed feminist clinics in an untenable position. Aside from the legal implications, the strength and naturalized status of gender norms and roles made any claim that masculinity contributed nothing to parenting appear 'loony' and unprofessional, drawing into question the centre's standing as a specialist body. At the same time, clinical affirmation of a child's need for a close male role model[29] placed centres in tension with feminist clients who rejected paternalist assumptions.

Beyond its impact on progressive clinics, the Right's legislative intervention can also be seen as assisting those who wished to discriminate – legitimizing their practice, and obstructing pressure for liberalizing change. Although S. 13(5) did not significantly transform the *extent* of provision to lesbians, it did affect the style and rhetoric of clinical practice. For instance, among clinics refusing lesbians' access, several cited the Act as a way of strengthening or validating their position.[30] Such a discursive tactic functions to negate the notion that clinics are simply acting out of prejudice. Rather they are following the terms of the legislation, itself a product of professional expertise and knowledge.[31]

Although in the main clinics interviewed tended to discount the legislation having any substantive effects, and to argue that the position for lesbians seeking donor insemination had not significantly changed, their perception undoubtedly differs from that of lesbians contemplating insemination. Although there is little formal research in this area, it appears from anecdotal evidence that the publicity given to HFEA, combined with the oppositional discourses of the lesbian community, conveyed to many prospective mothers that insemination through clinics would subsequently be much harder, if not impossible, to obtain. Their concerns would not have been ameliorated by contacting clinics, many of whom, from my telephone survey, expressed outright hostility to the notion of lesbian insemination. Even among more sympathetic clinics, provision for lesbians was identified as a highly sensitive issue. PAS, which provides access, does not make lesbian access clear in their leaflet. Although the leaflet states donor insemination can help single women, there is no clear statement that this includes lesbians, while references to couples implicitly assume their heterosexuality.[32]

The cognitive realignment among prospective lesbian mothers in relation to clinics also reveals something of the identity change organizations undergo when their state nexus increases or intensifies. As long as clinics such as PAS were regarded as part of the voluntary sector, many lesbians deemed them less intrusive than the NHS. For women, fearful that their sexual status might be monitored, assisted reproduction – with its attendant conditions of confidentiality and vulnerability – appeared safer outside of state-run institutions. Not only could more trust be placed in such clinics as a result of their non-state identity, but, as well, fears that information would be passed on to other government agencies seemed less practically and ideologically likely. While the Authority's Code of Guidance does stress confidentiality and the protection accorded to sensitive information (part 10), the new disciplinary regime enacted by HFEA (in conjunction with the institutionalization of paternalistic discourses) undoubtedly persuaded some women, at least, to seek alternative insemination sources.

Arrangements beyond HFEA

> A hospital last night launched an inquiry into allegations that a man was running a sperm bank for lesbian couples from his home . . . He said he embarked on the scheme . . . because he felt lesbians were not getting fair treatment from sperm banks . . . '. . . I know there is a great need for the service that I perform,' he said.
>
> (*The Independent*, 18 November 1993)

According to *The Independent*'s story, the donor had provided sperm for approximately 10 women. Although the scale is small, it does indicate a willingness on some women's part to consider alternative provision beyond the scrutiny and perceived judgementalism of state regulated clinics. Yet the lesbian community has never seen clinics as the only possible source of access to insemination (e.g. see Williams, *The Observer*, 25 April 1993; Saffron 1994). Many lesbians and single heterosexual women have preferred, or for other reasons chosen, private or community arrangements, often with gay men wishing to be donors or to adopt a parenting role. While ascertaining an increase in such agreements as a result of HFEA is difficult, I wish to explore the implications of 'informal' negotiations in order to consider the limits of regulatory law as a technology of power.

Informal insemination practices create a dilemma for conservative forces. On the one hand, the British government laid down access criteria in an apparent attempt to limit reproductive provision to women within conventional familial structures. At the same time, the nature of donor insemination meant clinics could never be the only point of 'entry'.[33] To what extent have lesbians been able to avoid the paternalist requirements of HFEA through setting up their own informal arrangements? Do private agreements offer a way of constructing families that challenge the hegemony of traditional values?

Informal arrangements operate in a range of ways. While some are anonymous – that is, prospective mothers do not have contact with donors, receiving their sperm through a third party mediary – in other cases lesbians and gay men decide to parent together, working out in advance their respective responsibilities and rights (Weston 1991). This latter has become a developing pattern in American cities, such as San Francisco, where children may have several parents in close geographical proximity. Yet although such domestic arrangements can involve a male figure in a child's upbringing, and thus at one level more closely mimic heterosexuality than the lesbian couple receiving anonymous sperm from a clinic,[34] the nature of the male role model – an (openly) gay man – remains undoubtedly a problematic one for many conservatives.

Equally problematic is the emergence of (potentially) stable, extended families. Informal arrangements enable a range of parenting structures that challenge the rigid hierarchy of dominant state discourse. Instead of claiming there is a single right way to parent, the variety of frameworks adopted by lesbians and gays offer the possibility of fluidity and adaptability. Different approaches are suitable for different people, change is not in itself bad, and children can be happy and healthy in a variety of households.

In constructing the arrangement that suits them best, lesbians in western countries have drawn on a range of resources. Yet their agency is structured and limited by the ideological and disciplinary forms of power operating. For instance, many women choose to negotiate and enforce their agreement with the donor through contract (O'Rourke 1985:158–61). However, while contracts may allow the expression of individual choice and variety to a greater extent than other legal mechanisms, not only is the contractual structure itself skewed to produce particular kinds of outcomes, but the status of such contracts is also uncertain (concerning the USA, see Kritchevsky 1981; Ettelbrick 1993). In Britain, courts may accept them as reflecting the intentions of the parties at the time they were made, nevertheless such intentions will not be allowed to supersede judicial perceptions of the child's 'best interests', in particular their right to two parents of different sex.[35] This may mean, for instance, reinterpreting the sperm donor as father, giving him more rights than was originally stated within the contract or agreement.[36] Alongside goes the demoting of the non-biological mother, since western courts have tended to be unable to conceptualize lesbian parenthood as a joint decision and venture engaged in by two women each of whom may be identified as mother by the child (Ettelbrick 1993).[37]

Consequently even if lesbians or heterosexual single women 'choose' to distance themselves from HFEA's regulatory framework, the more general reproductive values and norms conveyed within it pervade the wider legal arena. This is hardly surprising since paternalist values have a much wider remit than HFEA, reflecting a broad state/professional consensus. Women may be able to obtain DI informally without having to demonstrate a father figure. However, if subsequent problems arise and one party goes to court, paternalist requirements are likely to seep back in. Indeed, they can never be fully absent, since knowledge or predictions of possible legal outcomes casts a shadow over initial reproductive negotiations.

In attempting to restrict this alternative, procreative economy, HFEA comprised only one of several mechanisms utilized by the Right.[38] It also offered an at best ambivalent technique. In a context where access cannot be definitively limited, specific regulatory provisions catch only those already allowed within its terrain. While the Right may have intended, by excluding lesbians, to discourage them from procreating and to withdraw the benefits of state regulated provision, the other side is a distance from the monitoring, scrutinizing and confessional aspects of the legislation.[39] Part of the difficulty facing the Right was their own limited political power, illustrated by their inability to outlaw informal DI altogether. Despite influencing British legislation during the late 1980s, winning support for amendments such as S. 13(5), HFEA 1990 and S. 28, Local Government Act 1988, their agendas were incorporated – co-opted even – within legislatory enactments that minimized or undermined their efficacy.

Discursive impact

Finally I wish to turn to the discursive effects of the Right's intervention. Coming in the midst of injunctions to be sexually 'careful', the 'virgin mothers' débâcle played a somewhat ironic role in its reiteration of a penetrative imperative, albeit within the narrow parameters of a nuclear, reproductive economy. Just as the gay penis had become hailed as the weapon of death, so the heterosexual penis's life-giving properties were affirmed. Even the sterile vaginas of lesbians and virgins could bud when saturated by its nourishing rain. Yet in this currency of sperm, allocation was to remain unequal. The threat that men might be reduced to their 'lowest' common denominator provided for many the necessary impetus to restrict semen to the 'deserving'. Or perhaps it was that despite the curative properties claimed, sperm by itself lacked the strength to re-gender the disarticulated woman.

At the same time, the virgin mothers' upheaval, and the debate over access to insemination had other, somewhat contrasting, discursive effects. First, it familiarized a tabloid and broadsheet reading public with donor insemination: the possibility that women, including lesbians, can and do have babies without male partners.[40] From its situation as a rather obscure practice, donor insemination joined the mainstream – a topic for sitcoms and popular literature. Although HFEA enacted the undesirability of lesbian procreation, the process of its passage and the surrounding debates gave lesbian mothers a discursive presence. Two terms, usually identified as oxymoronic, became linked together (Weston 1991:168–9).[41] Beyond that, lesbian reproduction gained some small legitimacy as a public policy concern, an issue to be taken into account when decisions were made. Yet the permanence of lesbian visibility within public policy discourse should not be overstated. The sudden focus on lesbians in this instance of DI can be contrasted with their invisibility within state AIDS discourse (see Chapter 4), as well as in debates over the child maintenance responsibilities of biological fathers.[42]

Moreover, the inclusion of donor insemination within a bill on reproductive technology affirmed the conventional notion that insemination without the presence of a physical penis was a complex and difficult procedure, requiring up to date instruments of modern technology. In an article in *The Independent* (18 November 1993) on a man who sold lesbians his sperm, Dr Neuberg 'described the donor's service as "a mini con-trick" because *without medical knowledge the chances of success were remote*' (emphasis added). Thus, *self*-insemination became discursively marginalized, not only a biological but also a technical impossibility.

Finally the discourse of 'virgin mothers', with its semantic play on, perhaps, the most famous 'virgin mother' of all, can be seen as a secular provocation – a tease to the proponents of immaculate conception.[43] Or is it more than an ironic joke? For we might also interpret the outcry as the resistance of rational, secularized modernity to a new (postmodern) reproductive order. The Fordism of a society where reproduction adopts a unitary style, and where sexual desire and practice have become the rationalized subjects of scientific examination and knowledge is fundamentally challenged by the post-Fordist possibilities of an order where the reproductive method of one's choice becomes an option, where sexual 'truths' are deconstructed, and where modernist notions of the intercourse–procreation couplet are discarded. In the allusion to that most pre-modern birth, we can identify the cyclical nature of social possibility. We have moved away from a modernist world to one where once again anything is possible, where rational standards and values no longer provide the means of measurement and closure.

In making this point, however, we also need to remember that the 'virgin mothers' outcry occurred in the context of legislation to regulate reproductive *technology*. HFEA both reflected and offered a response to the intense growth of scientific possibility, an evolution based on reason, modernist practice, and male achievement over women (Franklin 1990:224). Thus, the concept(ion) of 'virgin mothers' also represents the pinnacle of secular achievement.[44]

Conclusion

In this chapter, I have explored the Right's attempt to utilize state power to restrict non-conventional reproduction. Through exploring the meaning and impact of regulatory law in this area, I have sought to problematize the notion that the state can shape or control sexual activity or practices in a coherent, predictable manner. In particular, I have drawn attention to four complications.

First, developing my analysis of the previous chapter, I have sought to problematize the notion of state intentionality and agency. As the implementation of HFEA demonstrated, conflicting agendas and politics existed within the state which worked to undermine a right-wing agenda. These were evident in the liberal interpretation granted S. 13(5) by the Licensing Authority, and in the continued support for lesbian parenting offered by several clinics.

In addition, there are problems in identifying a conservative reproductive economy as part of a long-term state project. While this may be the dominant ideology among certain state actors or within particular state apparatuses, there are also contradictory tendencies. For instance, in 1994, a lesbian couple, using the Children's Act 1989, obtained a court order granting parental responsibility for the non-biological mother (Gibb, *The Times*, 30 June 1994).[45] At the same time, the Official Solicitor confirmed his office had been involved in and *supported* two other cases where lesbian couples were granted joint residence orders under the same Act (Dyer, *The Guardian*, 6 July 1994). While it would be misleading to overstate current support within the state for lesbian mothers or the benefits recent legislation has produced, assumptions of absolute closure seem equally untenable.

The notion of a coherent state exercising agency to advance a specific agenda is thus perhaps better understood as a discursive and disciplinary *effect*. To the extent it is achieved it represents a victory for the hegemonic faction. In this instance, although the Right could not produce the degree of suturing required, they proved at least partially able to reinscribe the state with their own notion of 'welfare': paternalistic, moral interventions validated by professional, scientific and common-sense knowledges. To the extent, then, that professional voices gave credibility to the state's identity as representative of moral value, they also legitimized their own intensified regulation. Yet achieving an input into the development of a statutory regulatory framework does not necessarily mean desired effects will follow. To what extent were the Right successful in their deployment of regulatory law?

The concept of regulation not only implies a coherent project, but also a degree of control or effectivity that the state does not easily possess. In the context of HFEA, the 'child's need for a father' amendment had little impact either on clinics currently rejecting lesbian applicants or on more progressive centres. While it may have affected the climate within which donor insemination occurred, the impact on lesbian mothers seems to have been less to discourage them from having children than to seek alternative methods.

In claiming that lesbians were able to withdraw from the regulatory framework of HFEA, however, I nevertheless argued that they did not have the power to remove themselves from reproductive disciplinary relations. Thus my third point is to problematize the notion that we can be outside of disciplinary frameworks. This is not an inherently pessimistic statement. As I argued in Chapters 2 and 3, discipline can be conceptualized simply to identify the ways in which our use of time and space is socially structured. Thus I would argue it is not a question of more or less discipline, so much as the character of the discipline in question. For this reason, I chose to con- sider the networks of power within which lesbians constructing their own arrangements operated, and to question briefly whether these provided greater potential for oppositional or pluralist relations. Yet it is important not to see these networks or webs as static. While they reflect the intersec- tion of dominant and counter-hegemonic discursive and disciplinary forms, they also reflect the possibility of change as communities such as lesbian mothers deploy the resources to which they have access socially and politically.

Finally, I examined the discourses produced by the 'virgin mothers' débâcle and the arguments over HFEA S. 13(5). In doing so, my aim was to demon- strate the contradictory effects of discourses generated by right-wing activism. In attempting to restrict eligibility for reproductive assistance, conservative forces called forth a range of other voices. Not only did this produce popular knowledge about donor insemination for lesbians and single heterosexual women, but the express articulation of a child's need for a father made a range of competing discourses possible. While these remained subordinate during the period explored, the long-term effects of putting into public dis- course this key patriarchal tenet are less easy to quantify.

Notes

1 Some of the early research upon which this chapter was based was carried out by myself and Didi Herman in 1991 and published in Cooper and Herman (1991).
2 Ann Winterton, MP, claimed treating single women with donor insemination 'reduces children to the status of consumer goods', quoted by Mihill, *The Guard- ian*, 12 March 1991.
3 Quoted in *The Guardian*, 12 March 1991.
4 See *The Guardian*, 12 March 1991.
5 Considerable confusion is apparent in the press concerning the meaning of 'vir- gin' births. Some use it to describe women reproducing without intercourse, others to describe 1) women who have never had penetrative sex with men, 2) those who have never had relationships with men, or 3) women who have never been in a sexual relationship with anybody.
6 See *The Guardian*, 11, 12 March 1991; *The Times*, 11, 12 March 1991.

7 Report of the Committee of Inquiry into Human Fertilisation and Embryology, para. 2.11 (HMSO, 1984, 1988 edition).

8 Human Fertilisation and Embryology (Warnock Report), Commons, 23 November 1984: 577.

9 See debates in the House of Lords, 6 February 1990.

10 The strength and nature of Christian belief also influenced the approach adopted by a number of conservative peers. On other disagreements, and lack of consensus generally over HFEA, see Montgomery (1991).

11 Lord Ashborne, Lords, 6 February 1990: 756; Lady Saltoun of Abernethy, ibid., 789.

12 For instance, see the speeches of the Lord Chancellor, 20 March 1993: 209.

13 A key component of this section is the welfare of the child principle. However, the focus of this chapter is on the paternal requirement. While HFEA makes explicit the child's need for a father, who the father actually is proves a complex issue. Under S. 28, HFEA, the child's father is the husband of the (biological) mother or, where unmarried, her partner if they were treated as a couple. The emphasis on identifying a father also needs to be seen in the context of ongoing concerns about the 'drain' single mothers make on the welfare state. Thanks to Judith Masson for this point.

14 See the Working Party of the Council for Science and Society (1984), who claimed providing single women and lesbians with infertility treatment increases social problems in child care and welfare, and is a threat to normal family life. See also St Clair Stephenson and Wagner (1991:46–47) on the medical profession as moral gatekeepers in relation to reproductive technology, and the ways in which they have influenced public, political bodies.

15 See discussion in Oddie (1991:16–17), also Persaud, Institute of Psychiatry, quoted by Mallin, *The Guardian*, 12 March 1991, who argued that women might need psychological help.

16 Now University of East London.

17 Spallone (1987:181) for instance, in her designation of the 'scientific state', fuses together medical professionals and the state corpus.

18 This can be compared with the considerably more limited and partial status of local government policy in representing state intentionality (see Chapter 6).

19 Breaches of the code were taken into account when deciding whether to vary or revoke the licence (interview with employee of Authority). See also *The Guardian*, 22 March 1993.

20 Montgomery (1991:528) nevertheless identifies the change as one of the clinics losing autonomy to a regulatory authority.

21 Even without these developments, DI regulation may still have been needed for married couples in order to designate fatherhood, and to regulate inheritance, subsequent (potential) incest, litigation, and insemination practices.

22 So too does 'deregulation' (see Johnson 1993:139), although perhaps this is better conceptualized as the construction of new regulatory forms which restructure the relationship between the state and civil society.

23 See generally on this point Dixon (1991), who discusses the extent to which regulation implies state acceptance of the area regulated, in his example, gambling.

24 See Gusfield (1963) on status movements and symbolic politics, particularly pages 147–8.

25 This is not to suggest that regulation is always or even generally unsuccessful, although it raises questions as to the complexity of identifying what regulation is intended to achieve. For examples of apparently successful regulation, see Sunstein (1990:408–10). However, his article focuses on progressive regulation that seeks to transform social and economic practices. Conservative regulation that aims to reinforce, rather than challenge, the status quo may raise quite different issues.

26 However, even if people behave 'rationally', this might not be in the manner anticipated by the legislators; see Sunstein (1990).

27 This was based on a short telephone interview. Undoubtedly, what clinics were prepared to say on the phone about lesbian access to donor insemination is likely to be cautious. According to the director of Midland Fertility Services in 1991, most clinics provided for single women although they would not admit this over the phone (quoted in an article by Dyer, *The Guardian*, 13 March 1991). However, if women ringing get a hostile or negative response to the question, 'Do you provide insemination for lesbians or single women?' they may be unlikely to pursue the matter further.

28 An article by Braidwood in *The Observer*, 23 July 1989, argued that the majority of clinics were hostile to single women receiving donor insemination and that there had been little change between 1989 and 1985 when a survey was carried out to this effect; see Steinberg (1987).

29 For example, since the Act, to fulfil the conditions of their licence, PAS ask during counselling whether a father figure exists. However, this is interpreted liberally, in accordance with the Authority's Code of Practice, to include other men in a child's life.

30 See Kritchevsky (1981:17–18), where she argues that in the USA, many doctors refused to inseminate unmarried women, deploying the grounds of illegality as an explanation. A similar response to legislation is evident in relation to S. 28, Local Government Act, 1988. Where authorities were sympathetic to lesbian and gay equality, they interpreted the legislation liberally to argue they came within it; where they were opposed they used the legislation as grounds for refusing to provide support; see Cooper and Herman (1991).

31 Arguably, in taking such a narrow approach, clinics were ignoring the more liberal interpretation of the Authority (see also the quotation of Wittall, spokesperson for the Authority in *The Daily Telegraph*, 2 July 1994: 'The authority has never taken regulations in the Act to mean that single or lesbian women should be excluded from treatment'). It is also not clear whether clinics can restrict themselves legally in advance by policies which stop them from considering the merits of each case. The Authority however has suggested they will not intervene where clinics refuse to provide lesbians with donor insemination. They would however intervene to stop clinics that attempted solely to provide insemination for lesbians (interviews).

32 See back of leaflet on donor insemination: 'If you are married and your partner has consented to the treatment then he is regarded as the legal father of the child.

The same applies to a single woman cohabiting with a regular partner who consents to the treatment'. This assumption of heterosexuality is even more explicit in the leaflets produced by the Human Fertilisation and Embryology Authority which assume that a woman's partner will be male. This is despite the Authority's apparent openness towards lesbian donor insemination.

33 Some right-wing politicians suggested outlawing non-clinical donor insemination. However, partly perhaps because of the implementation difficulties involved, this proposal was not incorporated within the legislation. In Victoria, Australia, in contrast, self-insemination has been criminalized; see Infertility (Medical Procedures) Act, 1984. The same has also occurred in parts of the USA. Kritchevsky (1981:20) discusses the statutory position in Oregon in the late 1970s where 'artificial insemination' could only be performed with medical supervision.

34 However, this form of two-parent arrangement can be seen as more congruent with a nuclear family structure than the extended family of both lesbian and gay parents; see Arnup and Boyd (1995) for further discussion.

35 However, see the discussion in Arnup and Boyd (1995) of a US court decision estopping a gay man from a declaration of paternity on the grounds that the family as the child knew it consisted of two mothers (*Thomas S* v. *Robin Y*, 599 NYS 2d 377 [family court 1993]).

36 This occurred in the USA, where the courts refused to recognize attempts to create alternative family forms and treated the donor as the father (O'Rourke 1985:141). Robson (1992:180) argues that some gay men used this ruling to obtain visitation orders from the courts on the basis of paternity, despite original agreements with the mother(s). The approach of different courts to the rights of donors in the context of informal agreements has led to tensions within and between the lesbian and gay community.

37 See though Gibb, *The Times*, 30 June 1994 on a lesbian couple in Britain who obtained a court order giving the non-biological mother parental responsibilities for 'a child whose birth they organised with a surrogate father'.

38 Others include Section 28, Local Government Act 1988; the expectation on fathers to support children through the Child Support Agency; and the attack on local government equality policies.

39 Regulation of assisted insemination benefits the state by structuring and making visible the outcome of particular reproductive transactions; however, many of its provisions are also helpful to the parties concerned since they set out the parties' legally determined and enforceable rights, duties and expectations in advance. Clinical provision also means getting sperm tested for HIV. Informal arrangements, on the other hand, rely on considerable trust. Thus to the extent more single heterosexual women and lesbians seek private arrangements, government policy in this area conflicts with their explicit drive to both lower and monitor contracting of the human immunodeficiency virus.

40 What seems to be remarkable is the number of journalists who treated reports of DI in 1991 as a unique occurrence. For instance, see Clancy, *The Times*, 11 March 1991: '[T]he woman, who is in her 20s, could become the first modern mother to conceive without having had sex'.

41 One can see, however, in expert interrogations an attempt to uncover which is women's inner truth: lesbian or mother? This uncovering is facilitated by questions about the child's best interests, since if she is after all a (potential) mother, she will want to ensure her child has a father-figure in its life.

42 In this debate, the whole issue of donor insemination was marginalized or ignored by state participants who tended to assume that all fathers were identifiable and that their status occurred through an act of intercourse. Women unable to identify the biological father were assumed to be irresponsible and promiscuous. However the debates in the House of Lords, 14 March 1991, do raise questions about tracing fathers in the context of anonymous 'virgin births' outside of clinics.

43 See discussion in House of Lords, 14 March 1991: 367, 383. See also Oddie, *The Spectator* (1991) 267:16–17; Armstrong, *The Times*, 12 March 1991.

44 For instance, *The Daily Telegraph* headline: 'Woman on course to claim science's first virgin birth'. See also, Duce, *The Times,* 11 March 1991, on 'the concept of a scientific virgin birth'.

45 However, the progressive implications of this judgment were quickly undermined by a demand from the Child Support Agency (CSA) that the donor provide maintenance. According to a spokesperson from the Agency, only men who give sperm to licensed clinics are exempted (Lightfoot, *The Sunday Times,* 3 July 1994). This response of the CSA demonstrates the ways in which the implications of the court judgment will predominantly benefit middle-class women. Mothers on welfare benefits, in contrast, may fear seeking such a residency order in case it leads to the CSA demanding the donor provide child support. A further repercussion may be men deciding not to offer their sperm for women on (or likely to be on) benefits.

6

Access without power: Gay activism and the boundaries of governance

Introduction

Entryism has always possessed an ambivalent reputation. Can oppositional forces enter the state without becoming co-opted? Is there anything to gain by a presence within the state's terrain? Despite conflicting opinions within lesbian and gay communities, in different countries lesbian and gay organizations and activists have attempted to gain access to state power.

In the 1980s in Britain, lesbian and gay forces turned their attention to local government. As councillors, activists and officers, they positioned themselves within and at the boundaries of municipal decision-making, determined to use local government power to confront anti-gay discrimination and prejudice. As a result of their work, a number of predominantly London-based councils incorporated sexuality within their equal opportunity policies, while a smaller handful still introduced formal bureaucratic structures.[1]

The origins of lesbian and gay municipal entry lie in the changes that took place within British urban politics from the late 1970s onwards. In this way, the fate of sexuality as a legitimate political concern followed the more general fortunes of the new urban Left. In the early 1980s, Labour left-wingers seized control of a range of key urban councils intent on institutionalizing a new, radical, communitarian politics (Boddy and Fudge 1984; Gyford 1985; Stoker 1988; Lansley *et al.* 1989). Two objectives stand out: the defiance of central government, and the prefiguration of a national socialist administration. In furtherance of these goals, policies clustered around a range of projects that included decentralization, anti-poverty strategies, solidarity gestures, environmental work and equal opportunity policies (EOPs). Initially, EOPs focused on race and gender (Goss 1984;

Halford 1988; Solomos 1989; Nelson 1990). However, the discourse of non-discrimination was such that its boundaries could never be conclusively sutured. In the 1980s, people with disabilities, the young, and lesbians and gay men slowly began to gain access (Otitoju 1988; Tobin 1990; Jeffery-Poulter 1991; Cooper 1994a).

Municipal attempts to eradicate anti-lesbian and gay discrimination epitomized for right-wing forces the escalating lunacy of local government (Jeffery-Poulter 1991:203–4). Homosexuality, a phenomenon that should, at best, have remained a marginal private practice was becoming acclaimed as a legitimate subject of proactive public policy. Local government was overreaching itself, taking on a mantle not only ridiculous but one it had no right to possess. Right-wing forces and central government did not stop at critique. As I discuss below, using the political resources at their disposal, they attempted to destroy lesbian and gay policy work, while simultaneously exploiting its existence for their own political advantage.

Despite the high profile opponents attained, however, they did not represent the only, or even the main, constraint facing progressive initiatives. Alongside overt opposition went the more subtle forms of discursive and disciplinary power endemic to bureaucratic practice that structure possible action. These operated to limit and repress more radical initiatives, generating others compatible with liberal discourse.

In this chapter, drawing on field research carried out between 1987–93, I critically examine the attempt to develop a lesbian and gay municipal project.[2] While Chapter 5 focused on the Right's exercise of state power in order to entrench restrictive access to donor insemination, this chapter focuses on progressive forces' endeavours to deploy state power. My argument is that even when lesbian and gay activists won access, state power was structured in such a way that its utilization by lesbians and gays remained constrained. However, as I discussed earlier, such social forces are not simply subjects of an overweening power. Thus I also wish to consider the ability of lesbian and gay actors to challenge the constraints they faced, and to refigure the discursive and disciplinary character of municipal government.

In discussing lesbian and gay municipal activity, it is easy to lose a sense of proportion. Indeed, the Right played on this very element to argue that lesbian and gay policy-making was becoming the paradigmatic activity of the municipal Left. However, only a minority of Labour councils responded to sexuality in any noticeable positive way; the majority, in common with those controlled by Liberal and Conservative councillors, remained at best uninterested but more often antagonistic or deeply hostile.

In order to analyse the efficacy of attempts to deploy municipal power on behalf of a progressive sexual politics, the chapter is structured as follows. The first section explores the different sexual politics of the forces involved. My objective in doing so is to problematize not only the idea of a coherent local government sexual politics but also the notion that lesbians and gays entering local government shared a common politics. While a liberal sexual discourse did predominate, this represented a complex and uneven condensation of several different political perspectives.

The second section of the chapter explores the relationship between liberal discourse and bureaucratic process. It examines the ways in which discursive and disciplinary technologies of power 'organized' out more progressive initiatives and ideologies. In the third section, I consider what happened when these forms of power failed to function successfully. In such instances, local residents, church figures, peers and tabloid press mobilized, deploying dominant sexual and constitutional discourses to contain and crush local government excesses, while central government reasserted its disciplinary authority. This capacity of central government to re-establish its position within a hierarchy of apparatuses contests the notion of the state as an entirely fragmented terrain. So too does the theme explored in the final section of the chapter, that of the discursive construction of local government. Here I show how discourses *about* local government impact upon the discourses possible to generate *within* it.

Competing municipal sexual politics

Despite opponents' claims that lesbian and gay municipal policies represented a coherent ideological project, considerable differences and discrepancies existed (Lansley *et al.* 1989; Carabine 1994; Cooper 1994a). Approaches varied both between and within individual authorities. Not only did councillors tend to hold different perspectives from community activists, but, among lesbian and gay participants, whether as community representatives, politicians, or council employees, political attitudes also varied. Perspectives ranged from 'countering heterosexism' (Lansley *et al.* 1989), which focused on the institutionalized nature of gay oppression, through to more radical, feminist approaches (Cooper 1994a).[3] Yet despite differing sexual politics, in most instances lesbian and gay participants came together, united around a minimalist set of shared objectives.[4]

> Lesbians and gay men worked well together. Lesbians were more organized but had no problem working with men. In part it was because they were fairly small in numbers and because the council was seen as something to be grappled with. They didn't feel they should organize separately.
>
> (London council leader)

Where disputes did arise, they often concerned the relationship between sexuality and other social relations. For many white, gay male participants, lesbian and gay initiatives constituted a response to the needs of a discrete, subordinated sexual identity. Thus homosexuality could be considered separately from issues of race, gender and class.[5]

> There was a gay councillor into homosexual equality, but he ignored sexism, racism and ableism. Generally, he was into pity, rather than a more political approach.
>
> (specialist lesbian officer)

> Gay men had problems understanding heterosexism because they didn't understand sexism.
>
> (lesbian policy officer)

Lesbians, on the other hand, *tended* to have a more developed analysis of the relationship between sexuality and gender, and to see lesbianism as a positive choice that could not simply be equated with heterosexuality or bisexuality.[6] According to one policy officer, 'lesbians were more politically sussed' (a view which many gay male participants resented).

The differences between lesbian and gay activists are important if we are to problematize the notion of local government responding to a single unified pressure group. As I have discussed elsewhere (Cooper 1994a, 1994c), councils responded in varied ways to the demands placed upon them, finding some political perspectives and agendas easier to incorporate than others. Yet in identifying a 'local authority response', the coherence of local government also requires interrogation. Politicians and management in progressive Labour authorities held (and to a degree expressed) a range of views about homosexuality and the appropriate role of local government, their attitudes shaped by class, gender, race, party affiliation and sexuality.[7] Some adopted a multicultural perspective, arguing that homosexuality was as valid as heterosexuality.[8] According to one London council leader,

> Lesbian and gay initiatives are about multiculturalism, but they are also about freeing the homosexuality in people, to understand their own sexuality, bodies, pleasures.

Others preferred a more minimalist position: homosexuals should not be discriminated against but nor should their sexuality be presented as a viable alternative to heterosexuality.[9] Yet not all Labour councillors in authorities developing policies proved even that supportive. According to one Labour councillor, 'Many Labour councillors were anti-gay; while some were open, others were quieter'.

Given the broadly less radical sexual politics of senior councillors and managers, to what extent were they able to constrain lesbian and gay policy development? A conventional account might certainly expect such actors' politics or preferences to prevail on account of their greater formal power.[10]

For instance, in one Labour administration, an unsupportive council leader was able to use her authority to demand that all lesbian and gay reports be presented to her prior to committee to screen out any 'embarrassing' topics from discussion in a public arena.[11] However, I wish to problematize this account of senior power in several ways.

First, the municipal process, in its condensation of different sexual perspectives, did not generate a single discourse; rather at different junctures, different approaches dominated. The affirmative sexual politics of consultative meetings with community activists, for example, diverged from the discourses of departmental reports which tended to construct gay relationships as unstable, and homosexuality as uncertain in its effects.[12] To the extent that dominant ideologies represented the preferences or interests of powerful actors, the identity of the powerful varied at different organizational junctures.

Second, while senior actors were better able than more marginalized participants to inscribe their politics within the policy process, their own attitudes did not exist in a vacuum. Not only were senior politicians and bureaucrats pragmatic in the views they expressed, but even their 'personal' opinions did not function as some kind of fixed, 'inner truth'. Rather, they were shaped by a range of different discourses, including the arguments and rhetoric of equality emanating from the lesbian and gay movement. However a key influence on senior actors' discourse was local government's own language of equality.[13] Equal opportunity, rights, fairness, justice – the articulations of citizenship – were applied by local government to a range of different communities, including lesbians and gay men, often with little thought as to what such frameworks in these differing instances might entail.[14]

The cross-fertilization of gay, equality and municipal discourses is apparent in the term 'heterosexism'.[15] Although it refers specifically to the oppression of lesbians and gay men, its construction of a homology of 'isms' based on institutional disadvantage places it within the municipal politics of the mid-1980s. Yet the use of heterosexism highlights a third complication. Despite senior politicians' and officers' use of equality concepts, considerable discrepancies or disjunctures existed between these discourses, and the ideologies embedded in the policy recommendations actually developed and implemented. These latter tended to convey a considerably more minimalist politics centring on bureaucratic incrementalism and limited civil rights (Cooper 1994a: Ch. 4). Thus the character of policy recommendations cannot be assumed to reflect the ideological politics of any particular actors – or if they did, such preferences remained substantially at odds with the public discourses many of these actors conveyed.

Finally, I wish briefly to mention the relationship between senior actors' ability to hegemonize their politics and the resources at their disposal. This was not a one-way determination in which the level of resources determined political success. The impact of particular actors did not depend solely on their (in)formal status, for, at the same time, their behaviour shaped the resources to which they had access. The ability of politicians to define which sexual discourse dominated substantially depended on the character and content of the politics they advocated. Councillors championing non-hegemonic ideologies found themselves (almost) as marginalized and politically ineffectual as community activists voicing similar perspectives.[16]

As a result, although the sexual politics of senior actors played a part in constraining lesbian and gay municipal activism, their impact cannot be separated from the disciplinary and discursive forms of power to which they were also subject. Despite their own personal politics which were, in many instances, sympathetic to lesbian and gay equality, their structural location placed them in the role of agents – mediating and reproducing external opposition and internal pressures.[17] In the main, rather than proactively initiating lesbian and gay work, senior councillors and officers functioned to channel concerns: financial cut-backs, hostile local residents, the press, legislation, the pressures of other departmental agendas – in ways that restrained lesbian and gay policy development.

Struggling on the state's terrain

Internal constraints on lesbian and gay power

Within local government lesbian and gay initiatives adopted bureaucratic forms that largely mirrored structures established to deal with gender and race equal opportunity initiatives. At its most formally institutionalized, lesbian and gay work involved specialist staff, council committees, regular consultative forums, and staff working groups. At its least developed, it formed an additional category within an ever-growing equal opportunities list, itemized on the bottom of job advertisements or in policy documents.

Although authorities with the most developed organizational frameworks tended to be the ones instigating the greatest number and range of initiatives, the correlation was imperfect (see Cant 1991:164–5). In several authorities with poorly developed structures, front-line and departmental staff energetically initiated affirmative action work, attempting to ensure the allocation of municipal resources incorporated lesbians and gay men. This took the form of library stocking, adult education classes, youth groups, AIDS work, cultural events, and support to gay housing and community projects. Other initiatives included anti-heterosexism training for council staff, the facilitation of adoption and fostering by lesbians and gay men (so far as was legally permitted), developing school curriculum policies, introducing structures to deal with anti-gay harassment, expanding staff leave policies, public housing succession rights and campaigning for anti-discriminatory codes in other public bodies (Cooper 1994a: Ch. 3).

While lesbian and gay municipal work engineered a range of positive changes, my research highlighted the disillusionment of many lesbian and gay actors who had hoped that exercising state power would generate more substantial results. Above, I problematized the presumption that the principal constraint facing lesbian and gay work was the opposing ideologies of senior council actors. Such a presumption is grounded not only in an individualist, but also in a hierarchical view of power which sees control concentrated at the top. Despite criticism from a range of academics and activists, this presumption still pervades dominant political discourse which identifies municipal power as residing with a body of elected politicians and perhaps a few chief officers. It also informed many of the forms lesbian and gay activism in the 1980s took, in particular the focus on establishing formal committees and the production of policy documents.[18]

While I in no way wish to deny the resources senior actors possess(ed) or to suggest that power within local government is (or was) radically dispersed, a key failing in the development and implementation of equality initiatives was the inability successfully to utilize 'street-level' power exercised by workers engaged in direct contact with the 'public' (Prottas 1978; Lipsky 1980; Maynard-Moody et al. 1990). While many front-line staff were supportive, often taking a lead role in the initiation and progression of lesbian and gay work, where this was not the case, policies could flounder.[19]

> Things happened if services wanted them to. Not because the [lesbian and gay] working party directed it.
>
> (Labour councillor)

> There was a range of responses from front-line workers. Some people saw it not as a priority because they were fighting for basic services. They didn't see lesbian and gay issues as the responsibility of local authorities. It was the icing on the cake.
>
> (lesbian policy officer)

Alongside varying degrees of discretion in the allocation of resources (money, attention, expertise) departments and front-line officers also controlled the form of interactions with service users and street-level staff. As 'implementers' they engaged in crucial policy interpretation, determining what the proposal or initiative demanded often in a manner congruent with personal or departmental agendas. Thus even when outright resistance or rejection did not occur, what the policy meant and entailed was consciously or unconsciously re-formed within the dominant discourses of the officers concerned.[20]

Street-level implementation problems were exacerbated by the fact that where difficulties were recognized, the response was often to deploy disciplinary power to contain or penalize 'inappropriate' discretion (see generally Lewis 1984). Not only did this prove counter-productive, generating resentment and localized resistance, but, as well, it proved extremely hard to operationalize effectively.

> Bureaucracies attempted to cope with discretion via more regulation, renewed efforts to assert hierarchical control, more information gathering and monitoring . . . in other words, by more bureaucracy. So the spiral continued.
>
> (Hoggett 1991:247)

Front-line discretion could not always be scrutinized (e.g. see Prottas 1978) nor entirely regulated; these problems were exacerbated by limited resources, and exploited by ambivalent or unsympathetic management.[21]
Implementation is easy to identify as the weak link in an otherwise healthy chain. However, the problems experienced there reflect difficulties running through the entire policy development process.[22] Lesbian and gay actors' ability to deploy state power to develop initiatives was impeded by a range of factors. In some instances, as I have said, senior actors used their structural location to repress, water down or reject initiatives. In other cases, discipline functioned more anonymously – an effect of complex bureaucratic processes. For example local government culture defined lesbian and gay work as a non-service based, high risk initiative. Consequently any proposal was required to undergo extensive consultation – with 'line management', service departments, trade unions, community activists and politicians – slowing proposals down or causing substantial delay.

> Over-bureaucratic management and procedures minimizes risk but takes away energy from work. I wanted to circulate a poster for a meeting of lesbians working for the council. I could have done it myself. Instead, I had to go to all chief officers' meetings and ask them to do the circulating. I was told to do it for safety. Maintaining the lines of command made management feel better.
>
> (specialist lesbian officer)

Not only did torpidity dilute the sustained interest and attentiveness of community activists, but it also gave time for opponents to organize.[23] Extensive consultation produced policy documents that were meaningless or insipid through trying to appease a range of interests. It also produced bifurcated reports in which progressive language was used to placate activists, while the actual recommendations remained more in line with conservative departmental and trade union wishes (Cooper 1994a).
In understanding the ways in which lesbian and gay municipal power was constrained, however, we need to consider not only the opposition of different actors and the implications of bureaucratic organizational forms, but

how these factors were overdetermined by 'external' considerations as well, in particular, lack of resources, media hostility and electoral unpopularity.

In June of 1987 came the first realization of major budget reductions. This led to a change in climate that carried through the setting of the 1988/9 budget. By 1990, no one was progressing work. Lesbian and gay policies ceased to be an issue after a climate of cuts.

(Labour councillor)

There was a fear of councillors being labelled 'loony left', a fear of voters and media responses. The local MP picked up everything and raised it in the House. This was seen as a problem by the council.

(lesbian officer)

To what extent however did councillors *use* these considerations and anxieties simply as a way of legitimizing their own opposition (see Carabine 1994)?[24] Certainly, in many authorities, councillors relied on generalized discourses of electoral hostility to a degree that seemed to go beyond any 'evidence' of real opposition or the council's own electoral vulnerability.[25] However, in other instances, the expression of anxiety or restraint was more directly reactive. In Southampton, for example, the Labour Group publicly opposed a grant to Pink Pride, a lesbian and gay festival, in order to contradict 'premature' inferences in the local press of their support.[26]

It was not only politicians and senior officers who internalized opponents' concerns. Lesbian and gay municipal actors too developed a panoptic gaze. As several specialist gay officers said when interviewed, initially they had to be told by management to halt work in the six months' run up to an election, but after a short period in local government most knew what would be permitted. Lesbian and gay officers learned how to rephrase controversial proposals to avoid opposition, and to develop work away from public committees. To the extent they had internalized municipal values – what made good sense – they no longer needed to be told. According to one lesbian policy officer,

Working for the council, there was a pressure to soften one's politics, to become more realistic and sympathetic to the problems of working within the state, to the importance of compromise.

Indeed, several expressed criticism of those lesbian and gay specialist employees who never became fully socialized, continuing to act as if they were working in the voluntary sector rather than for local government.

Some people weren't sure whether they were paid to be an officer or an activist. But if you didn't absorb municipal values, you would be constantly in conflict.

(lesbian policy officer)

In addition to these constraints, work suffered from another more basic problem. The political overload endemic within local authorities during the mid-1980s caused initiatives, however supported in theory, to take a back seat in practice. This limitation, experienced by many of the new progressive policies emerging in this period, reflected the tension of attempting prefigurative work in an era of public cut-backs, retrenchment and attack. As a result of trying to please various different and often competing interests, local authorities passed more commitments than they could ever hope to develop or implement. Although their political promises had a symbolic effect, bringing marginalized issues into the public realm, restrictions in terms of time, funding, legal power, staff and implementation systems left councils unable to adopt even a fraction of their agendas. Forced to concentrate on the ever-growing burden of statutory requirements, initiatives which appeared complex, unpopular and equivocal in their effects found themselves discarded at the bottom of the priority heap.

External opposition intervening

These internal processes of containment meant that, in the main, the Right did not need to mobilize to quash gay municipal policies. I want to stress this point since the high profile nature of central–local conflict has often led to more subtle forms of power being ignored. Nevertheless, while internal processes proved a significant means of constraining lesbian and gay municipal activism, the effects of external forces should not be minimized. Not only did opponents play an important role independently of council processes, but also, their hostility became absorbed within local authorities to shape the character and culture of municipal decision-making processes.

In discussing the role of external forces, I also wish to consider central government's deployment of power. Although, on one level, such power operated as an external force *upon* local government, the discourses surrounding it emphasized its domestic(ating) character. Central government, through ministerial dictates, legislation, funding control and departmental instructions, reasserted local government's embeddedness *within* the apparatus of state. Not only were government measures concerned to emphasize a state nexus, but more particularly, a *subservient* nexus. In contrast to municipal discourses which identified the state as a set of linked public bodies legitimized through their accountability to different constituencies, central government emphasized the state's hierarchically articulated identity. Within this framework, local government was a creature of statute, not an independent political body.[27]

Thus as lesbian and gay social forces attempted to situate themselves at the heart of local state power, central government reasserted the origins and location of local power within its own terrain. Local government might *manage* the power residing within it, but such power originated, and in the last analysis was controlled, from elsewhere. Lesbians and gays may have been drawn into the apparatus of the local state; they had not, however, won command of its power.

Central government discourse retained contradictory elements however. At the same time as asserting local government's lack of autonomy, central government distanced 'undemocratic' left-wing councils from the (functionally-identified) representative state. By this I mean that a state defined by its representative function must by nature exclude bodies hijacked by 'undemocratic' interests. Lesbian and gay local power constituted for central government such an interest. Articulated as a key symbol of 'loony leftism' it became the signifier of an unhinging from the broad ship of state; thus it could only be illegitimate. Moreover, the ascendancy of lesbian and gay forces within local government cast the councils themselves as without credibility.

To explore the impact of 'external' and state pressure more fully, I wish to use the case study of Haringey council, a north London borough, led in the mid-1980s by a left-wing leadership formally committed to lesbian and gay equality (see Cooper 1989; Cant 1991; Durham 1991: Ch. 6; Cooper 1994a: Ch. 6). During the period 1986–7, Haringey became one of the most public authorities to develop policies in this area (Durham 1991:111), largely as a result of events which surfaced in the summer of 1986.

That June, the council's newly established lesbian and gay unit sent a letter to headteachers of local schools informing them of a fund established by the council to promote educational equality initiatives that included lesbians and gay men. The letter, advising heads to put together grant bids, fell into the hands of local Conservatives; from there it was conveyed to government ministers, sparking off a storm of protest at both national and local level.[28] The main group to mobilize in Haringey during the summer of 1986, against what was to become known as 'positive images', was the Parents' Rights Group (PRG). Using a discourse of parental status, they mobilized residents against 'the council's policy to promote among children the belief that homosexuality is an acceptable alternative to heterosexuality'.[29] In the months that followed, others joined in the protest: local churches, a breakaway group from the PRG, the New Patriotic Movement and national conservative, Christian lobbies (Cant 1991: 168–9; Durham 1991: 112–14).

Under pressure from the media, as well as from parliamentary, church, and local opponents, the council expressed public disapproval towards the lesbian and gay unit for sending out the letter without the knowledge or involvement of the education department. Nevertheless, they were also compelled to respond to the political pressure intensifying among progressive forces that the council make good their electoral commitment to lesbian and gay equality. Caught between opposing forces, the council spent the autumn months of 1986 drawing up reports which would begin the long process of policy development aimed at challenging institutionalized educational heterosexism.[30] At the same time, a leaflet, 'What every parent needs to know', and a form letter were issued from the chief education officer to all parents. Both were intended to allay fears by assuring parents that nothing would happen quickly, and that, in any event, the authority had no intention of 'promoting' homosexuality.

This process of bureaucratic recontainment was not sufficient to appease right-wing and religious opponents who continued to mobilize, forcing the council further onto the defensive. The power deployed by the Right included grass-roots protests, symbolic demonstrations, electoral threats, ridicule, unsympathetic media narratives and hostile editorials. In addition, they used their discursive influence effectively to depict 'positive images' as a highly interventionist policy intended to promote homosexuality and proscribe heterosexuality. Together with asserting the ultimate authority of the Education Minister (Cooper 1994a: Ch. 6),[31] protestors also challenged Haringey's authority as an organ of government. Opponents proudly burnt library books, withheld children from schools,[32] and accused the authority of lying without public censure.

Having placed its authority as a state apparatus in jeopardy through the development of illegitimate policies, Haringey became discursively constructed by opponents as a quasi-pressure group, an institution of civil society, covertly run by activists who had never stood for public election. According to one opponent speaking at a deputation to Haringey council, 20 October 1986:

> We have seen sneaking . . . moves by the council coupled with frequent denials by council officials and employees as to exactly what is going on. Not only are we concerned about what the council states is going to take place, *we are even more concerned about what has remained unsaid.* I heard a member of [the community group] Positive Images on the local radio recently talking about mothers and fathers as unhelpful role models. Unhelpful to whom? Unhelpful to the 90 per cent of children who will one day grow up to be parents themselves, or unhelpful to the members of Positive Images in their present campaign? . . . *It is this underlying attitude of the people who are to implement the policy.* [Emphasis added]

Yet Haringey council's delegitimization was both partial and contradictory. Although public attention focused on the illegitimate nature of 'positive images', most services within housing, social services and even education remained untouched by the council's loss of political credibility. In these areas, Haringey continued to act, indeed had no choice but to act, within national regulatory frameworks, as a suborgan of the nation state. In addition, despite the government's dismissal of Haringey as a legitimate state body, it was not allowed to remain within civil society. Instead, its non-negotiable location *within* state structures was deployed as a means of achieving its unqualified return.

So far I have explored some of the ways in which lesbian and gay state activism was constrained through external pressure and the discursive reconstruction of Haringey council. I now wish to turn to a final, key limitation. This both underpinned right-wing challenges to Haringey's legitimacy, but also provided a culture within which such challenges did not generally have to be made. My argument is that a major factor stopping progressive local authorities from generating a more radical sexual politics concerned a pre-emptive 'mobilization of bias'. The result of intensely powerful perceptions of local government's appropriate role and remit, it prevented radical ideas and preferences from being contemplated by municipal actors, or, where contemplated, led them to be rejected without serious consideration. I call this mobilization 'local government discourse' since it concerns the production and framing of knowledge about appropriate local government practices. Although my focus is its impact on municipal sexual discourses, other aspects of local government practice can be analysed in similar ways.

Discursive boundaries to state possibility

> Given the modern policy context . . . the power of certain discourses to define the domain of possible thought is more significant than ever.
> (Shapiro et al. 1988)

Before discussing discursively constituted, 'structural' limitations to local government radicalism, I want to make explicit that I am not pre-emptively rejecting the *possibility* of change. As the 1980s demonstrated, discursive boundaries have been as much subject to struggle and contestation as other aspects of the local state. However, while British local government discourse adapted to accommodate new roles and responsibilities in the area of service provision and 'information' communication, it proved much more resilient in two basic areas. These were first, local government functioning explicitly as an agent of ideological change, and second, its ability legitimately to convey counter-intuitive meanings.

While both censorship and overt discouragement of more radical proposals occurred in local councils during the 1980s, these were not the only ways through which municipal discursive boundaries were preserved. Equally important was the ability of local government discourse to *produce* more 'acceptable' suggestions. However, proving this occurred as a result of power is difficult, for the pre-emptive 'organizing out' of a more radical sexual politics precipitates little evidence. Discursive injunctions or boundaries tend to become apparent only when breached. While they are working successfully, it is hard to demonstrate the 'non-event' of a particular sexual politics being unexpressed or not communicated. The existence, however, of a few counter-factuals – the Right's mobilization against Haringey's 'positive images' letter, for example – do suggest such boundaries exist; so too does the fact that more radical politics were expressed by *municipal* lesbian and gay activists *outside* of local government.[33] In exploring why more radical meanings or approaches tended to remain unthought or unverbalized within the domain of local government I am concerned, as I have said, with two discursive boundaries. Let me take each of them in turn.

An explicit project of ideological change

> The job of a politician is to change people's hearts and minds.
>
> (London council leader)

To say that councils were constrained from following a project for ideological change may seem a surprising point. The *conscious* communication of progressive ideas formed a major aspect of a new urban Left politics which aimed to use the local state to create a counter-hegemony around alternative values and norms including those of anti-racism, peace and collectivism. Within this context, lesbian and gay initiatives had an explicit ideological role: to transform people's attitudes towards same-sex object choice.

Clearly such attempts to create ideological change did not go unchallenged. Opposition concerned not only lesbian and gay policies; antiracist and anti-sexist strategies also came under attack (Gyford *et al.* 1989:310–12). However, what became increasingly evident was that opposition was not principally directed at the *substance* or content of the policies, a content firmly rooted within equal opportunities and liberal pluralism. Rather, the opposition was directed at the *purposive* character of the initiatives, their conscious attempt to use local government in an ideological way. Why?

To address this question we need to consider the discursive construction of local government's identity – the meanings generated as to its role and purpose. Within the wider British polity, according to Leach (1989:103), local government's role was identified as provider and promoter of public services. Other roles included representing local residents, responding to their needs, and helping to maintain or regenerate the local economy.[34] Within any of these projects, conflict was deemed inevitable, even acceptable (Gyford *et al.* 1989:299), providing it was kept within certain bounds. Even the Widdicombe Committee on local government considered it appropriate for councils to have a political function with regard to conflicting perceptions as to how and which public services should be provided (Gyford *et al.* 1989:4).

Explicit attempts to achieve ideological restructuring were, however, another matter. Mather (1989:214) describes how 'the Thatcher government [was] vigilant to police the borders of what it [saw] as acceptable local policy innovation'. And the Thatcher government was not alone. Not only the Right but others also perceived the role of local government as something less than an agent of ideological change.

In identifying the reason for this prohibition, some socialist academics have pointed to the relationship between local government and political power (e.g. Miliband 1984). At this historical juncture, they argue, one of local government's tasks is to mystify and depoliticize social relations, thereby hiding both the constellation of power that exists and the ways in which it is facilitated and reproduced by state machinery. It is crucial therefore that local government's identity constitutes it as beyond the realms of ideological machinations, a basically apolitical, non-partisan apparatus. This assists the local state and hence the state itself to maintain legitimacy and hegemony.

While this argument may accurately point to some of the *effects* of state practice, to see mystification and depoliticization as the local state's *role* appears unduly functionalist. It reduces local government to a single, coherent core upon which a series of functional but illusory identities have been constructed. It also conceptualizes the state as an apparatus organized through a single or dual social relationship, that is, class (and perhaps gender). In this book, I have challenged the a priori privileging of any particular organizational framework. I have also questioned the notion of a coherent, functionalist state, demonstrating not only the tensions and contradictions within and between different state bodies, but also the multidimensional nature of the state itself (see Chapter 4).

If the explanation does not lie within a broad, transhistorical notion of the capitalist state's 'role', how else can we explain local councils' inability publicly to advocate policies and political opinions that could be expressed with relative ease within civil society? One possible answer concerns the operation of liberal discourse: the generation of knowledge and signification through which the dominant identity of local government is currently constructed. Within liberal political frameworks, local government's identity is constituted within a hierarchical framework of state apparatuses, its role to administer local services, represent electors, and provide limited, local governance. The advocacy of a specific version of the 'good life' is deemed, in contrast, to be a 'misuse' of its state power, a breach of the border between state and civil society.[35]

Dominant liberal discourses depict the state as (potentially) forceful and dominating. Thus society requires boundaries to be placed on the exercise of its power. The discursive construction of a 'private' sphere highlights areas of life the state should stay well clear of (see Chapter 4).[36] Two sites defined within liberal discourse as particularly private are sexuality and personal belief. Lesbian and gay policies penetrated both of these. Not only were they about that most concealed of sexual practices[37] – 'homosexual deviance' – but, in addition, they targeted for intervention and transformation people's personal, private attitudes.[38] The appearance of intensified intervention facilitated conservative evocations of a particular kind of state identity. Councils were described as both 'Stalinist' and 'fascist', as Conservative councillor, Pat Salim, put it at a Haringey Full Council meeting (20 October 1986).

> If these people [the Labour leadership] are in power in the land as a government, believe me, you in the gallery [left-wing and gay activists] will be the first to be kicked into line. You won't be allowed to behave by them as you are behaving now . . . I repeat, I thought the 1930s were behind us, but I see we have a good fascist mind in the people opposite.

The articulation of non-common sense

Alongside the prohibition on ideologically purposive activity went a second and, I would argue, even more powerful boundary that targeted the *substance* of meanings conveyed. The strength of this interdiction can be seen in the fact that although the new urban Left *did* attempt to deploy local government power in a purposive or instrumental, ideological manner, almost no examples exist, as far as I know, of councils conveying oppositional, non-common sense meanings – that is ideologies which were not only progressive but, more importantly, outside of the parameters of generally acceptable meanings.

Again, this is perhaps a surprising point. Lesbian and gay policies, in particular, were lambasted by the mass media and opponents for proposing 'loony' nonsense. Yet, I would argue, the policies and initiatives referred to in this way, such as gay men's swimming sessions or anti-heterosexism training, whilst possibly unusual, were situated within broadly liberal paradigms. Their emphasis on formal equality, citizenship and non-discrimination did not constitute oppositional meanings beyond the realms of common sense. But perhaps this is putting the point too strongly. Such policies did entail the articulation of homosexuality with liberal precepts, a conjunction which may have given previously mainstream notions a radical tint. Indeed, identifying the point at which social meanings relinquish the bounds of common sense cannot be conclusive; not only is there no clear dividing line, but different actors' perceptions will vary. Nevertheless, lesbian and gay actors themselves deemed some meanings to be too transgressive for local government.

In part, their perceptions were motivated through feelings of inappropriateness; equally powerful though was the perception of *latent* opposition. The opposition that mobilized against purposive ideologies, such as lesbian and gay equality, was significant, however, many municipal actors feared such opposition would drastically intensify if more radical discourses were articulated. At least with the former, municipal actors could point to the *common-sense* nature of the ideas being conveyed within hegemonic liberal discourse. However, if *radical*, counter-intuitive ideologies were communicated, both 'injunctions' would have been breached, since such a public project could only function instrumentally, that is, entail the conscious promotion of social change.

While caution in the face of potential right-wing opposition is understandable, the power of inappropriateness requires more explanation. Again, my starting point is the relationship between local government's identity as democratic, and hegemonic liberal discourse. In its general limited critique of common sense, liberal discourse tends to assume the basic validity of dominant meanings. Even when dominant discourses or ideologies are challenged, western liberal discourse is reluctant to prefer oppositional formulations, at least not until they command popular acceptance. From this it follows that a state should convey the common sense. In contrast, articulating counter-intuitive beliefs involves undemocratic behaviour, since oppositional ideologies are, by their very nature, marginal – unrepresentative of 'general' opinion.

At the same time, communicating radical ideas exploits, while simultaneously undermining, local government's identity as an authoritative constructor of reality. Their promotion by a state body, gives controversial ideas 'unfair' assistance while undermining a fundamental aspect of local government's identity, as a democratic, *credible* state organ. Thus, non-common sense ideas are defined as dangerous, putting not only the *status* of local government in jeopardy, but potentially its existence as well.

In this section I have explored one of the more subtle limitations on the power of lesbian and gay municipal actors. This goes beyond the explicit suppression of particular demands or politics, and even beyond the general bureaucratic steer within local government. Rather, it concerns the limitations engendered by discourses about local government upon 'internal' policy discourses.[39]

In exploring the constraints generated by dominant state discourse, my analysis has focused on two injunctions or boundaries. First, it was deemed inappropriate for local government to conduct itself as a political actor advocating a prescriptive social vision. Second, councils were not to convey ideologies which challenged or went outside of an existing common sense.

In attempting to find reasons for these injunctions, I have focused on the operation of liberal discourse – its generation of certain knowledges and perceptions of local government's identity and role. Yet this explanation is not by itself enough. We need to ask why liberal discourse provides the dominant framework for understanding British state identity. How do such discourses link with organizing frameworks of class, gender and race, and with terrains such as the economic and civil society? These are substantial questions which I do not have the space to address here. I raise them as a reminder that rooting explanations in discourse theory as an antidote to Marxist functionalism can leave us with a description or analysis of what is occurring, but without a real sense of 'why'.

Conclusion

In this chapter, I have taken my discussion of the relationship between sexuality and the state further by exploring the capacity of lesbian and gay municipal actors to further their agendas through the deployment of local government power. In doing so, I have focused on various operating constraints, and on the ways state practice and discourse shaped the production of policy proposals and initiatives.

Lesbian and gay municipal initiatives encountered criticism not only from right-wing opponents, but from radical lesbians and gay men as well. Lesbian feminists expressed concern that the dominant municipal discourse of equal opportunities and 'heterosexism' was unable to distinguish between the different gender politics of lesbians and gay men (Cooper 1994c). Sex radicals argued homosexuality was becoming desexualized. The character of local government discourse and policymaking combined with the focus on 'oppression politics' was transforming homosexuality into a purely social identity. In many ways, the subsequent 'in your face' approach of queer politics provided an antidote for British lesbians and gays intent on counteracting the new, seemingly hegemonic culture of municipal respectability and insipidness.

Despite the limitations and problems faced by lesbian and gay municipal policy development, however, success stories exist. I want to conclude by considering some of the successes, as well as the ensuing tensions municipal activism generated. At the level of provision, achievements occurred in the development of AIDS policies, adoption and fostering initiatives, housing rights, outreach, and the funding of social and cultural events (ALA 1990; LGIU 1991:18–19; Cooper 1994a). Lesbian and gay structures also provided a 'state' base from which to support community campaigns in Britain and abroad. Few lesbian and gay actors considered municipal activism simply as a discrete site of activity, rather they perceived it as linked to wider equality struggles. Lesbian and gay council committees used their bureaucratic status to demand that bodies reliant on, or regulated by, local authorities abide by municipal non-discrimination policies. In Southampton, for instance, the lesbian and gay committee raised the question of controlling anti-gay jokes made by comedians in acts on council premises.[40] The committee also asked for an investigation into local hotels' policy on providing rooms for lesbian and gay couples.[41]

Perhaps, though, the most important achievement was lesbian and gay work's very existence – the visibility generated, and the experience participants gained from entering the local state *as* lesbian and gay, albeit in most cases for just a short while. This point is eloquently summarized in Femi Otitoju's rephrasing of an activist's words, following the abolition of the GLC:

> 'But think about it,' he said, 'We've all been here working together and soon we're going to be scattered, into other boroughs, and into the voluntary sector, scattering far and wide like the seeds of a single dandelion that eventually cultivates a whole field.'
>
> (Otitoju 1988:231)

However transient and politically precarious, the lesbian and gay municipal project was an attempt to deploy state power in an innovative, contentious way that challenged past truths and certainties. Within this context, perhaps one of the work's most interesting aspects was its contestation of disciplinary relations. This practice was not unique to lesbian and gay work. It can also be found in race, gender, disability and anti-poverty initiatives (Gyford *et al.* 1989:266–74), where the participative frameworks established – committee co-options, public meetings, outreach, consultation – began the complex, difficult process of constructing new relationships between state and civil society (Cant 1991:164–5).[42]

In the case of lesbian and gay municipal work, grass-roots relationships emerged as strong and exciting. Actors drew on these links to stop or, at least, impede the ability of the state to discipline their work. Supported by and politically acccountable to diverse communities, lesbian and gay officers and councillors (not always consciously) developed a range of resistance strategies. Unpredictability, insubordination, cheek, taking risks – these were some of the practices or tactics that gave lesbian and gay work its high profile, controversial identity. As time wore on, however, such challenges to state disciplinary power lessened. As specialist lesbian and gay staff became more socialized – absorbing bureaucratic culture and processes – their accountability to, and reliance upon, communities weakened.

In Haringey, as new employees, the council's lesbian and gay unit could claim they were unaware of the protocol that meant all education matters went through the education department. Several months later, their professional and social induction, combined with the criticism and censure received for their earlier 'mistake', made a repeat incident unlikely. Nevertheless, as a unit they continued to resist some of the manifestations of bureaucratic hierarchy and municipal process. According to one unit member:

> The leadership tried to have a containing role . . . but because our politics were beyond a lot of them, they couldn't take us on effectively. One time Bernie Grant [the council leader] demanded to see the unit in his office. We said we couldn't come because his office wasn't accessible. So he had to come down to the unit, onto our territory where there was eight of us and one of him.
>
> (lesbian and gay training officer)

Nevertheless despite such challenges, at a broader level Haringey's unit, in common with other lesbian and gay specialist officers, faced ongoing uncertainty as to their role. Should they, as activists, continue to challenge the disciplinary character of local government power, or, as professionals, use available resources to develop affirmative action provision for the benefit of lesbian and gay communities? This question lies at the heart of struggles to deploy state power (see Smart 1989), raising in turn an important problem: can state power transform the organization of sexuality if its technologies of power do not themselves change? Indeed, how static can such technologies remain when state power is deployed on behalf of new, oppositional objectives?

As I go on to argue in my final chapter, I would dispute any polarization of strategy into one of using or undermining state power. Rather, I would like to argue both can coexist as valid. While the state controls particular resources, attempts to gain access to them to further oppositional agendas is important. At the same time, state culture and process will limit and re-form their utility as I have here explored. Neither process is static, however. The use of state power by oppositional forces will often provoke (intentionally or not) changes to the character and content of its power technologies. Similarly, attempts to undermine state power, for instance, through contesting social services intervention within the home, or local government control over educational provision, may well lead to transformations in its access.

Exploring lesbian and gay state activism raises a further more basic question what values, norms and objectives provide the basis for engaging with dominant power? Is resistance to heterosexual domination sufficient reason, or should lesbian and gay state activism be linked to a more developed political project? These are questions I explore in the afterword which considers the role of an 'ethics of power' in providing a foundation for political action. First, in the chapter that follows, I wish to examine the nature of strategy within postmodern theory and activism. In particular, I critically explore the current emphasis on resistance, linking it to an argument for a proliferation of strategy and struggle within both counter-hegemonic and anti-hegemonic projects.

Notes

1 Key authorities to develop lesbians and gay equality policies included the London boroughs of Camden, Ealing, Haringey, Islington, Lambeth and Southwark. Authorities outside London included Manchester, Nottingham and Southampton.

2 For a more detailed and extensive analysis of lesbian and gay municipal activism, see Cooper (1994a).

3 Amongst a few of the older gay councillors a civil rights perspective prevailed.

4 In a minority of authorities, joint working was less apparent. However, even where lesbians and gay men organized separately and had distinct committees, they tended to be constructed within a common discourse (Cooper 1994c).

5 See Cooper (1994c) for further discussion of these tensions.

6 Tensions between gay men's and lesbians' approach to sexuality blew up in Nottingham over the language to be used in equal opportunity logos. Gay men were happy with the term 'sexual orientation' which they argued included heterosexuals as well as gays. Lesbians, however, argued that the phrase was an 'umbrella term' which 'lumps lesbians together with male practices with which they have nothing in common' and 'which suggests lesbianism is only about who we have sexual relationships with'; see Nottingham Lesbian Sub-Committee, *Minutes*, item 33, 6 November 1986.

7 Unusually, in London during this period, at least two council leaders were 'out' as lesbians, and several others had close links with the lesbian and gay community. There were also senior officers and other councillors who were 'out'. Thus one cannot construct a neat distinction between the lesbian and gay community, and council officers and politicians. However, although the politics of some senior gay actors was shaped by their identification with the lesbian and gay movement, their political decisions were also shaped by their municipal position. As a result, the conflicting agendas and imperatives generated, in some instances, caused tensions in their relations with the lesbian and gay activist community.

8 In certain instances, Labour councillors' backing was seen as a pragmatic rather than ideological decision – a way of maintaining political credibility.

> Initiatives were supported through opportunism. It became 'the line' that was supported and then later dropped. The Left care about credibility, appearing to take lesbian and gay voices into account, 'scoring' points; 'I'm more radical than you' posturing.
>
> (London council leader)

9 See Carabine's (1994) study of sexuality and policy-making in Sheffield. There she argues that a 'civil liberties' stance was adopted by some Labour councillors because it was compatible with a Labourist framework. However, she argues

that even this approach was not adopted consistently, and councillors' positions would depend on the political context. Thus where it was about contesting Tory policy they might be more willing to advocate a 'civil liberties' agenda than where the issue concerned young people's social and sexual education.

10 Progressive council leaders, for instance, when interviewed stressed the difference their support for lesbian and gay equality made, particularly when no formal policies were in existence.

11 See letter to this effect from the city secretary of Nottingham City Council to the committee secretary of the Gay Men's Sub-Committee, 25 July 1986.

12 See, for example, the report to Lambeth Working Party for Gay Men and Lesbians, *Item* 7(b), 21 May 1984:

> There is very little research available to answer even basic questions related to the ability of gay people to provide good parenting.

13 In progressive authorities, this was a mixture of liberal and socialist ideology.

14 However, municipal lesbians and gays had to work hard to hold onto their place within the equal opportunity litany. The prevailing perception among heterosexual municipal actors that homosexuality's right to be included was marginal, meant lesbians and gays had to reaffirm the legitimacy of their inclusion constantly.

15 Heterosexism is the belief and practice that heterosexuality is the only *natural* form of sexuality . . . [It] also teaches people to regard lesbians and gay men as 'queer', as 'perverted' . . . *because of the way these attitudes have beeninstitutionalised*, lesbians and gay men are subject both to serious discrimination . . . and harassment.

Haringey Labour Party (1986) *Manifesto*, section 5; emphasis added

16 Arguably, if such councillors had support from the majority of Labour politicians on their council they would have been less marginalized; however, in such instances, as I argue later, other processes might well intervene to limit the impact they could have.

17 In considering why senior actors adopted this role we need to consider not just their sexual politics, but a wider range of ideologies, objectives and motivations. These included maintaining control and legitimacy, 'empire building', long-term political ambitions, anxiety, and an unwillingness to make lesbian and gay equality a priority.

18 However, municipal lesbian and gay work was also more contradictory, as I explore later, in the way it emphasized community participation and lateral organizational systems. For a discussion of the shift from 'vertically integrated' to more 'decentralized' methods of public management during the 1980s, see Hoggett (1991).

19 I use the term 'policy' to refer to specific programmes for action or for structuring action embedded within discursive/normative frameworks.

20 Although lesbian and gay structures comprised part of the formal policy-making processes of local government, their newness, different discourse, organizationally central location and lack of a departmental structure meant the links between them and departments were often not clear-cut or straightforward; thus

the implementation problems experienced mirrored some of those encountered in policy coordination between different agencies, as well as those between different levels within the same agency (see generally Lewis 1984).

21 Because of the need to gain support from workers in services, some councils concentrated on training policies, using specialist resources to confront and alter the attitudes and/or practices of departmental and front-line staff.

22 On similar problems facing women's initiatives, see Halford (1992:165–6).

23 The repeated inattendance of key people at meetings could also impede proposals from being developed. In some authorities, ongoing inquoracy was a serious problem.

24 Bureaucratic procedures were also used politically to lessen the impact of lesbian and gay work. Extensive consultation, for instance, was used to minimize criticism that policies were being implemented without adequate opportunity for opponents to make their feelings known, as well as to postpone a controversial decision.

25 Councillors were also influenced by the Right and media's construction of similar narratives of frightened, provoked local residents (Cooper 1994a). While councillors may have exaggerated or overestimated the threat of opposition, this was not necessarily done intentionally but rather reflected their absorption of dominant municipal and political discourses. Thanks to Susan Halford for this point.

26 See Southampton Standing Advisory Committee on Lesbian and Gay Rights, *Item* 6, 11 June 1985.

27 This was made clear in letters from the Department of Education to Haringey education service in response to their 'positive images' of lesbians and gay men policy. The DES's letters set out to remind the authority of its obligation to operate within the statutory framework and its lack of political independence (25 July 1986, 29 January 1987, 31 July 1987).

28 See discussion in the House of Lords, 28 July 1986: 552–4.

29 Parents' Rights Group leaflet, summer 1986.

30 See 'Equal opportunities – lesbians and gay men', *Report*, Education Committee, 30 September 1986.

31 Letters from the Department of Education and Science to Haringey council's chief education officer, 25 July 1986, 29 January 1987, 31 July 1987.

32 For example, see *The Daily Mirror*, 15 October 1986; *The London Standard*, 19 March 1987; *The Haringey Independent*, 23 April 1987.

33 For some, this ideological bifurcation was a conscious process based on the realization that given local government in the 1980s only certain things were possible. For others, the process was more subliminal, rooted in an 'instinctive' sense that local government was not an appropriate arena for the promotion of, for instance, lesbianism or the contestation of marriage.

34 The municipal Left can also be seen as entrenching this kind of interpretive framework by using these roles as a means of challenging central government incursions. In particular, they focused on local government as the site of local democracy and provider of local services. Others on the Left, however, argued this discourse romanticized local government and reinforced a liberal political perspective on the local state.

35 While reproducing status quo social relations and norms is no less political, the

naturalized nature of these relations and norms tends to render them less visible.

36 This is not to suggest that the state does not penetrate so-called private realms in ways perceived as legitimate.

37 The extent to which homosexuality is actually 'concealed' or invisible within liberal discourse is explored more fully in Chapter 4.

38 One of the interesting ironies here is the way in which right-wing opponents also structured their opposition around the local state's identity within liberal discourse.

39 In considering possible strategies we need to ask: in what ways do local government and other (state) institutions reinforce or reproduce specific discourses *about* local government? Do these sites also offer the possibility of generating new state discourses that highlight or produce more oppositional state identities?

40 The leisure department responded by saying they could only ensure acts fell within the law by not offending public decency. Implicit in this statement was the provision that homophobia would be tolerated while the promotion of lesbian and gay equality might not be.

41 Both issues were raised under *Item* 4, 14 November 1985.

42 Lesbian and gay officers can also be seen as partially circumventing the authority and sphere of control of service-based street-level workers. Their own knowledge and embeddedness within lesbian and gay communities as well as their brief to carry out community development and individual case work meant they often possessed greater legitimacy as workers in the area of sexual equality (and as 'representatives' of the lesbian/gay community in ways that challenged politicians' representative legitimacy). Strong community contacts in some instances meant they could also monitor and override front-line officers' interactions.

7

Beyond resistance: Political strategy and counter-hegemony

> Resistance is directed at not being a docile or useful body . . . resistance
> happens when we stop the search for our 'truth', when we fight against
> the experts telling us who and what we are, when we refuse to be docile
> bodies. *If power is targeted at the body, then it is the body that is the site of
> resistance.*
>
> (O'Connor 1993; emphasis added)

Introduction

Throughout the 1980s, conservative governments in Britain, the USA and
Canada witnessed local and institutional opposition to a range of different
policies. Government agendas were challenged, obstructed, and sometimes
simply ignored as progressive communities attempted to carve a space for
initiative within civil society. At the same time, the international evapora-
tion of neo-communist regimes exacerbated growing local doubts and disillusionment in the potential of a transcendent, socialist project. At a
theoretical level, postmodernists proclaimed the death of the 'grand narrative' (Lyotard 1986), advocating instead micro-analysis and resistance. Yet
despite intensified political uncertainty, activists and writers continue to
champion specific, particularized strategies towards progressive change.[1]

In *Power in Struggle*, I have explored some of the debates over strategy in
the area of sexuality, in particular between radical lesbians and radical
pluralists. The nomenclature of the 'sex wars' only begins to identify the
intensity of struggles to define the 'authentic' feminist response to pornography, sexual violence, and sado-masochism. In the very different terrain
of political organizations such as the British Labour Party, similar energy
was spent battling over *the* correct response to Thatcherism in a way that

denied the possibility or validity of different approaches. Even postmodernists have not been immune from a desire to privilege specific terrains, forms of power, and normative frameworks despite the apparent contradiction with their political analysis. For instance, at the same time as arguing, 'Those who are committed to progressive action in a post modern world must resist the temptation to seek theoretical closure and enforce practical dogma', Alan Hutchinson states (1992:786) 'postmodernism is the only critical resource that a progressive activist can have and want'.

In this concluding chapter, my aim is to contest the a priori privileging of particular political strategies, and to argue instead for the proliferation of challenges to systemic inequality throughout social life. I defend this advocacy of diversification and strategic pluralism for reasons that become apparent as the chapter progresses.[2] It is important, however, from the start to distinguish this approach from analytical or normative pluralism – whether we do or should live in a pluralist society. In earlier chapters, I disputed the notion of social pluralism, that is, that power is significantly dispersed in ways that operate against systemic inequality. In the afterword – where I outline a particular ethic of power – I critique pluralism as a normative ideal.

In arguing for a diversification of strategy, this chapter explores the following issues and questions. First, what is the relationship between power and resistance? Here I wish to develop my earlier argument (see Chapter 2) that resistance is not, as many Foucauldians suggest, power's antithesis. This discussion raises a second question or theme: the connection between resistance and other social struggles. Much (post)modern theory has tended to reduce struggle to resistance. In this section I discuss this development and explore its implications.

The following section continues my argument for diversified strategy by focusing on three issues. First, I argue that since no spheres or technologies of power should be granted primacy a priori, there is no inherent closure nor a single route to the good life. Second, strategies need to be situated and specific. In making this point, I critique certain feminist poststructuralist theorists who praise or condemn abstract 'progressive' concepts. Instead, I argue that different concepts or principles may 'work' in diverse contexts. However our ability to predict the outcome and effects of specific strategies is limited, since overdetermination and the interventions of a range of social actors mean strategies may generate disparate and unexpected consequences. As a result, I argue third for an open, non-judgemental consideration of different political approaches, since those we might condemn or consider misconceived *may* prove more 'effective' in retrospect than we imagined.[3]

The final section draws these issues together by considering a key strategy of the (late) modern era: counter-hegemony. Counter-hegemonic projects aim to link together diverse communities, strategies and terrains to win consent for a new cultural order. In comparing counter-hegemony to its new postmodern counterpart – the anti-hegemonic project – I explore some of the advantages and problems of each.

Power and resistance within oppositional struggle

> Wherever there is power there is resistance.
>
> (Laclau and Mouffe 1985:152)

Foucauldian feminism has tended to equate power with varied and pervasive forms of domination rather than with liberation. At the same time, as I discussed in Chapter 2, there is no simple freedom beyond power; we cannot ignore force relations through an illusory attempt to construct a power-free society. The only hopeful prospect is ongoing and constant resistance, a possibility that exists wherever power takes hold, since power always involves agency, that is, the capacity of a subject to behave differently (Foucault 1988:123).[4]

Within this framework, resistance has come to be conceptualized as *the* means by which subjugated forces act, counterposed to power within an apparently secure dialectic.[5] De Lauretis (1991:iii), for instance, states,

> [L]esbian and gay sexualities may be understood and imaged as forms of *resistance* to cultural homogenization, counteracting dominant discourses with other constructions of the subject in culture.
>
> (emphasis added)

Not all feminist writers adopt this approach, and many have criticized Foucauldian perspectives on resistance (see Ramazanoglu and Holland 1994). Here, I wish to focus on a particular problematic that emerges as a result of identifying subjugated forces' actions as resistance. This problematic has two aspects: first, it *assumes* conflict (even if none is apparent) since resistance functions as an antagonistic response to a dominant form of power; second, such conflict is conceptualized as resistance rather than other kinds of struggle. However, if we analyse the actions of 'subjugated' forces as *deploying* rather than simply resisting power, conflict cannot be assumed. Power, as I have conceptualized it, does not inevitably involve opposition. It may be present, but its existence requires closer analysis. Let me provide an example of what I mean.

In his 1992 presidential address to the American Law and Society Association, Joel Handler (1992:713–15) discusses postmodern writing which tells stories of protest 'from below'. One concerns a narrative, based on research by Ewick and Silbey (1992), about a 'middle-aged African-

American woman'. This woman, Simpson, was erroneously sentenced to 15 hours' community service for a traffic crime for which she was subsequently acquitted. Unbeknownst to the court, she elects to do it in a church in which she already works as a volunteer, an action identified as resistance to power (Handler 1992:714).

> In Simpson's story, there is acquiescence, resistance, and contestation . . . The authors' emphasize the resistance. In arranging for the community service, Simpson 'successfully insinuated her life into the space of the law and . . . reversed for a moment the trajectory of power . . .'

Yet what is it about the act that makes it 'resistance'? Arguably, Simpson is simply utilizing the legal resources – the power she possesses – to choose where to perform her community service. Such a choice is not only permitted but actually facilitated by the criminal process. To what extent is it then resistance, 'an infiltration of the dominant text' (Ewick and Silbey 1992:27)?

According to Handler's narrative (1992:714), Simpson feels that she has won a victory against the institution. She has used the provision to 'elect' her place of community service to limit the effects of the penalty, and thereby to undermine what she perceives as the institution's intentions and objectives. But if, hypothetically, unbeknownst to Simpson, the court was aware she carried out voluntary work at the church and either did not care, or else believed that such knowledge on their part did not negate her right to choose, would it still be resistance? Does resistance simply depend on the subjective interpretation of the resister, that is, their perception that conflicting interests exist and that their behaviour impedes the wishes of opposing forces? Does it require recognition on the part of the other actor or institution? Or does it necessitate *actual* resistance – the obstruction of dominant projects – hence (possibly multiple) 'external' readings to determine whether it has taken place?

In many instances, these different interpretive standpoints come together; however, their merging cannot be assumed. For instance, Section 28 of the British Local Government Act 1988 may have been obstructed most effectively not by protestors arguing for its withdrawal, but by those solicitors in progressive authorities who claimed the section was unworkable. In the main, however, this was not done out of a desire to frustrate the law but rather to provide councillors with the desired interpretation. Can such a reading of the legislation be defined as resistance? What does it mean to call it such?

As with debates in cultural studies over meaning and standpoint, these questions are difficult to resolve satisfactorily. Indeed, in this discussion, an answer is not really the objective. Although we could choose to identify resistance as intentional disruption, this would still not deal with the varied motivations causing people to obstruct different processes. In any event, I am more concerned with emphasizing the conceptual ambiguity resistance as a term possesses. Currently a fashionable expression to be thrown at a myriad of social engagements, 'resistance' by itself tells us little of what is actually taking place.[6]

Constructing resistance as an overarching category counterposed to power is both grounded in, and also facilitates, a division of people into the dominant and dominated (e.g. Hartsock 1990; cf. Faith 1994). In the telling of Simpson's story, the dominant becomes a coherent grouping (Ewick and Silbey 1991:12). The assumption of conflict in describing her action as 'resistance' elides together the interests of law makers, judges and court into a unified, strategic project at odds with Simpson's wishes. As I have discussed in Chapters 4, 5 and 6, however, state agency is much more complex and contradictory. Thus we could examine the diverse agendas and processes which led to the provision allowing defendants to choose their place of community service. We might guess that while some within the criminal justice system approved, others found it too liberal. Defining Simpson's action as resistance not only suggests a coherent, powerful state but also one with sufficient agency to enforce its will. Simpson is the mouse, searching for cracks and crevices in the elephantine drive of institutional power. But where does this place more progressive state voices? How does it acknowledge the nuances of their position – opposed to conservative agendas, yet implicated within state practice?

Simpson's story also raises the question of resistance's effects. Does resistance do more than simply impede the reproduction or generation of domination – in Simpson's case, the relentless onslaught of state power? A problem with resistance is that it tends to operate as an essentially negative term, underestimating, as a result, the changes that *do* frequently emerge. That is, two options are assumed: either the (re)production of dominant social relations if resistance fails, or else, if successful, the return to a pre-existing individual, collective or institutional situation.

However, if we understand resistance as the deployment of power by oppositional forces, motivated to oppose a particular (new) practice or form of institutional power, rather than as simply naming a response to power, outcomes are rarely as clear-cut or fixed. Even if resistance is successful, it does not precipitate a return to some pre-existing status quo but rather generates a new, precarious equilibrium – a fresh context within which subsequent actions will be played out. For instance, the anti-poll tax movement in Britain in the late 1980s may have aimed simply to 'stop' the poll tax, and on one reading it achieved this. However, it also played a part in the emergence of a new tax (that did not fully replicate its rates predecessor); generated inventive local knowledges of legal defiance; informed the reshaping of municipal tax collection practices, and, perhaps most significantly, paved the way for Margaret Thatcher's overthrow as British Prime Minister.

As well as generating multiple outcomes, resistance is often not the exclusive objective within a particular struggle. The mobilization against Section 28, for instance, was not just an attempt to stop a particular legislative enactment. Woven into 'Stop the Clause' campaigns were discourses of lesbian and gay pride and affirmation, support for local council lesbian and gay work, and the publicization of lesbian and gay contributions to the arts (see Carter 1992:222). Whilst some of these may have been strategically advanced to emphasize the dangers of S.28, and thus part of a discourse of resistance, to *reduce* the campaign to resistance not only marginalizes other objectives, but also minimizes participants' conflicting perspectives as to the purpose of their struggle.

One of the dangers of focusing on resistance, therefore, is that it can shift attention away from the diverse values and objectives of social movements as their agendas become defined through their opposition to 'power'. Identified as lacking power themselves, such movements are only capable of *resisting* the oncoming force. Thus they become constituted through this singular relationship of opposition.[7] A similar trend is apparent in the conceptual popularization of the term 'oppositional' (e.g. Fraser 1989:173; Terry 1991:57); now often used as a substitute for 'progressive', 'socialist' and 'feminist', 'oppositional' emphasizes what social movements share, that is, a rejection or hostility to the status quo. Used to describe a social movement or political agenda, 'oppositional' risks marginalizing and homogenizing the substantive heterogeneity and aims of the groups involved.[8] This may paradoxically cause problems for coalition building since the substantial differences between 'oppositional' organizations and movements are not given adequate attention or respect. Sawicki (1991:44), for instance, illustrates this point in her injunction that lesbian feminists support other 'sexual minorities':

> Lesbian feminists . . . new self-understandings are not immune to cooptation within dominant power relations. For example, lesbian feminists could be tempted to capitulate to more conservative forces by disavowing their affiliation with other oppressed sexual minorities rather than engaging in efforts to further articulate their connections with the sex fringe . . . This would require that we continue to provide detailed historical analyses of the ways in which sexuality has become a pivotal target in strategies of domination.

In Chapter 3, I explored these tensions more fully. The point I wish to highlight here is that the value dissension between some lesbian sadomasochists and radical lesbians is as fundamental as their shared opposition to dominant sexual hierarchies and compulsory heterosexuality. Whilst both forms of lesbian politics may exist in an antagonistic relation to the status quo, they remain irreducible to such a relation. Oppositionality alone does not render them compatible. Indeed, as I discussed in Chapter 3, what each finds objectionable in, or even definable as, the status quo may be quite different.

None of this is to deny the possibility or desirability of coalitions or joint working. Within the lesbian and gay community, various forces have co-alesced on issues such as homelessness, health care, racism and state violence. Whether these alliances can or should become more formalized or any less contingent is uncertain. In the final section of this chapter, I explore the problems and benefits of strategies that seek to bring together disparate forces within a counter-hegemonic project. However, before considering the possibilities for coherent, articulated strategies, I wish to argue for political diversification. I begin by considering some of its constituent elements.

A proliferation of struggles

Targeting technologies of power

So far I have argued that resistance is just *one* political method or motivation for struggle; to treat it therefore as an umbrella term for other kinds of struggle is, I suggest, problematic. Equally contentious is holding resistance up as the antithesis of power. Technologies of power are deployed by all forces in their struggles, it is what gives them the *capacity* to struggle. At the same time, different forms of power operate to structure the terrain, objectives and manner of struggle. Thus I am not arguing for a framework which treats power simply as a resource different forces possess to varying degrees. As the means by which outcomes are generated, it is considerably more (Chapter 2).

Engagement with status quo power can take many forms, involving a range of objectives and practices other than resistance. Let me briefly outline four discussed in more detail in earlier chapters. Considering these strategies provides us with a glimpse of what an ethics of power might mean, as I explore in the afterword. To begin with, strategy can aim at *deploying* institutional power. For instance, in British local government in the 1980s, lesbians and gay men took up municipal office as local government officers and councillors (see Chapter 6). Key here is a transformation in the *identity* of the agents exercising power, although changing this will often lead to other alterations as well. Thus deploying power cannot simply be dismissed as a limited, reformist tactic that does not impact upon the character of the power in question (see Chapter 6). Moreover, in some instances, concerns may focus more on *who* is exercising power than with the *kind* of power being deployed.

Second, social change strategies may involve transforming the particular *form* power takes, its content, or the pervasiveness of certain technologies.

For instance, it could involve democratizing decision-making processes within industry, or minimizing (containing) the strength of particular power techniques such as physical might, *laissez-faire* economics, and militarism. I have discussed certain possibilities for transforming power technologies elsewhere in this book. For instance, in Chapter 3, I explored the possibility of reconstituting desire as a form of disciplinary power along less asymmetrical lines. Similarly, in Chapter 5, I discussed the 'alternative' reproductive arrangements established by lesbian mothers as a result of their access difficulties to state regulated provision.

Political strategy might involve redistributing *access* to resources, through anti-poverty strategies, community education, and rights-based struggles. The municipal strategies discussed in Chapter 6 included attempts to reallocate municipal funds to lesbians and gays trying to establish community centres or to assist them in holding cultural events.[9] However, other kinds of resources, such as education, cannot be meaningfully reallocated without changes to their content.[10] For instance, giving young lesbians and gay men access to sex education would not constitute a particularly useful resource if it ignored their own sexuality.

Finally, struggles may aim to make dominant power forms visible: to 'name' and reinterpret them. Anti-heterosexist strategies have not just been about challenging the nature of institutionalized sexual power but also, at a more basic level, to identify the social processes involved in the construction of sexual orientation and hierarchy. In this way, heterosexuality is shown to have 'origins' within power rather than nature.

Transforming the mechanisms of power raises the question of whether effects and outcomes bear any relationship to the power-struggles adopted. For example, if municipal funds are reallocated, will this empower the communities affected? Or will they be disempowered by a possible backlash, subsequent change of political will, dependency, co-option and so on? While we may be able to look back at such a reallocation of resources and consider its diverse effects, to what extent can these be 'known' or accurately guessed in advance? Much current theory asserts the radical indeterminacy or contingency of social life. In this section, I argue for a midway position which recognizes the riskiness of prediction and the uncertainty of strategy without claiming that power generates totally chaotic and unexpected effects. In taking this approach, I suggest that strategy should be multiple, diversified and ongoing.

Negotiating uncertainty

Politicians and theorists who advocate single strategies, claiming the possibility of prediction, tend to start from the premise of a primary relation of domination or form of power. If the deep structure of social life operates according to a single dynamic, it seems possible to analyse its workings and effectively to designate strategies of transformation. However, if there is no primary determinant, if social life is overdetermined by the constant articulation and rearticulation of different elements, the effects of political strategy are both more complex and uncertain. For instance, the outcome of British lesbian and gay municipal policies was shaped by political, economic and cultural changes. These changes included the reduction in municipal resources, central government's legislative agenda, the growing visibility of lesbian and gay politics, and an expansion of multi-culturalism. The outcomes of such municipal policies were also shaped by the specific interactions of public officials, right-wing opponents, lesbian and gay activists, and advocates of other local initiatives who dismissed sexual politics as a waste of municipal time and resources (see Chapter 6).

The concept of overdetermination as I am using it not only contests the primacy given by orthodox Marxists to the economic sphere and to the role of the working class, but as well the textual privileging of some current theorists who claim signifying systems determine what can be thought and known (e.g. Ebert 1991:294). This latter approach has become highly influential in relation to sexual strategies as I discuss in Chapter 3. Theorists such as Bensinger (1992:83) and Butler (1990:30) argue we cannot envisage or live new sexual choreographies but must simply recirculate those that currently dominate. To put it another way, within a 'phallic economy', lesbians can reinterpret the phallus, claim it as their own in a project that attempts to denaturalize any links with the penis. What they cannot do, however, is reject it.

It may be idealist to pretend we can live at a distance from dominant ideological representations. At the same time, in recognizing that such representations are not the primary determinant of social life, it becomes possible to identify a way beyond current hegemonic ideologies, namely, through engaging with the modes and terrains which *shape* dominant representations (see Chapter 2). Challenging male economic authority and the legitimacy of military and street-level aggression may be as successful a way of contesting the hegemony of the penile phallus as lesbians packing their trousers with dildos.

Adopting an overdetermined framework, which recognizes the determinancy of varied terrains and forms of power, highlights the value of a diversified approach to strategy. At the same time, sensitivity to context is crucial. This is both a reason for strategic pluralism – no one approach can be appropriate in all circumstances – and as a way of tempering a blanket approach which assumes so long as there is variety, subtlety does not matter.

> Political strategies . . . rest on analyses of the utility of certain arguments in certain discursive contexts . . . There are moments when it

makes sense for women to demand consideration for their social role, and contexts within which motherhood is irrelevant to women's behaviour . . . meanings are always relative to particular constructions in specified contexts.

(Scott 1988:47)

Within recent theory, considerable effort has been made to provide situated accounts of norms and truths (Hutchinson 1992:779). However some normative theory, in its desire to advocate particular strategic frameworks, has lost sight of this contextualization. Concepts such as justice and equality have become reified as good or bad without adequate consideration of their different impacts according to their articulation in particular situations.

Post-modernists do not seek 'equality', whether this is understood as 'equal treatment for equals' or due process for all. Feminists have begun to question whether 'equality' can mean anything other than assimilation to a pre-existing and problematic 'male' norm.

(Flax 1992:146)

Flax (1992) argues that justice is a more useful concept than equality because, while the latter implies sameness, justice is grounded in difference. Although she acknowledges that the relative value of justice is context-dependent, her conceptualization of justice is so broad that it is hard to envisage circumstances in which it would not be of benefit.

Drawing on deconstructive methodologies, Young (1990) adopts a similar approach. She argues for the normative rejection of the concept 'community' on the basis of its 'deep' meaning:

The ideal of community . . . privileges unity over difference, immediacy over mediation, sympathy over recognition of the limits of one's understanding of others from their point of view . . . The dream (of community) is understandable but politically problematic . . . because those motivated by it will tend to suppress differences among themselves or implicitly to exclude from their political groups persons with whom they do not identify.

(Young 1990:300)

While critiquing community as an ideal may in certain circumstances be appropriate, it understates the value in other contexts of a communitarian framework. In some situations, community, like equality, may prove a useful discursive strategy; there may also be value in trying to rearticulate it in ways that avoid some of its limitations. While terms do have histories and thus can never be fully freed (Butler 1993a:229), some, such as justice, citizenship and equality may prove relatively malleable within progressive political praxis (Cooper 1993a; Herman 1993).

One danger in arguing for a contextualized approach is its potential to revert to a position which declares that at any juncture *one* right strategy exists. Can we be both nuanced and pluralist? Is there such a thing as a 'dangerous' strategy? Sheila Jeffreys certainly suggests there might be in her book *The Lesbian Heresy* (1994:102–107). There she attacks the postmodern feminist strategy of mimicry, arguing that feminists parodying femininity insults women in its intellectual élitism, as well as acting to reinforce traditional feminine stereotypes.

While mimicry *may* have these effects, it is also conceivable that its exaggerated performativity helps to denaturalize femininity. Before examining this further, however, let me address a prior question: how desirable or significant is such denaturalization? Whether mimicry is seen as useful or counter-productive depends on this question. Sheila Jeffreys's approach, for instance, seems to discount the importance of gender's common-sense status:

> If male supremacy only managed to carry on because little lightbulbs of realisation of the falsity of gender were failing to be illuminated in the heads of men and women, then Butler's strategy might be destined for success.
>
> (Jeffreys 1994:103)

By focusing on gender as a conflict of interests, the benefits of denaturalization appear less substantial. Men do not care whether women are born or made inferior, their aim is simply to maintain their advantage. Thus the potential harm mimicry can cause to women's self-esteem outweighs the uncertain benefits of disrupting what it means to be a woman.

The approach I adopt, however, acknowledges the significance of common sense in the perpetuation of systemic inequality. Strategies that attempt to dislodge traditional forms of knowledge are, therefore, in theory, worthwhile. Let me then return to my initial question: how likely is mimicry to disrupt successfully gender assumptions (or prove beneficial in other ways)? Can this be even answered or does it require, albeit within a specific context, too high a degree of prediction, of guessing, of estimates? There may also be a difference between asking whether gender parody will generate particular concrete effects in the short term, and whether it will lead to hazy, diffused, long-term changes in the organization of gender. As I go on to discuss in the context of prefiguration, political predictions are a fraught business in their suggestion that we can 'know' the future. That is, not only can we identify whether one practice will lead to another, but also what such subsequent practices might look like.

In using the concept of overdetermination, I argue that future effects can neither be fully predicted nor fully understood. The interaction of different sites and technologies, the practices and activism of diverse forces, the likely time lag between strategy, practice and effects in a constantly changing climate mean effects may be unanticipated and possibly surprising. At the same time, politics and strategy depend on a degree of predictability and strategic learning. Moreover, as I have explored in earlier chapters, outcomes often do reflect the expectations of strategists and critics. For instance, while the emergence of British lesbian and gay municipal policies may have seemed to many to be surprising, their subsequent disappearance as conventional municipal forces reasserted themselves could have been (and was) expected. History and learning offer techniques of anticipation. Terrains, actors and forms of power operate according to principles that can often be surmised. While the character and impact of various combinations is often difficult to identify (within the short, medium or long term), to ignore the extent of 'systematicity' would be to live in a perpetual world of chance and surprise.

How does this ambivalence assist in engaging with the postmodern (strategic) practice of parody and mimicry? First, I would argue it requires generosity, the recognition that strategies and struggles may prove beneficial (within certain time-frames and junctures) even if they are not the ones we ourselves would choose. At the same time, theorists defending parody or mimicry need to explore carefully the drawbacks critics raise, critically considering the situated usefulness of their strategy.

In this section, I have argued for the need to go beyond resistance to embrace a diversified approach towards strategy, one that entails the politicization of many different terrains, and the deployment of various power technologies. However, while it may be impossible to ascertain conclusively the most effective strategy, just as it is impossible to predict the range of short and long-term outcomes, this does not make planning redundant. Rather, like prefiguration, political planning deploys a fictional future in order to reorder a less contingent present. Planning or strategic learning does not have to adopt a monopolistic tone. Carried out within a spirit of recognition for the contingency of effects, dogmatism and hostility towards alternative approaches can be, if not transformed into engaged, interested support, then at least markedly more muted.

Counter-hegemony, anti-hegemony and prefigurative practice

So far I have argued for the diversification and proliferation of political action, but to what extent can and should different strategies be integrated into one corporate project? While advocates of counter-hegemony argue that difference should be articulated to form a common, united front, anti-hegemonic supporters stress the benefits of fragmentation. Oppositional politics, they argue, cannot be consolidated except at considerable cost to diversity and initiative. In this section, I wish to explore these two competing frameworks: one which attempts to consolidate difference, the other to fragment and expand it. My focus here is on 'progressive' projects, however, counter-hegemonies can also come in the form of right-wing challenges to the status quo (e.g. see Herman 1994a).

The framework for counter-hegemony derives from the work of Gramsci (1971). However, in its recent popularization, the Italian Marxist's original ideas have been refigured in a number of ways. Gramsci's argument concerned the problematic of revolutionary change in developed capitalist societies where the ruling class governed through consent as well as force (Gramsci 1971; Buci-Glucksmann 1982; Showstack Sassoon 1982). Within this context, the state functioned as the complex of activities through which justification, domination and the winning of active consent occurred (Gramsci 1971). Gramsci's work explored the possibility of disarticulating consent from the status quo in order to reformulate it around a different political project (Showstack Sassoon 1982). This process, as Gramsci envisaged it, placed the working class at the centre linked to other classes whose support would be gained through material concessions (Mouffe 1979: Ch. 5; Buci-Glucksmann 1980: Ch. 3). Thus a new historic bloc would form making possible a challenge to the dominant state power (Showstack Sassoon 1982).

In Gramsci's exploration of hegemony and the reformulation of consent, he identified the economy as a privileged site of determination. In recent years, however, the notion of counter-hegemony has been deployed by theorists such as Laclau and Mouffe (1985; Mouffe 1988) within a paradigm which refuses to prioritize any site of action or particular social force.[11]

> There is no *unique* privileged position from which a uniform continuity of effects will follow, concluding with the transformation of society as a whole . . . There is therefore no subject . . . which is absolutely radical and irrecuperable by the dominant order.
> (Laclau and Mouffe 1985:169)

Laclau and Mouffe's work focuses on creating linkages – articulations – between different social struggles within a democratic project based on radical notions of citizenship (see also Mouffe 1992a; 1992b; Smith 1994). It has been criticized from the Marxist Left (e.g. Wood 1986). However others, adopting a more postmodern perspective, have also questioned Laclau and Mouffe's expectation of a chain of equivalences forged between different struggles.

> There is a temptation to think that there must be some master code or 'monologic' that tells us what to do . . . Even thinkers like Laclau and Mouffe . . . fall back on the idea that there must be a 'chain of equivalences' that links the various struggles in which we must engage.

. . . There may *be* no equivalences . . . The truth is that we want and
need many things . . . we need many politics, many political practices,
many political communities, many political spaces.

(Magnusson 1992:79)[12]

In the introduction to *Organizing Dissent* (1992), William Carroll sets
out several approaches to counter-hegemony. He describes the approach
adopted by Magnusson and Walker (1988) as the advocation not of moving
beyond the fragments to create an oppositional hegemony, but rather of
multiplying the fragmentary effects of different campaigns.

Such postmodern movement politics can be called counter-hegemonic
only in the sense that they oppose and strive to destabilize the
hegemonic discourses that sustain subordination.

(Carroll 1992:14)

This third approach, then, I will call anti-hegemonic (see also Hutchinson
1992:775, who describes it as non-hegemonic). It aims to contest and de-
construct the status quo from diverse positionings without putting any
single project in its place.[13] Thus anti-hegemony not only opposes the status
quo but is also antipathetic to the concept of hegemony more generally (see
also Weeks 1993:90).[14] This does not mean that an anti-hegemonic approach is purely deconstructive. Magnusson and Walker (1988:63, 58), for
instance, stress the importance of 'exploration . . . of new political spaces,
political practices . . . and political communities', undertaken by 'critical
social movements' as well as the possibility of 'global solidarities'. Nevertheless, in defining critical social movements by their *oppositional* character, 'their challenge [to] the structures and practices of bourgeois society'
(Magnusson and Walker 1988:60), it appears that what is valued in anti-
hegemonic struggles is their contestation of the status quo, rather than the
new truths of certainties different movements may proffer.

Magnusson and Walker's (1988) focus on a proliferation of destabiliza-
tions and alternative political spaces parallels the strategic pluralism developed in this chapter.[15] Counter-hegemonic projects can prove limiting
when they denounce or reject oppositional tactics outside of their umbrella.
In the desire to create an integral, broad-based social movement, counter-
hegemonic movements invent an 'outside' – those forces or values excluded
from the project – as well as diminishing or marginalizing the work of
progressive social forces who do not wish to join. This creation of margins
and boundaries is something an anti-hegemonic approach *seeks* to avoid.[16]
Moreover, the fragmented character of anti-hegemonic political activism
renders the construction of pervasive new norms and dominant actors less
likely than a counter-hegemonic approach which seeks to constitute itself as
the new force or project.

The tendency to establish norms and standards, which then become rules to be policed, has proven a central problem for counter-hegemonic projects. Criticism and ridicule thrown at current 'political correctness' by those on the Left, while often revealing internalized prejudices and hierarchies of importance, nevertheless highlights the opposition generated by attempts to mandate a new hegemony. Engaging with power's *effects* through prescriptions, orders and injunctions – the construction of a forbidden – seems more likely to incite opposition and obstruction than the alternative of intervening in power's *processes* – the creation and (re)production of desires, practices, knowledges and interests.[17]

This is not to suggest that prescriptions and prohibitions can be completely avoided. The criminal law, for example, which tends to adopt this form has a role that progressive forces may rightly wish to extend to deal with 'hate speech' or discrimination (Matsuda 1989). However, as well as generating resentment and non-compliance, not only do legal prohibitions tend to avoid more complex forms of harm or inequality – the outcomes of government policy for example – but, as has been extensively demonstrated, they also do not necessarily generate the beneficial anticipated effects (Petersen 1991). This is not just a question of non-compliance. Rather it goes to the overdetermined relationship between legal enactments and their environment, including the discourses and agendas of implementers and legal subjects.

In saying counter-hegemony should focus on the processes of production, however, to what extent is it possible to distinguish between these processes and power's outcomes? To take one example, the *effects* of gender inequality in turn provide the mechanisms for its reproduction; thus they cannot easily be separated. However, while engaging with both the results and processes of gender may raise similar concerns, for instance, employment policies, childcare, pornography, rape, the character of strategy can differ according to which is centred. For example, focusing on the role media images play in relation to the *production* of gender inequality, rather than simply as gendered effects, makes possible a more reflexive approach that continuously reconsiders the impact of strategies to ensure they do not become counter-productive.

Locating struggle at the level of power's productivity may also create greater diversity of political engagement. Campaigns aimed at producing alternative images, teachers deconstructing sexist texts in classes, boycotts of particular media companies or products can be linked in ways that may prove less feasible when counter-hegemonic forces focus on prohibition. A less censorious approach also recognizes that problematic practices are socially constructed, and it is to deal with that social production for which strategies are required. Arguably this is less exclusionary and less dictatorial. By highlighting the social connectedness of life, it provides space for different social forces to engage with dominant discourses, asymmetrical disciplinary power, and the unequal allocation of resources in ways that, while diverse, still maintain a sense of political connection on the basis of (potentially) shared norms and values.

A counter-hegemony which focuses on power's processes rather than just its effects also makes possible the development of prefigurative practices. Prefiguration entails 'hiving off' fragments of terrain which can then be restructured according to futuristic, normative ideals. Within this newly bounded arena, prefiguration requires the intense deployment of resources, in particular time, energy, and commitment, to transform specific discplinary and discursive forms.

Prefiguration, however, has encountered criticism from postmodern theorists on the grounds that not only can we not know the future but we also cannot escape those current power relations in which we are enmeshed. Prefiguration is therefore both idealist and utopian in its suggestion that we can voluntarily enact elements of future practice in ways that will help precipitate that future. Yet, while criticism may be valid in acknowledging the fictive nature of any prefigurative practice, this alone does not provide sufficient reason for its rejection.

The extent of people's agency is such that to varying degrees we can *attempt* to conduct social relations differently. While these attempts may not prefigure a 'brave new world', they may provide a better quality of life in the here and now. The notion of prefiguration, however illusory, offers an important element for a counter-hegemonic project, for it provides a way of convincing people that different practices may be preferable. The argument that we persuade people primarily through debate, in its idealism, loses sight of the importance of material change to shaping people's values and perceptions. Practical examples, therefore, of alternative practices can provide such a foundation.

Both counter-hegemonic and anti-hegemonic strategies have advantages and drawbacks. Moreover, there may be no need to identify one as *the* way forward.[18] Both have a place within a radical politics, that is, both the development of an alternative cultural and social project and the proliferation of more fragmented challenges to the status quo. However, as I have argued, the benefit of challenging the status quo depends on the values and practices being contested, and (to a lesser degree) the ideological perspective from which such an attack is generated; not all change is progressive.

Conclusion

In this chapter I have focused on strategy – the planning of political action on the basis of objectives, values and operational traditions. Yet there is a danger of reducing all activism to strategy, to see every challenge, resistance or oppositional deployment of power as part of a coherent operation. This would miss a crucial element of both protest and change (one which postmodernists tend to emphasize), the intuitive, expressive, unprepared action.

While non-strategic actions are important to understanding political practice, paradoxically their theoretical fetishization transforms them into elements within a broader strategy. If the unplanned, expressive response to domination is an effective way of dodging or undermining its mark, then it must take its place within the panoply of strategic responses.[19] This is the tension anti-hegemony faces. Is it a description/analysis of current political practice or a normative framework? If the latter, are social forces to be *encouraged* to practise unpremeditated, expressive activism? The paradox of mandated spontaneity crystallizes the contradictions of an intellectual politics which lauds (but also at times infantilizes) the resistance of the subjugated.

Let me end by briefly summarizing the chapter's argument. I began with a critique of resistance as the antithesis of power, and therefore as *the* strategy of opposition. Instead, I argued that resistance could be conceptualized as one specific kind of strategy that aims to halt or disrupt the (re)production of particular forms of domination. Yet in highlighting the ambiguities of even this formulation, I questioned the conceptual clarity of resistance, without further elaboration, in offering an account of political activism.

In the central section of this chapter, I suggested that progressive forces need to draw on a range of political strategies and approaches, privileging a priori no particular terrain nor power technology. In part, my argument is based on the uncertainty of effects, thus the impact of particular strategies cannot be predicted. However, it is also grounded in the recognition that if no site is privileged as ultimately determinative, no realm can offer by itself a comprehensive locus of change.

In exploring the pluralization of political strategy, I argue for a nuanced, situated approach which recognizes that diverse strategies are needed to respond to radically different circumstances. At the same time, there is rarely a single perfect strategy for a given political context. Therefore, I argue for a generosity towards different strategic responses, while suggesting such responses need themselves to remain open to their own potential counter-productiveness.

Finally I considered the question of how different struggles or strategies might relate to each other. Should they be articulated within a single project or is fragmentation more desirable? Counter-hegemony, which seemed one of the most promising approaches in the early and mid-1980s, in Britain and elsewhere, subsequently encountered criticism for its attempt to weld people together around a single oppositional project. In this chapter I argued that counter-hegemony has a place (albeit not a monopolistic one) within progressive struggles. It does however have its problems. While all hegemonies are likely to create an 'outside', a radical hegemony requires the reflexivity constantly to interrogate its own borders.

To argue for a politics that encompasses both anti- and counter-hegemonic strategies may appear contradictory. Can we support both the establishment of a new commonsense and its contestation? Perhaps that is what is required, however. While counter-hegemonic projects encourage the transformation of structures on the basis of an aspirational future, anti-hegemony reminds us that such a future can only remain a strategic narrative.

Notes

1 By strategy, I mean a programmatic, linked combination of objectives and means of action that can be developed or acted upon by dominant or subordinate forces. I do not therefore use the term in its Foucauldian sense (e.g. see Hunt 1992:13).

   As identified earlier, I use the term 'progressive' to refer to political projects that advocate a more egalitarian, less asymmetrical society. These include projects that might themselves reject the notion of 'progressive' for its teleological implication that societies inevitably move 'forward'.

2 In using the concept of pluralism, I do not mean that struggles on different terrains or in relation to different power technologies operate automatically, unaffected by struggles elsewhere, nor do I assume that struggles should have a discrete existence. This last point is explored below in my discussion of counter-hegemony.

3 However, as I go on to argue this does not mean all strategies are equally likely to achieve specific results. We can therefore still engage in discussion about appropriate choices. Yet in recognizing the lack of certainty in any given choice, we can be more open to the possibilities offered by others.

4 Yet while it may be possible to resist the 'gaze within' through a process of externalization – that is by recognizing its 'otherness' – in the case of desire or interests, power's ability to shape what we want makes resistance appear a much less likely possibility. Those who resist tend to be those for whom the production of particular desires, for example heterosexuality, has failed to succeed. However in other instances, desires are resisted, not because of their general lack of efficacy, but because other principles or values, such as asceticism, prevail. This can alternatively be seen as resistance generated by a conflict of desires.

5 For theoretical work which focuses on resistance, see Laclau and Mouffe (1985:152); Woodhull (1988:168); Aladjem (1991:284); Sawicki (1991:43); McNay (1992:39–40).

6 Ewick and Silbey (1991) use resistance to identify a particular kind of response that can be differentiated from a public (oppositional) engagement with power.

Their focus is on resistance as an evasive tactic, an anti-disciplinary technique that operates through 'poaching, appropriation, silence' (1991:13).

7 The emphasis on resistance rather than social transformation is also linked to two other trends. The first, also drawn from Foucault, focuses on micro- rather than macro-interactions: mental health patients/clinic, pupils/school, inmates/ prison. Within this framework the notion of impeding or stopping the processes of dominant forces may seem more likely than grander possibilities. The second is a more general tendency within feminist (post)modern work.

The shift away from analysing class relations and capitalism has led to a shift in conceptualizing the possibilities for change (Harvey 1993b:104). Marxism was based on a clear notion of social transformation by a revolutionary class, not simply on resisting the status quo. However, current feminist work on subjectivity, race and sexuality, with some exceptions, has not tended to see lesbian and gay, or other black actors as the agents of a new social order. In part this is a result of questioning both the ability to foresee, and the desirability of achieving a new social (order). It is also due, however, particularly in relation to sexuality, to a tendency to identify the problem faced by new social movements as oppression which needs lifting rather than the transformation of an entire sexual matrix.

8 See similar point in Laclau and Mouffe (1985:182) in their discussion of the 'logic of equivalence'.

9 This can also be seen as deploying institutional power although at a more dispersed level than that of senior politicians and management.

10 This is also true for money, although perhaps to a lesser extent. For instance, the ways in which groups could spend state funds was structured by legislation, by their own attitudes and expertise, by other parties involved in the exchange relationships, and by the norms/gaze of the wider political community.

11 See also Ferguson (1991:48, 124, 245) who argues for the development of a counter-hegemonic culture against the triad of capitalism, patriarchy and racism.

12 Magnusson's (1992) interpretation of Laclau and Mouffe on this point may not be quite fair, since both Laclau and Mouffe (1985:178) make it clear that articulations are not pre-given. There is no necessary link between anti-capitalism and anti-sexism, rather it needs to be forged. This they argue can only happen on the basis of separate struggles.

13 For a critique of this approach, see Phillips (1994).

14 However, while an anti-hegemonic politics may not aim to create an alternative common bloc, the political drive to win consent raises the question whether any political perspective or tactics can be truly anti-hegemonic.

15 However, I disagree with the privileged place Magnusson and Walker (1988) give to capital which they appear to treat as the key organizing principle of modern history and current society.

16 Identifying an anti-hegemonic approach may appear somewhat paradoxical, since an 'approach' suggests a cohesive normative framework potentially at odds with the concept of anti-hegemony. While it is doubtful whether anti-hegemony can form a voluntaristic political project, I use it here to refer to normative work which highlights and acclaims the fragmentation and deconstructive character of current social movement activism.

17 This draws on and parallels Foucault's (1988:118) argument that the interdiction

signifies power's limits – its extreme or frustrated form (see also Dreyfus and Rabinow 1982).

18 Indeed the rejection of counter-hegemony by theorists such as Magnusson and Walker (1988) may be to restrict the range of new forms and identities since, arguably, counter-hegemony can be identified as one such form.

19 Unless one argues it can only work when intuitive and unpremeditated.

Afterword:
An ethics of power

> By *equality* we mean not merely formal equality or even equality of
> material resources, but rather a commitment to the idea that substantial
> differences in levels of power and well-being themselves raise central
> issues of social justice.
>
> (Frazer and Lacey 1993:190–1)

An ethical engagement with power technologies

In this final section, I wish briefly to explore some elements of an ethics of
power. This is an afterword in the sense that my discussion is tentative and
largely preliminary; however, developing and deploying an ethics of power
is central to the book's argument. As I stated in my introduction, once
power is conceptualized as normatively polysemous – as simply the generation of effects – a range of strategies becomes relevant. These strategies do
not principally seek to eradicate power, but to change the forms and processes through which social relations and practices are (re)produced. In
some instances, this *may* involve attempts to eliminate specific power technologies, nuclear weapons for example, or to contain and control others.
But strategies can also seek to expand, encourage and develop alternative
forms, whether they be democratic systems in the workplace, or oppositional discourses.

My focus on transforming technologies of power is anchored in an evaluation of anticipated outcomes. Whether public funding should be reallocated or state disciplinary structures reconstructed depends on the likely
effects of these changes.[1] Thus an ethics of power can be seen as revolving
around three interconnected elements that together comprise *Power in
Struggle*'s terrain of analysis. They are: first, the resources social forces (can)
deploy in political engagement with dominant forms of power; second, the
sites and technologies that constitute the target of interventions; and third,

the effects.[2] This last provides the prism through which the relationship between activist resources and sites of intervention come to be scrutinized.

In my exploration of 'power in struggle', I have examined a range of political resources and strategic engagements, from the prefigurative narratives of radical lesbians to the 'perversity' affirmation of sex radicals. In relation to the specific site of the state, I have surveyed both regulatory strategies of the new Right and the attempted deployment of municipal power by lesbian and gay activists. Including the new Right in my discussion highlights the problem of considering all 'oppositional' struggle beneficial. However, even if we bracket or reject the Right's oppositionality, to what extent should resistance and opposition be validated simply because they pose a challenge to the status quo?[3] In Chapter 7, I considered in some detail the problematic of strategy. While my argument emphasized the benefits of proliferative strategies and struggles within a political framework that did not privilege a priori any particular terrain or social relationship, I distinguished this form of strategic pluralism from the advocacy of a pluralist notion of the good life. Indeed, in arguing for a diversity of political engagements, an ethical basis or framework for activism becomes crucial.

In setting out an ethics of power my aim is not to argue that struggles *only* have value to the extent they are grounded in or promote a particular ethical principle. Nevertheless, in as much as value coherence is required to develop a counter-hegemonic project or bloc (see Chapter 7), I wish to consider several elements that might form the basis for such an articulation linking together a range of strategic political engagements.[4] This notion of a counter-hegemonic articulation comes from the work of Ernesto Laclau and Chantal Mouffe (1985). In her later work (1992a, 1992b, 1992c, 1993), Mouffe explores more fully what such an articulation might mean within the context of a radical democratic project (see also Cooper 1993a). Her writing emphasizes two principles: liberty and equality:

> [O]nce we acknowledge that what constitutes modern democracy is the assertion that all human beings are free and equal, it becomes clear that it is not possible to find more radical principles for organizing society.
>
> (Mouffe 1992a)

Yet despite the importance Mouffe places on democratizing social life, it becomes apparent that in situations of conflict, the 'good' does not necessarily take priority over the 'right' (Mouffe 1992a, 1992b:229–30).

Problematizing difference

Mouffe's emphasis on freedom mirrors a widespread feeling within left-wing normative theory that socialism has proved too interventionist and paternalistic a creed. Weeks (1993) also explores the importance of individual liberty for any progressive transformation. In an article entitled 'Rediscovering values', he (1993:208) advocates a framework of limited intervention based on 'protecting and enhancing the lives of others, without violating the other's negative freedom, the freedom from interference'. Eisenstein's (1994) work, in which she stresses the centrality of a reconstituted notion of privacy, reveals a similar focus. A key theme within *The Color of Gender* is Eisenstein's argument for an affirmative but noninterventionist state:

> [W]e need freedom from the state in order to be free to choose, and we need equality . . . I inscribe the liberal notion of privacy with an egalitarian text that does not assume sameness as a standard, but rather recognizes a radically pluralist individuality.
>
> (Eisenstein 1994:175)

Attempts to articulate liberty and equality as central principles within a political ethics highlight a range of problems none of which are new. Despite what is seen as the postmodern attractiveness of liberty/equality, these are principles which have been exhaustively thought, critiqued, reworked (and critiqued again) within modern liberalism. Postmodernism no doubt provides a new spin or twist, but analogous questions and tensions arise: what balance should be struck between freedom and intervention in the name of equality? Which institutions or actors are to be trusted to regulate or mediate people's choices, desires and preferences? Finally can liberty be achieved *without* intercessions into people's choices and actions? While the first question raises important issues of value, and the second highlights the need to differentiate between different institutional and collective actors,[5] I wish briefly to consider the third dilemma.

The postmodern accent on 'difference' draws attention to the social preconditions of liberty. Can freedom or diversity be meaningfully achieved without extensive action to ensure certain differences do not lead to marginalization and discrimination? Furthermore, to what extent does the validation of difference mean ensuring everyone has access to the same diversity of choice? If action though is called for to *enable* difference, does it not also *interfere* with difference by intervening in the social processes that shape the range of differences possible? Radical conceptions of diversity seem to require – or at least to produce – the restriction of certain activities, and the facilitation of others. Yet does this undermine a radical pluralist project of difference?

The impossibility of allowing/enabling all forms of diversity is not new. Rather than trying to resolve this particular problem, I wish to approach the question from a different ethical direction: one that focuses on power. As I stated earlier in this chapter, the epicentre of my discussion is power's effects, in particular, the impact of situated power technologies upon people's deployment of power. I am therefore concerned with the ways in which access to power is constrained or facilitated as a result of age, race, class, gender and nationality. Yet the ability to deploy power is more than a matter of access; the ways in which terrains and technologies of power are shaped by organizing principles also requires consideration. As I discussed in Chapter 2, the gendering or racialization of particular knowledge forms shapes the output of such knowledge in ways that may perpetuate systemic asymmetries despite the fact that knowledge is 'produced' by women and black people.

Equality of power and the construction of subjectivity

In exploring an ethics of power, my starting point is the normative judgement that people should have an equal capacity to make an impact – whether in the home, workplace or community.[6] This draws on the liberal formulation of 'equal respect', but goes further. Not only is a greater redistribution of resources necessary for people to achieve parity of respect – few living on the street or begging receive much respect for instance – but as well, if we accept equal respect as a basic principle, the presumption exists that it should apply to people's goals and views. Here, formal parity of respect is not enough. For it to have any meaning people need to have an equal capacity to *achieve* their notion of the good life and to contribute to the ways in which civil and political society are shaped.

The presumption of equal respect for people's goals and views is a rebuttable one, however. Desires and preferences are formed and lived within communities. Affirmation therefore must be contingent on the implications such goals have for others. As I go on to discuss, this is more than an issue of harm. I am not simply asking that the needs of others provide the boundaries to an individually-centred liberty. By focusing on equality within an ethics of power, my concern is rather to explore how we engage with desires, needs and interests in ways that empower the disempowered. Thus it is not a matter of allocating power equally from our current asymmetrical baseline, but of challenging that baseline.

Talk of equality, however, highlights a key problematic: how do we identify (in)equality of power within a framework which treats power as something that cannot be quantified? Clearly asymmetrical practices exist, whether in the form of economic exploitation or cultural marginalization, that then produce uneven access to power. Yet this becomes difficult to measure in relation to communities or classes where individuals experience a range of (often) conflicting, over-determined social locations that do not fit into any neat classification. In some instances, the position is more clear-cut, either because a grouping is disadvantaged through its location within several organizing frameworks, or else because there is a strong correlation between a particular organizing framework and the structuring of a specific terrain, race and the economy, for instance. However, focusing on equality between groups can construct a static, oversimplified schema which under-estimates both the complexity of people's experience and the often dispa-rate, uneven relationship between organizing principles and technologies/ sites of power.[7]

Instead of attempting to classify, measure and then arithmetically equal-ize different groups' ability to deploy power, a preferable approach, as others have argued, is to consider how diverse technologies or sites of power (combine to) *produce* asymmetries. This also acknowledges the fact that inequality is not simply a historical phenomenon that generates current need, but a practice of power that is ongoing and reproductive.[8] Public space, for instance, is clearly organized around – and hence continues to empower – certain physiques: 'medium' height,[9] sighted, pedestrian rather than wheelchair mobile and so on, to the detriment of others. These effects are repetitive irrespective of any new *exercise* of power. Thus people are systematically (dis)advantaged as a result of the way organizing principles (class, gender, race, nationality, age) are inscribed within sites and tech-nologies of power,[10] without any necessary intention or agency on the part of those who benefit.

Focusing on the ways in which certain practices produce disempower-ment also provides a basis for problematizing the enactment of particular desires or interests. While the emphasis of an ethics of equal power is on creating parity in people's ability to achieve their wants, preferences cannot be unquestioningly affirmed if their achievement entrenches or reproduces social asymmetries. This proposition involves two things: first, it undercuts the notion of equal respect or equal striving for all preferences; second, it suggests that certain choices or desires might form the site of political engagement. Interrogating people's personal desires and interests is, however, a messy business. In the main, the focus of this book has been on the process of preference construction. Interference, in this context, involves engaging with preferences as they are formed and reformed so that ine-quality does not become fetishized, eroticized or facilitated. However, not only is this process an uncertain one, it also does not deal with those 'problematic' preferences that already exist. On what basis should existing desires be constrained or prohibited?

Curbing or penalizing the enactment of certain desires is not *per se* a contentious claim. Most progressive and radical theorists accept that racial or sexual violence/abuse, for example, should not be deemed a legitimate preference or choice. Many would also agree that actions based on discrimi-natory inclinations ought to be discouraged if not prohibited. A refusal, for instance, to employ lesbians and gay men would be considered by many to be an unacceptable exercise of economic power. In both contexts of sexual/racial abuse and employment discrimination, the progressive response can be identified through a 'harm' paradigm. In the first instance, women and black men are harmed, in the second, lesbians and gays. But, as I discussed in Chapter 3, harm is a problematic concept. Not only does it conceptualize people as separate, autonomous individuals impacting upon each other in limited, knowable ways, but, as well, what we define as harm often depends on the behaviours we wish to circumscribe. For instance, other interpreters might argue that firms are harmed through employing lesbians and gay men. Thus choosing not to appoint them is a legitimate way of avoiding damage. In saying this, I do not intend to *advocate* a relativist notion of harm. However, what is defined as harm – the movement of its parameters – is not self-evident but rather constitutes a site of political and discursive struggle.

Instead of focusing on harm, I wish to use the concept of equality of empowerment as a way of exploring the difficulties the enactment of certain preferences poses. Problematic activities include those that maintain or reinforce systemic forms of disempowerment. This might be to the detriment of others (directly or indirectly involved) – the case of employment discrimination for instance – to the participants themselves or at a more general level generating the reproduction of power asymmetries. Yet arguing that the enactment of preferences requires examination does not necessarily mean that people should be 'protected' from their *own* decisions, whether it be smoking, sado-masochism or dangerous sports. 'We know best' elements within feminist and socialist politics which told people they had been duped, or proscribed the acting out of 'problematic' desires often disempowered subjugated forces or identities more than the reverse. Telling women, for instance, that their heterosexual feelings are naïve, masochistic or simply misplaced may reinforce women's self-perception as stupid and out of control (Hunt, M. 1990).

Do other means exist of contesting disempowering desires or wants[11] in ways that do not reinforce disadvantaged subject positions?[12] In order to address this question, I wish first to consider a key issue that it highlights. I mentioned above that the targets for an ethics of equal empowerment are the technologies and sites of power that interact with organizing principles to maintain systemic disadvantage; yet in challenging these processes *who* are we trying to empower? This question is difficult to answer because writing in recent years has tended to equate the social relations that are the target of political struggle such as gender, religion, sexual identity, with the identities that are to be affirmed. Simply arguing for the empowerment of particular groups underestimates the complexity and productivity of social power. At the same time, to divorce the subjects of empowerment from the social relations and communities within which they are embedded may be to resurrect the conventional notion of personhood as an abstract, ungendered and unracialized entity. This latter is the transcendent subjectivity feminists have rejected, both on normative and analytical grounds, since within the abstraction, various characteristics are assumed: white, male, middle-class and ablebodied.[13]

While the (formal) identities that gender and race frameworks currently produce *may* need to be inscribed within the subjectivities of empowerment, questions become more complex when we include within identity or subjectivity, sexual preferences and other desires. If people feel that their sexual identity is as important to who they are as their class or race, can anyone else say that this should not be treated as an integral aspect of their personhood? Moreover, when sexual preferences and desires form the grounds of discrimination or marginalization, should this not be sufficient to constitute them as the basis of affirmation? Or should we (continue to) interrogate aspects of identity and subjectivity, refusing to assume that all causes of disadvantage are necessarily wrong?

Recent sex radical writing has expressed an intense unwillingness to problematize desires, treating them as constitutive of identity, subjectivity and community. With the exception of radical and revolutionary feminists such as Jeffreys (1990, 1994), theorists have tended to focus on equality *between* rather than *within* sexual communities. Movements too (as discussed in this book), have focused on external forms of discrimination, taking identities themselves as given legitimate subjects for empowerment. However, if preferences are to be problematized, this also necessitates engaging with the ways in which desires becomes interiorized within the construction of personhood and subjectivity.

An identity or preference which illustrates some of the tensions running through this area is that of lesbian sado-masochism, a sexual positioning that has attracted criticism for seeming to legitimize and accentuate sexual inequality (see Chapter 3). Yet, proponents argue, both parties are affirmed. Violence and abuse are contained within the cathartic arena of the sexual act, and even there the masochist – the apparently disempowered actor – is able to set boundaries, identify her desires in the joint mapping out of the scenario, and retain a 'stop' word. Whether or not sado-masochism exacerbates existing (or creates new) inequalities of power between the parties concerned is an issue I wish to bracket, for the basis upon which I have problematized sado-masochism concerns its eroticization of ritualized domination and inequality.[14] The sexual parodying of abuse and humiliation, while it may not entrench or reproduce *specific* forms of inequality, nevertheless symbolically affirms asymmetry *per se*. Yet if we accept the contention that sado-masochism is an inherent aspect of some lesbians' identity, that it is linked to systemic forms of class, gender and racial disadvantage, as well as itself providing a basis for marginalization, subjugation and discrimination (see

Rubin 1989), to what extent can we – should we – struggle to empower sado-masochists while not empowering or affirming sado-masochism?[15]

The approach I wish to adopt suggests that such a separation is possible on the basis of the contingency of desire and identity. As Butler (1990) persuasively argues in relation to dominant identities, these are not constructed once and for all, but have to be constantly reproduced. If this also applies to subordinated identities, people cannot be reduced to their *current* set of preferences since these are liable (or able) to change. In arguing, therefore, that 'people' should be equally empowered, we *can* disarticulate the possibility of personhood from present forms of disempowering identification. In doing so, we might choose to distinguish those identities that seem inherently disempowering from those where the disadvantage they generate is caused by social location. The category of woman, for instance, may not be intrinsically disempowering; moreover, it offers a location from which to challenge gender as an organizing principle. Yet even 'woman' might eventually disappear, if the practice of gender became fundamentally reframed.

At the same time, in considering whether strategies are likely to accentuate or diminish inequality, we need to acknowledge the investment people may have in their current identification. As Harvey (1993b:117) argues in the context of homelessness,

> The identity of the homeless person . . . is vital to their sense of selfhood . . . A political programme which successfully combats homelessness . . . has to face up to the real difficulty of a loss of identity on the part of those who have been victims of such forms of oppression.

Identification not only concerns a sense of belonging, but also, in many cases, an experience of accompanying discrimination and marginalization. For lesbian sado-masochists, their perception of disadvantage as a result of their sexual identity needs to be respected and taken into account. Strategic responses to sado-masochism which exacerbate people's sense of subjugation or disadvantage may simply have the effect of further disadvantaging sections of a community already marginally inscribed as a result of gender, class, ethnicity and/or education.

Respect does not necessarily mean supporting campaigns which assume the validity of sado-masochist identity and practices, however. Rather, it suggests the possibility of pragmatic acceptance of lesbian sado-masochism in specific contexts. The distinction between these two approaches is apparent if we consider the refusal of several London feminist and progressive bookshops to stock sado-masochist literature on the grounds of its offensiveness to women (Smith 1993). From a pragmatic perspective, the shops' decisions to use their ordering and stocking power to further a political policy is legitimate. Sado-masochism does not have to be affirmed morally. However, the refusal, in some cases, to process individual orders for books may do little to challenge the eroticization of domination but simply function symbolically to reinforce particular lesbian communities' perception of exclusion or exorcism.[16]

I have explored the question of identity in some detail because it has become a significant mechanism for legitimating, and hence closing off from discussion, problematic practices or preferences. If the latter are to be critically examined, identity (or community) cannot become the means of their evacuation. At the same time, identity and community are central to the ways in which aspirations are constructed and choices made. Identification cannot therefore remain transparent within political strategy. In approaching the issue in this way, I rebut the either/or framework constructed by sex radical theorists such as Margaret Hunt (1990) who argue (or imply) that if we do not wish to be paternalistic and authoritarian, all sexual minority preferences and identities need affirming. Instead, my argument is that preferences and identities, like other social phenomena, form legitimate terrain for progressive debate and strategy. The challenge for an ethical approach is to find strategies that engage with 'disempowering' preferences and identities in ways that work against, rather than to accentuate, existing principles of systemic (dis)advantage.

Sustainability and counter-hegemony

Interrogating the character of desires, practices and identities highlights a further element within an ethics of equal empowerment: sustainability. While equal empowerment focuses on the factors that unequally structure people's social capacity or agency, and on the impact their exercise of power may have on other social relations and organizing principles, sustainability concerns the long-term effects of empowerment strategies. It also fundamentally problematizes the very notion of empowerment. Is it a good thing that people are able to impact upon the world? Should we normatively privilege the generation of effects? While sustainability does not undermine the concept of equality, it does force us to consider in which direction equality should go.

Within the ecological and environmental literature, the notion of sustainability has come up against criticism. This has focused on the conservative connotations of 'sustainability' that current ecosystems or needs should be maintained, that only developments which do not disrupt the present equilibrium be developed (see Harvey 1993b:40; Braidotti *et al.* 1994:131–7). Here, however, I am using the term in a slightly different sense to ask whether particular empowerment strategies over a given time period are likely to lead to an intensification of social (in)equality. This may be for the individual or class concerned, for other communities, or for future life.[17]

Sustainable equal empowerment is not intended to designate an attainable goal – a static, futuristic society in which, with equality achieved, nothing need change – but rather offers a paradigm for an ongoing, reflexive process. As a normative element within a counter-hegemonic political project, it provides a basis for strategy, a mean by which current practice can be evaluated. As Mouffe (1992b:235; see also Mouffe 1993:81) argues in her discussion of citizenship,

> [W]hile politics aims at constructing a political community and creating a unity, a fully inclusive political community and a final unity can never be realized since there will permanently be a 'constitutive outside', an exterior to the community that makes its existence possible.

In theory, if everyone was a citizen, the concept would have no meaning. The same may be true for equality. Equality only has meaning in the context of inequality. Indeed, it is this conceptual relationship between the two terms which provides the interpretive framework for constructing and highlighting particular problems.[18]

A discourse of equal empowerment will not by itself generate consensus. In any situation, views will differ as to the likely effects of a particular strategic intervention – whether equality will be furthered – and even over what sustainable equality might mean. But the inevitability of contestation does not make ethical discussion redundant. The point of developing an ethics is to help frame the questions – the arena of debate – not to provide pre-emptive answers to a range of specific concerns. Indeed, once we relinquish linear, causal chains, prediction becomes a risky business. Economic democratization, the proliferation of multicultural sexual discourses *may* further equality of empowerment. They may also in certain circumstances backfire, generating a range of antagonistic responses. This is not an argument for rejecting radical approaches *because* of the eventuality of such a backlash. Backlashes often precipitate in turn the mobilization of progressive forces, as materialized during the passage of Section 28, Local Government Act 1988, in Britain. What an ethical engagement with power requires is a sensitivity and reflexivity towards a constantly changing situation, a willingness to recognize the possibility or likelihood of undesirable consequences evolving from particular political engagements and to develop strategic, nuanced responses.

As a broad political principle, equal empowerment provides a basis for prefigurative projects that aim to transform, not stifle, variety. It also offers an interrogative foundation for anti-hegemonic activity that endeavours to challenge the reproduction of inequality. But does ethical activity negate the role of a deconstructive politics which aims to contest, rather than produce or constitute itself through, new truths? In Chapter 7, I argued that the notion of anti-hegemony as truly non-hegemonic was misleading since politics relies on value-trumping – the privileging of particular ethical frameworks – whether these take the form of radical pluralism or feminist interventionism. Thus if values are always present, the character of those underlying progressive political practice – whether of the anti- or counter-hegemonic variety – form a crucial area for debate (see Connor 1993).

Equally important is recognition and engagement with the values inform-ing *dominant* practices: the social processes through which interests, preferences and desires are constituted and formed. While a mechanistic praxis which expects specific effects to follow from particular power engagements seems likely to be disappointed, to assume that preferences – both oppositional and conventional – emerge in a chaotic, unpolitical man-ner is to evacuate an important arena for social struggle.

I have focused in this afterword on the construction of preferences and identities because this is an area from which radical intellectuals have tended to shy away in recent years. At the same time, it is important not to fixate on the construction of desires. The danger of so doing is to forget or to neglect the social, cultural and economic processes which structure our relative capa-city to attain our preferences, whatever they might be. The democratic foun-dations of equal empowerment can also end up marginalized. Empowerment, as I conceptualize it, goes beyond the (subjective) fulfilment of desires to highlight the scope and character of decision-making processes whether in the home, community or workplace. Democratic participation and involvement is thus privileged both as a good in itself as well as a mechanism for achieving more equal preference attainment in other areas. Yet the character of prefer-ences – the demands they make upon decision-making processes – are not fixed, but alter as decision-making structures change. Attempts to generate equality of empowerment through more symmetrical organizational struc-tures re-form the nature of our preferences and desires. At the same time, the changing character of our aspirations and interests informs the discourses and practices through which our participation occurs.

As the *fin de siècle* approaches, sexual minorities intensify their struggles to participate in political forums, to achieve a fairer distribution of resources, and to reshape cultural boundaries. The ethics explored in this afterword are rooted in this political mo(ve)ment, this politics of presence and productivity that constitutes itself in the right to impact, to make a difference. Given the historical conditions of current western states, is this identification of politics inevitable? Will it always be the turn of another subordinated community demanding a right to participate, to achieve their notion of the good life? Is politics inherently about who gets to shape society? Or is there another political ethic, so different it remains unimaginable, awaiting its (performative) turn in the wings?

Notes

1 Progressive practice, however, tends to curtail this process assuming that the effects can be read off from the technologies of power themselves. Often this

proves possible. For instance, funding for lesbian and gay community projects is likely to be more empowering than lack of funding. Yet while reading off from the technologies is an important shorthand practice, it is not conclusive.

2 These in turn can include the resources activists have access to. For instance, lesbian and gay utilization of equality discourse in order to gain entry to local government and thereby to impact upon local government sexual discourses had, as an effect, the legitimization and growing hegemony of equality discourse in the area of sexuality. This strengthened the resources lesbians and gay men could deploy.

3 This is a position certain queer advocates have adopted which seems to ignore the complex character of society and the ways in which certain progressive values have become incorporated within it.

4 Other possible ethical principles developed by different writers include care (e.g. Tronto 1993) and responsibility (Seidman 1992).

5 The focus in much of the literature on state interventions (e.g. Eisenstein 1994) does not necessarily address the question of community intervention and interrogation.

6 People's capacity to make an equal impact depends on the relationship between power technologies and effects. Thus access and the character of different technologies might change but this does not necessarily mean that the effect will be one of 'equal impact'. Certain terrains may also make equal impact impossible. Utilizing the framework developed here, that raises the question whether the terrains themselves are problematic.

7 This conception of equality has also been rejected by feminist theorists such as MacKinnon (1991) on the grounds that it creates a norm, for example, men, against which the 'other' is measured.

8 One of the problems I have with Tronto's (1993) interesting book on an ethic of care is her limited problematization of why people have needs and the ways in which these are reproduced by current social structures and practices.

> Care arises out of the fact that not all humans or others or objects in the world are equally able, at all times, to take care of themselves . . . care is not an activity that occurs between equal and autonomous actors . . . but between those who have needs and those who can provide for those needs.
>
> (Tronto 1993:145)

9 The notion of medium height is also racialized, since some ethnic communities appear taller than others. Western space tends to be designed for the average Aryan build.

10 In saying this I do not wish to suggest that only people who are disadvantaged racially or sexually experience disempowerment. Anyone can find themselves without access to particular resources. However, in this afterword, my focus is on the ways in which systematic organizing principles and power technologies/ terrains interact.

11 These desires may be disempowering for those whose preferences they are as well as for others. Who is being disempowered as a result of the enactment of specific desires or choices is clearly an important political and strategic issue.

12 Disempowering preferences can obviously also be articulated to socially powerful positions. However this raises fewer problems of the sort being explored here.

13 Similar arguments are made within communitarian studies where it is argued that people are constituted by and within particular communities. For a very useful feminist analysis of the communitarian literature, see Frazer and Lacey (1993).

14 In this sense I am claiming that acts carry with them moral significance (cf. Seidman 1992:201), although clearly the precise meaning depends on context (Herman 1994b).

15 This raises the question: on what basis are empowerment arguments being made? The approach I am adopting is to argue for empowerment, not on the basis of disadvantage as a result of being sado-masochist, but because of people's positioning as working-class, black, lesbian and female. However, as I discuss, people's experience of disadvantage on the basis of being sado-masochists has to be taken into account.

16 It is arguable that processing orders does affirm the eroticization of domination or generate cultural alienation on the part of bookshop staff who feel the literature is racist or misogynist. Whether sado-masochist literature *per se* is sexually or racially oppressive is a contentious issue. It also forms an important terrain for debate in its exploration of racialized and sexualized representations, although currently it tends to end in a slanging match between two antagonistic sides.

   Bookshops may also choose to refuse orders on the grounds that purchases support particular publishers. However, since much of the literature is currently being produced by small lesbian publishers, this in itself may not be a strong basis for refusal.

17 This issue raises the environmental impact of particular aspirations, policies and engagements with power. Radical chic, with its fetishization of black leather, conspicuous consumption and fashionability, has constructed itself in opposition to a cultural ethic of recycling, second-hand clothes, non-leather fabrics and natural dyes. This is not to deny the significance of environmental concerns among proponents of radical chic. However the critique of naturalism as itself socially constructed – while valid – is in danger of entrenching an even more acute dichotomy between culture and nature (or of eradicating nature altogether).

   This shift is compounded by a postmodern politics of indeterminacy which perceives the future as so unknown and uncertain that current responsibility to subsequent generations cannot but be misconceived. However while it would be a mistake, I think, to reify current ecosystems in the way sustainability can do (i.e. our obligation to the future is to maintain the present ecological equilibrium), acknowledging that there is likely to be life after us creates a relationship of power with future generations. While we may not know (all) the forms such life will take, to limit or constrain its possibilities seems to perpetuate a problematic privileging of the present.

18 This does not mean that without a concept of equality the 'problem' would not exist, but rather that it might be understood differently.

Bibliography

Adam, B. (1987) *The Rise of a Gay and Lesbian Movement*. Boston, MA: Twayne.

Adam, B. (1989) The state, public policy, and AIDS discourse, *Contemporary Crises*, 13, 1.

Adam, B. (1992) Sex and caring among men: Impacts of AIDS on gay people, in K. Plummer (ed.) *Modern Homosexualities*. London: Routledge.

Adams, M. L. (1989) There's no place like home: On the place of identity in feminist politics, *Feminist Review*, 31, 22.

Adkins, L. (1992) Sexual work and the employment of women in the service industries, in M. Savage and A. Witz (eds) *Gender and Bureaucracy*. Oxford: Basil Blackwell.

ALA (1990) *Lesbian and Gay Equality Now*. London: Association of London Authorities.

Aladjem, T. (1991) The philosopher's prism: Foucault, feminism, and critique, *Political Theory*, 19, 277.

Allen, J. (1990) Does feminism need a theory of the state? in S. Watson (ed.) *Playing the State: Australian, Feminist Interventions*. London: Verso.

Almond, B. (1988) Women's right: Reflections on ethics and gender, in M. Griffiths and M. Whitford (eds) *Feminist Perspectives in Philosophy*. Basingstoke: Macmillan.

Althusser, L. (1971) *Lenin and Philosophy and Other Essays*. London: New Left Books.

Altman, D. (1971) *Homosexual: Oppression and Liberation*. Sydney: Angus and Robertson.

Altman, D. (1980) What changed in the seventies? in Gay Left Collective (eds) *Homosexuality: Power and Politics*. London: Allison and Busby.

Altman, D. (1989) AIDS and the reconceptualisation of homosexuality, in D. Altman et al. (eds) *Which Homosexuality?* London: Gay Men's Press.

Amos, V. and Parmar, P. (1984) Challenging imperial feminism, *Feminist Review*, 17, 3.

Andrew, C. (1984) Women and the welfare state, *Canadian Journal of Political Science*, 17, 667.

Anthias, F. and Yuval-Davis, N. (1992) *Racialised Boundaries*. London: Routledge.

Arnup, K. and Boyd, S. (1995) Familial disputes? Sperm donors, lesbian mothers, and legal parenthood, in D. Herman and C. Stychin (eds) *Legal Inversions: Lesbians, Gay Men, and the Politics of Law*. Philadelphia, PA: Temple University Press.

Bachrach, P. and Baratz, M. (1970) *Power and Poverty: Theory and Practice*. New York: Oxford University Press.

Bakan, J. (1991) Constitutional interpretation and social change: You can't always get what you want (nor what you need), *Canadian Bar Review*, 70, 307.

Barker, R. (1990) *Political Legitimacy and the State*. Oxford: Clarendon.

Barrett, S. and Fudge, C. (1981) Examining the policy–action relationship, in S. Barrett and C. Fudge (eds) *Policy and Action*. London: Methuen.

Barrett, S. and Hill, M. (1986) Policy, bargaining and structure in implementation theory, in M. Goldsmith (ed.) *New Research in Central-local Relations*. Aldershot: Gower.

Barrett, M. (1980) *Women's Oppression Today*. London: New Left Books.

Barrett, M. (1991) *The Politics of Truth*. Cambridge: Polity.

Bartky, S. (1988) Foucault, feminism and the modernization of patriarchal power, in I. Diamond and L. Quinby (eds) *Feminism and Foucault: Reflections on Resistance*. Boston, MA: Northeastern University Press.

Bearchell, C. (1993) Gay porn censored from all sides, *Toronto Star*, 15 January.

Bech, H. (1992) Report from a rotten state: Marriage and homosexuality in Denmark, in K. Plummer (ed.) *Modern Homosexualities*. London: Routledge.

Beetham, D. (1987) *Bureaucracy*. Milton Keynes: Open University Press.

Bell, V. (1993) *Interrogating Incest: Feminism, Foucault and the Law*. London: Routledge.

Bensinger, T. (1992) Lesbian pornography: The re/making of (a) community, *Discourse*, 15, 69.

Berlant, L. and Freeman, E. (1993) Queer nationality, in M. Warner (ed.) *Fears of a Queer Planet: Queer Politics and Social Theory*. Minneapolis, MN: University of Minnesota Press.

Bhavnani, K. and Coulson, M. (1986) Transforming socialist-feminism: The challenge of racism, *Feminist Review*, 23, 81.

Boddy, M. and Fudge, C. (eds) (1984) *Local Socialism?* London: Macmillan.

Braidotti, R. *et al.* (1994) *Women, the Environment and Sustainable Development*. London: Zed Books.

Brazier, M. *et al.* (1993) Falling from a tightrope? Doctors and lawyers between the market and the state, *Political Studies*, 41:197.

Bright, S. (1993) A pornographic girl, in L. Frank and P. Smith (eds) *Madonnarama: Essays on Sex and Popular Culture*. Pittsburgh, PA: Cleis.

Brown, W. (1987) Where is the sex in political theory? *Women & Politics*, 7, 3.

Brown, W. (1992) Finding the man in the state, *Feminist Studies*, 18, 7.

Buci-Glucksmann, C. (1980) *Gramsci and the State*. London: Lawrence and Wishart.

Buci-Glucksmann, C. (1982) Hegemony and consent, in A. Showstack Sassoon (ed.) *Approaches to Gramsci*. London: Writers and Readers.

Bulkin, E. *et al.* (1984) *Yours in Struggle*. Ithaca, NY: Long Haul Press.

Burch, M. and Wood, B. (1983) *Public Policy in Britain*. Oxford: Martin Robertson.

Burrell, G. and Hearn, J. (1989) The sexuality of organization, in J. Hearn *et al.* (eds) *The Sexuality of Organization*. Los Angeles, CA: Sage.

Burstyn, V. (1983) Masculine dominance and the state, *The Socialist Register 1983*, 45.

Busby, K. (1994) Leaf and pornography: Litigating on equality and sexual representation, *Canadian Journal of Law and Society*, 9, 165.

Butcher, H. *et al.* (eds) (1990) *Local Government and Thatcherism*. London: Routledge.

Butler, J. (1990) *Gender Trouble: Feminism and the Subversion of Identity*. New York: Routledge.

Butler, J. (1991) Imitation and gender subordination, in D. Fuss (ed.) *Inside/Out: Lesbian Theories, Gay Theories*. New York: Routledge.

Butler, J. (1992) Sexual inversions, in D. Stanton (ed.) *Discourses of Sexuality*. Ann Arbor, MI: University of Michigan Press.

Butler, J. (1993a) *Bodies that Matter*. London: Routledge.

Butler, J. (1993b) Critically queer, *GLQ: A Journal of Lesbian and Gay Studies*, 1, 17.

Button, J. (1984) *Women's Committees: A Study of Gender and Local Government Policy Formation*, SAUS working paper, no. 45.

Cain, R. (1993) Disclosure and secrecy among gay men in the United States and Canada: A shift in views, in J. Fout and M. Tantillo (eds) *American Sexual Politics*. Chicago, IL: University of Chicago Press.

Cameron, S. and Welford, R. (1992) On the attitudes to and willingness to pay for artificial insemination, *International Journal of Sociology and Social Policy*, 12, 58.

Campbell, B. (1987) A feminist sexual politics: Now you see it, now you don't, in Feminist Review (ed.) *Sexuality: A Reader*. London: Virago.

Canel, E. (1992) New social movement theory and resource mobilization: The need for integration, in W. Carroll (ed.) *Organizing Dissent: Contemporary Social Movements in Theory and Practice*. Toronto: Garamond.

Cant, B. (1986) 'Outsiders and citizens', unpublished manuscript.

Cant, B. (1988) Normal channels, in B. Cant and S. Hemmings (eds) *Radical Records: Thirty Years of Lesbian and Gay History*. London: Routledge.

Cant, B. (1991) The limits of tolerance? in T. Kaufmann and P. Lincoln (eds) *High Risk Lives: Lesbian and Gay Politics After the Clause*. Bridport: Prism.

Cant, B. and Hemmings, S. (eds) (1988) *Radical Records: Thirty Years of Lesbian and Gay History*. London: Routledge.

Carabine, J. (1994) 'Sexuality, politics and policy making', paper presented at the BSA Annual Conference, University of Central Lancashire, March.

Carroll, W. (1992) Introduction: Social movements and counter hegemony in a Canadian context, in W. Carroll (ed.) *Organizing Dissent: Contemporary Social Movements in Theory and Practice*. Toronto: Garamond.

Carter, V. (1992) Abseil makes the heart grow fonder: Lesbian and gay campaigning tactics and S. 28, in K. Plummer (ed.) *Modern Homosexualities*. London: Routledge.

Champagne, J. (1993) Stabat Madonna, in L. Frank and P. Smith (eds) *Madonnarama: Essays on Sex and Popular Culture*. Pittsburgh, PA: Cleis.

(charles), H. (1993) 'Queer nigger': Theorizing white activism, in J. Bristow and A. Wilson (eds) *Activating Theory: Lesbian, Gay, Bisexual Politics*. London: Lawrence and Wishart.

Clark, G. and Dear, M. (1984) *State Apparatus: Structures and Language of Legitimacy*. Boston, MA: Allen and Unwin.

Cockburn, C. (1977) *The Local State*. London: Pluto Press.

Cocks, J. (1989) *The Oppositional Imagination*. London: Routledge.

Cohen, S. (1972) *Folk Devils and Moral Panics: The Creation of the Mods and Rockers*. London: Granada.

Collins, P. (1990) *Black Feminist Thought*. Cambridge: Unwin Hyman.

Connell, B. (1990) The state, gender and sexual politics: Theory and appraisal, *Theory and Society*, 19:507.

Connor, M. (1993) The necessity of value, in J. Squires (ed.) *Principled Positions: Postmodernism and the Rediscovery of Value*. London: Lawrence and Wishart.

Cooper, D. (1989) Positive images in Haringey: A struggle for identity, in C. Jones and P. Mahony (eds) *Learning Our Lines*. London: Women's Press.

Cooper, D. (1993a) The citizen's charter and radical democracy: Empowerment and exclusion within citizenship discourse, *Social and Legal Studies*, 2, 149.

Cooper, D. (1993b) An engaged state: Sexuality, governance and the potential for change, *Journal of Law and Society*, 20, 257.

Cooper, D. (1994a) *Sexing the City: Lesbian and Gay Politics within the Activist State*. London: Rivers Oram.

Cooper, D. (1994b) Productive, relational and everywhere? Conceptualising power and resistance within foucauldian feminism, *Sociology*, 28, 435.

Cooper, D. (1994c) A retreat from feminism? British, municipal lesbian politics and cross-gender initiatives, *Canadian Journal of Women and the Law*, (in press).

Cooper, D. and Herman, D. (1991) Getting the family 'right': Legislating heterosexuality in Britain, 1986–91, *Canadian Journal of Family Law*, 10, 41.

Cotterell, R. (1992) *The Sociology of Law*. London: Butterworths.

Coyle, A. (1989) The limits of change: Local government and equal opportunities for women, *Public Administration*, 67, 39.

Creet, J. (1991) Daughter of the movement: The psychodynamics of lesbian s/m fantasy, *Differences*, 3, 135.

Crenson, M. (1971) *The Un-politics of Air Pollution: A Study of Non-decisionmaking in the Cities*. Baltimore, MD: Johns Hopkins University Press.

Crimp, D. (1993) Right in, girlfriend! in M. Warner (ed.) *Fears of a Queer Planet: Queer Politics and Social Theory*. Minneapolis, MN: University of Minnesota Press.

Cummings, K. (1993) Of purebreds and hybrids: The politics of teaching AIDS in the United States, in J. Fout and M. Tantillo (eds) *American Sexual Politics: Sex, Gender, and Race Since the Civil War*. Chicago, IL: University of Chicago Press.

Daumer, E. (1992) Queer ethics; or, the challenge of bisexuality to lesbian ethics, *Hypatia*, 7, 91.

Day, P. and Klein, R. (1989) Interpreting the unexpected: The issue of AIDS policy making in Britain, *Journal of Public Policy*, 9, 337.

Dearlove, J. (1973) *The Politics of Policy in Local Government*. London: Cambridge University Press.

de Lauretis, T. (1987) *Technologies of Gender: Essays on Theory, Film, and Fiction*. Bloomington, IN: Indiana University Press.

de Lauretis, T. (1990) Eccentric subjects: Feminist theory and historical consciousness, *Feminist Studies*, 16, 115.

de Lauretis, T. (1991) Queer theory: Lesbian and gay studies, an introduction, *Differences*, 3, iii.

Delphy, C. (1988) Patriarchy, domestic mode of production, gender and class, in C. Nelson and L. Grossberg (eds) *Marxism and the Interpretation of Culture*. Basingstoke: Macmillan.

D'Emilio, J. (1983) Capitalism and gay identity, in A. Snitow *et al.* (eds) *Powers of Desire*. New York: Monthly Review Press.

Dews, P. (1987) *Logics of Disintegration: Post-Structuralist Thought and the Claims of Critical Theory*. London: Verso.

Diamond, I. and Quinby, L. (eds) (1988) *Feminism and Foucault: Reflections on Resistance*. Boston, MA: North Eastern University Press.

Dixon, D. (1991) *From Prohibition to Regulation*. Oxford: Clarendon.

Donzelot, J. (1979) *The Policing of Families*. London: Hutchinson.

Douglas, C. (1990) *Love and Politics: Radical Feminist and Lesbian Theories*. San Francisco, CA: Ism.

Dowding, K. *et al.* (1993) 'Rational choice and community power structures: A new research agenda', paper presented to the American Political Science Association Annual Meeting, Washington DC, September.

Dreyfus, H. and Rabinow, P. (1982) *Michel Foucault: Beyond Structuralism and Hermeneutics*. Hemel Hempstead: Harvester Wheatsheaf.

Duffy, A. (1986) Reformulating power for women, *Canadian Review of Sociology and Anthropology*, 23, 22.

Duhlerup, D. (1987) Confusing concepts – confusing reality: A theoretical discussion of the patriarchal state, in A. Showstack Sassoon (ed.) *Women and the State*. London: Hutchinson.

Dunleavy, P. and O'Leary, B. (1987) *Theories of the State: The Politics of Liberal Democracy*. Basingstoke: Macmillan.

Durant, R. and Diehl, P. (1989) Agendas, alternatives and public policy: Lessons from the US foreign policy arena, *Journal of Public Policy*, 9, 179.

Durham, M. (1989) The Thatcher government and 'the moral right', *Parliamentary Affairs*, 42, 58.

Durham, M. (1991) *Sex and Politics*. Basingstoke: Macmillan.

Durocher, C. (1990) Heterosexuality: Sexuality or social system, *Resources for Feminist Research* 19, 13.

Dworkin, A. (1987) *Intercourse*. New York: Free Press.

Eagleton, T. (1991) *Ideology: An Introduction*. London: Verso.

Eamon, C. (1992–93) The rhetoric of degradation, *Fuse,* 16, 16.

Ebert, T. (1991) Writing on the political: Resistance (post) modernism, *The Legal Studies Forum* 15, 291.

Ehrlich, C. (1986) The unhappy marriage of marxism and feminism: Can it be saved? in L. Sargent (ed.) *The Unhappy Marriage of Marxism and Feminism.* London: Pluto.

Eisenstein, Z. (1981) *The Radical Future of Liberal Feminism.* New York: Longman.

Eisenstein, Z. (1984) *Feminism and Sexual Equality.* New York: Monthly Review Press.

Eisenstein, Z. (1987) Liberalism, feminism and the Reagan state: The neoconservative assault on (sexual) equality, in R. Miliband (ed.) *Socialist Register.* London: Merlin.

Eisenstein, Z. (1988) *The Female Body and the Law.* Berkeley, CA: University of California Press.

Eisenstein, Z. (1994) *The Color of Gender: Reimaging Democracy.* Berkeley, CA: University of California Press.

Enloe, C. (1988) *Does Khaki Become You?: The Militarization of Women's Lives.* London: Pandora.

Enloe, C. (1993) *The Morning After: Sexual Politics at the End of the Cold War.* Berkeley, CA: University of California Press.

Ettelbrick, P. (1993) Who is a parent? The need to develop a lesbian conscious family law, *New York Law School Journal of Human Rights,* 10, 513.

Etzioni, A. (1993) Power as a social force, in M. Olsen and M. Marger (eds) *Power in Modern Societies.* Oxford: Westview.

Evans, D. T. (1989/90) Section 28: Law, myth and paradox, *Critical Social Policy,* 27, 73.

Evans, D. T. (1993) *Sexual Citizenship: The Material Construction of Sexualities.* London: Routledge.

Ewick, P. and Silbey, S. (1991) 'Negotiating subjectivities: Conformity, contestation and resistance accounts of legal consciousness', paper presented to the American Law and Society Conference, Amsterdam, June.

Ewick, P. and Silbey, S. (1992) Conformity, contestation and resistance: An account of legal consciousness, *New England Law Review,* 26, 73.

Faderman, L. (1992) *Odd Girls and Twilight Lovers: A History of Lesbian Life in Twentieth Century America.* Harmondsworth: Penguin.

Faderman, L. (1993) The return of butch and femme: A phenomenon in lesbian sexuality of the 1980s and 1990s, in J. Fout and M. S. Tantillo (eds) *American Sexual Politics: Sex, Gender, and Race Since the Civil War.* Chicago, IL: University of Chicago Press.

Faith, M. (1994) Resistance: Lessons from Foucault and feminism, in L. Radtke (ed.) *Power/Gender.* London: Sage.

Falk, P. (1989) Lesbian mothers, *American Psychologist,* 44, 941.

Felski, R. (1989) Feminist theory and social change, *Theory, Culture and Society,* 6, 219.

Feminist Review (eds) (1987) *Sexuality: A Reader.* London: Virago.

Ferguson, A. (1991) *Sexual Democracy: Women, Oppression, and Revolution*. Oxford: Westview.

Ferguson, A. *et al.* (1984) The feminist sexuality debates, *Signs*, 11, 106.

Ferguson, K. (1984) *The Feminist Case Against Bureaucracy*. Philadelphia, PA: Temple University Press.

Ferguson, K. (1987) Work, text and act in discourses of organisation, *Women and Politics*, 7, 1.

Findlay, S. (1987) Facing the state: The politics of the women's movement reconsidered, in H. Maroney and M. Luxton (eds) *Feminism and Political Economy*. Toronto: Methuen.

Findlay, S. (1988) Feminist struggles with the Canadian state, *Resources for Feminist Research*, 17, 5.

Fiske, J. (1993) *Power Plays, Power Works*. London: Verso.

Flammang, J. (1983) Feminist theory: The question of power, *Current Perspectives in Social Theory*, 4, 37.

Flannigan-Saint-Aubin, A. (1993) 'Black gay male' discourse: Reading race and sexuality between the lines, in J. Fout and M. S. Tantillo (eds) *American Sexual Politics: Sex, Gender and Race since the Civil War*. Chicago, IL: University of Chicago Press.

Flax, J. (1987) Postmodern gender relations in feminist theory, *Signs*, 12, 621.

Flax, J. (1992) Beyond equality: Gender, justice and difference, in G. Block and S. James (eds) *Beyond Equality and Difference*. London: Routledge.

Foucault, M. (1980) *Power/Knowledge*. New York: Pantheon.

Foucault, M. (1981) *The History of Sexuality*. London: Penguin.

Foucault, M. (1988) *Politics, Philosophy, Culture*. L. Kritzman (ed.). New York: Routledge.

Fox Piven, F. (1984) Women and the state: Ideology, power and the welfare state, *Socialist Review*, 14, 11.

France, M. (1984) Sadomasochism and feminism, *Feminist Review*, 16, 35.

Franklin, S. (1990) Deconstructing desperateness: The social construction of infertility in popular representations of new reproductive technologies, in M. McNeil (ed.) *The New Reproductive Technologies*. London: Macmillan.

Franzway, S. *et al.* (1989) *Staking a Claim: Feminism, Bureaucracy and the State*. Cambridge: Polity.

Fraser, N. (1989) *Unruly Practices: Power, Discourse and Gender in Contemporary Social Theory*. Cambridge: Polity.

Frazer, E. and Lacey, N. (1993) *The Politics of Community*. Hemel Hempstead: Harvester Wheatsheaf.

Frye, M. (1983) *The Politics of Reality: Essays in Feminist Theory*. Trumansberg, NY: Crossing.

Gamson, J. (1993) Rubber Wars: Struggles over the condom in the United States, in J.C. Fout and M.S. Tantillo (eds) *American Sexual Politics: Sex, Gender, and Race since the Civil War*. Chicago, IL: University of Chicago Press.

Gatens, M. (1992) Power, bodies and difference, in M. Barrett and A. Phillips (eds) *Destabilizing Theory*. Cambridge: Polity.

Gavey, N. (1993) Technologies and effects of heterosexual coercion, in S. Wilkinson and C. Kitzinger (eds) *Heterosexuality*. London: Sage.

Ginzberg, R. (1992) Audre Lorde's (nonessentialist) lesbian eros, *Hypatia*, 7, 73.

Gittins, D. (1985) *The Family in Question*. Basingstoke: Macmillan.

Golding, S. (1993) Sexual manners, in V. Harwood *et al.* (eds) *Pleasure Principles: Politics, Sexuality and Ethics*. London: Lawrence and Wishart.

Golombok, S. *et al.* (1983) Children in lesbian and single-parent households: Psychosexual and psychiatric appraisal, *Journal of Child Psychology*, 24, 551.

Goss, S. (1984) Women's initiatives in local government, in M. Boddy and C. Fudge (eds) *Local Socialism?* London: Macmillan.

Gramsci, A. (1971) *Selections from the Prison Notebooks of Antonio Gramsci*. London: Lawrence and Wishart.

Greenaway, J. *et al.* (1992) *Deciding Factors in British Politics: A Case-Studies Approach*. London: Routledge.

Griffiths, M. and Whitford, M. (eds) (1988) *Feminist Perspectives in Philosophy*. Basingstoke: Macmillan.

Grosz, A. (1991) Lesbian fetishism? *Differences*, 3, 39.

Gusfield, J. (1963) *Symbolic Crusade: Status Politics and the American Temperance Movement*. Urbana, IL: University of Illinois Press.

Gyford, J. (1985) *The Politics of Local Socialism*. London: George Allen & Unwin.

Gyford, J. *et al.* (1989) *The Changing Politics of Local Government*. London: Unwin Hyman.

Halford, S. (1988) Women's initiatives in local government . . . where do they come from and where are they going? *Policy and Politics*, 16, 251.

Halford, S. (1992) Feminist change in a patriarchal organisation: The experience of women's initiatives in local government and implications for feminist perspectives on state institutions, in M. Savage and A. Witz (eds) *Gender and Bureaucracy*. Oxford: Blackwell.

Hall, S. (1980) Nicos Poulantzas: State, power, socialism, *New Left Review*, 119, 60.

Hall, S. (1985) Signification, representation, ideology: Althusser and the post-structuralist debates, *Critical Studies in Mass Communication*, 2, 91.

Handler, J. (1992) Postmodernism, protest, and the new social movements, *Law and Society Review*, 26, 697.

Hart, J. (1992) A cocktail of alarm: Same sex couples and migration to Australia, 1985–90, in K. Plummer (ed.) *Modern Homosexualities*. London: Routledge.

Hartsock, N. (1990) Foucault on power: A theory for women? in L. Nicholson (ed.) *Feminism/Postmodernism*. London: Routledge.

Harvey, D. (1993a) The nature of environment: The dialectics of social and environmental change, *The Socialist Register 1993*, 1.

Harvey, D. (1993b) Class relations, social justice and the politics of difference, in J. Squires (ed.) *Principled Positions: Postmodernism and the Rediscovery of Value*. London: Lawrence and Wishart.

Hay, C. (1994) Crisis and the discursive unification of the state, in P. Dunleavy and J. Stanyer (eds) *Contemporary Political Studies*. Belfast: PSA.

Hearn, J. and Parkin, W. (1987) *Sex at Work: The Power and Paradox of Organisation Sexuality*. Brighton: Wheatsheaf.

Hearn, J. et al. (eds) (1989) The Sexuality of Organisations. London: Sage.

Held, D. (1989) Political Theory and the Modern State. Cambridge: Polity.

Heller, A. and Fehrer, F. (1988) The Postmodern Political Condition. Cambridge: Polity.

Henderson, L. (1993) Justify our love: Madonna and the politics of queer sex, in C. Schwichtenberg (ed.) The Madonna Connection: Representational Politics, Subcultural Identities, and Cultural Theory. Oxford: Westview.

Herman, D. (1993) Beyond the rights debate, Social and Legal Studies, 2, 25.

Herman, D. (1994a) Rights of Passage: Struggles for Lesbian and Gay Legal Equality. Toronto: University of Toronto Press.

Herman, D. (1994b) 'Law and morality re-visited: The politics of regulating sadomasochistic pornography and practice', paper presented to the Canadian and American Law and Society Conferences, Calgary and Phoenix, June.

Herman, D. and Stychin, C. (eds) (1995) Legal Inversions: Lesbians, Gay Men, and the Politics of Law. Philadelphia, PA: Temple University Press.

Hernes, H. (1987) Welfare State and Women Power. Oslo: Norwegian University Press.

Hindess, B. (1982) Power, interests and the outcomes of struggles, Sociology, 16, 498.

Hirst, P. (1979) On Law and Ideology. London: Macmillan.

Hoagland, P. (1988) Lesbian Ethics: Towards New Value. Palo Alto, CA: Institute of Lesbian Studies.

Hoggett, P. (1991) A new management in the public sector? Policy and Politics, 19, 243.

Hogwood, B. and Gunn, L. (1984) Policy Analysis for the Real World. Oxford: Oxford University Press.

hooks, b. (1990) Yearning: Race, Gender and Cultural Politics. Toronto: Between the Lines.

hooks, b. (1993) Power to the pussy: We don't wannabe dicks in drag, in L. Frank and P. Smith (eds) Madonnarama: Essays on Sex and Popular Culture. Pittsburgh, PA: Cleis.

Houston, B. (1992) In praise of blame, Hypatia, 7, 128.

Hoy, D. (1986) Power, repression, progress: Foucault, Lukes, and the Frankfurt school, in D. Hoy (ed.) Foucault: A Critical Reader. Oxford: Blackwell.

Humphrey, M. et al. (1991) Screening couples for parenthood by donor insemination, Social Science and Medicine, 32, 273.

Hunt, A. (1985) The ideology of law: Advances and problems in recent applications of the concept of ideology to the analysis of law, Law and Society Review, 19, 11.

Hunt, A. (1990) Rights and social movements: Counter-hegemonic strategies, Journal of Law and Society, 17, 309.

Hunt, A. (1992) Foucault's expulsion of law: Toward a retrieval, Law and Social Inquiry, 17, 1.

Hunt, M. (1990) The de-eroticisation of women's liberation: Social purity movements and the revolutionary feminism of Sheila Jeffreys, Feminist Review, 34, 23.

Hurtado, A. (1989) Relating to privilege, Signs, 14, 833.

Hutchinson, A. (1992) Doing the right thing? Toward a postmodern politics, *Law and Society Review*, 26, 773.

Isaac, J. (1987) Beyond the three faces of power: A realist critique, *Polity*, 20, 4.

Jan Mohamed, A. (1992) Sexuality on/of the racial border: Foucault, Wright and the articulation of 'racialised sexuality', in D. Stanton (ed.) *Discourses of Sexuality from Aristotle to AIDS*. Ann Arbor, MI: University of Michigan Press.

Jeffery-Poulter, S. (1991) *Peers, Queers and Commons*. London: Routledge.

Jeffreys, S. (1990) *Anti-climax*. London: Women's Press.

Jeffreys, S. (1994) *The Lesbian Heresy*. London: Women's Press.

Jessop, B. (1982) *The Capitalist State*. Oxford: Martin Robertson.

Jessop, B. (1985) *Nicos Poulantzas: Marxist Theory and Political Strategy*. London: Macmillan.

Jessop, B. (1990) *State Theory*. Cambridge: Polity.

Johnson, T. (1993) Expertise and the state, in M. Gane and T. Johnson (eds) *Foucault's New Domains*. London: Routledge.

Jonel, M. (1982) Letter from a former masochist, in R. Linden *et al.* (eds) *Against Sadomasochism: A Radical Feminist Analysis*. San Francisco, CA: Frog in the Well.

Jones, C. and Mahony, P. (eds) (1989) *Learning our Lines: Sexuality and Social Control in Education*. London: Women's Press.

Kaufmann, T. and Lincoln, P. (eds) (1991) *High Risk Lives: Lesbian and Gay Politics After the Clause*. Bridport: Prism.

King, M. and Pattison, P. (1991) Homosexuality and parenthood, *British Medical Journal*, 303, 295.

Kinsman, G. (1987) *The Regulation of Desire*. Montreal: Black Rose Books.

Kinsman, G. (1992) Managing AIDS organizing: 'Consultation', 'partnership', and the national AIDS strategy, in W. Carroll (ed.) *Organizing Dissent: Contemporary Social Movements in Theory and Practice*. Toronto: Garamond.

Kitzinger, C. (1994) Problematizing pleasure: Radical feminist deconstructions of sexuality and power, in L. Radtke (ed.) *Power/Gender*. London: Sage.

Kitzinger, C. and Wilkinson, S. (1993) Editors' Introduction, in S. Wilkinson and C. Kitzinger (eds) *Heterosexuality*. London: Sage.

Kline, M. (1992) Child welfare law, 'best interests of the child' ideology, and First Nations, *Osgoode Hall Law Journal*, 30, 375.

Kritchevsky, B. (1981) The unmarried woman's right to artificial insemination: A call for an expanded definition of family, *Harvard Women's Law Journal*, 4, 1.

Lacey, N. (1993) Theory into practice? Pornography and the public/private dichotomy, *Journal of Law and Society*, 20, 93.

Laclau, E. and Mouffe, C. (1985) *Hegemony and Socialist Strategy: Towards a Radical Democratic Politics*. London: Verso.

Lansley, S. *et al.* (1989) *Councils in Conflict: The Rise and Fall of the Municipal Left*. Basingstoke: Macmillan.

Lau, G. (1993) Confessions of a complete scopophiliac, in P. Gibson and R. Gibson (eds) *Dirty Looks: Women, Pornography, Power*. London: BFI.

Leach, S. (1989) Strengthening local democracy, in J. Stewart and G. Stoker (eds) *The Future of Local Government*. Basingstoke: Macmillan.

Leeds Revolutionary Feminist Group (1981) Political lesbianism: The case against heterosexuality, in Onlywomen Press (ed.) *Love Your Enemy? The Debate between Heterosexual Feminism and Political Lesbianism*. London: Onlywomen.

Lewis, D. (1984) Conclusion: Improving implementation practice, in D. Lewis and H. Wallace (eds) *Policies into practice*. London: Heinemann.

Lewis, J. with Cannell, F. (1986) The politics of motherhood in the 1980s: Warnock, Gillick and feminists, *Journal of Law and Society*, 13, 321.

LGIU (1991) *Priority for Equality*. London: Local Government Information Unit.

Linden, R. *et al.* (1982) (eds) *Against Sadomasochism*. San Francisco, CA: Frog in the Well.

Lipman-Blumen, J. (1994) The existential bases of power relationships: The gender role case, in L. Radtke (ed.) *Power/Gender*. London: Sage.

Lipsky, M. (1980) *Street Level Bureaucracy*. New York: Russell Sage Foundation.

Lukes, S. (1974) *Power: A Radical View*. Basingstoke: Macmillan.

Lumsden, I. (1984) Sexuality and the state: The politics of 'normal' sexuality, *Atkinson Review of Canadian Studies*, 1, 3.

Lyotard, J. (1986) *The Postmodern Condition: A Report on Knowledge*. Manchester: Manchester University Press.

McCann, M. (1992) Resistance, reconstruction, and the romance in legal scholarship, *Law and Society Review*, 26, 733.

McCaskell, T. (1988) The bath raids and gay politics, in F. Cunningham *et al.* (eds) *Social movements/Social change: The Political Practice of Organizing*. Toronto: Between the Lines.

McClintock, A. (1992) Screwing the system: Sex work, race and the law, *Boundary 2*, 19, 70.

McClintock, A. (1993a) The return of female fetishism and the fiction of the phallus, *New Formations*, 19, 4.

McClintock, A. (1993b) Maid to order: Commercial S/M and gender power, in P. Gibson and R. Gibson (eds) *Dirty Looks: Women, Pornography, Power*. London: BFI.

McClintock, A. (1993c) Confessions of a psycho-mistress, *Social Text*, 37, 65.

McCormack, T. (1991) Public policies and reproductive technology: A feminist critique, *Research in the Sociology of Health Care*, 9, 105.

Macdonnell, D. (1986) *Theories of Discourse*. Oxford: Basil Blackwell.

McGarrell, E. *et al.* (1990) Obstacles to seemingly simple reform: A case study of bail reform, *Policy Studies Review*, 9, 433.

McIntosh, M. (1978) The state and the oppression of women, in A. Kuhn and A. Wolpe (eds) *Feminism and Materialism*. London: Routledge and Kegan Paul.

McIntosh, M. (1993) Queer theory and the war of the sexes, in J. Bristow and A. Wilson (eds) *Activating Theory: Lesbian, Gay, Bisexual Politics*. London: Lawrence and Wishart.

MacKinnon, C. (1982) Feminism, marxism, method and the state: An agenda for theory, *Signs*, 7, 515.

MacKinnon, C. (1991) Reflections on sex equality under law, *Yale Law Journal* 100: 1281.

MacKinnon, C. (1992) Does sexuality have a history? in D. Stanton (ed.) *Discourses of Sexuality*. Ann Arbor, MI: University of Michigan Press.

McNay, L. (1992) *Foucault and Feminism*. Cambridge: Polity.

Maggenti, M. (1991) Women as queer nationals, *Outlook*, 11, 20.

Magnusson, W. (1985) Urban politics and the local state, *Studies in Political Economy*, 19, 111.

Magnusson, W. (1992) Decentring the state, or looking for politics, in W. Carroll (ed.) *Organizing Dissent: Contemporary Social Movements in Theory and Practice*. Toronto: Garamond.

Magnusson, W. and Walker, R. (1998) De-centring the state: Political theory and Canadian political economy, *Studies in Political Economy*, 26, 37.

Mahoney, K. (1992) The Canadian constitutional approach to freedom of expression in hate propaganda and pornography, *Law and Contemporary Problems*, 55, 77.

Mann, P. (1994) *Micro-Politics: Agency in a Postfeminist Era*. Minneapolis, MN: University of Minnesota.

Maroney, H. (1988) Using Gramsci for women: Feminism and the Quebec state, 1960–1980, *Resources for Feminist Research*, 17, 26.

Martin, B. (1992) Sexual practice and changing lesbian identities, in M. Barrett and A. Phillips (eds) *Destabilizing Theory*. Cambridge: Polity.

Mason-John, V. and Khambatta, A. (1993) *Lesbians Talk Making Black Waves*. London: Scarlet.

Mather, G. (1989) Thatcherism and local government, in J. Stewart and G. Stoker (eds) *The Future of Local Government*. Basingstoke: Macmillan.

Matsuda, M. (1989) Public response to racist speech: Considering the victim's story, *Michigan Law Review*, 87, 2320.

Maynard-Moody, S. *et al.* (1990) Street-wise social policy: Resolving the dilemma of street-level influence and successful implementation, *Western Political Quarterly*, 43, 833.

Mercer, K. (1990) Welcome to the jungle: Identity and diversity in post-modern politics, in J. Rutherford (ed.) *Identity: Community, Culture, Difference*. London: Lawrence and Wishart.

Mercer, K. and Julien, I. (1988) Race, sexual politics and Black masculinity, in R. Chapman and J. Rutherford (eds) *Male Order: Unwrapping Masculinity*. London: Lawrence and Wishart.

Merck, M. (1993) *Perversions*. London: Virago.

Michaud, J. (1992) The welfare state and the problem of counter-hegemonic responses within the women's movement, in W. Carroll (ed.) *Organizing Dissent: Contemporary Social Movements in Theory and Practice*. Toronto: Garamond.

Miliband, R. (1977) *Marxism and Politics*. Oxford: Oxford University Press.

Miliband, R. (1984) *Capitalist Democracy in Britain*. Oxford: Oxford University Press.

Miller, P. and Rose, N. (1993) Governing economic life, in M. Gane and T. Johnson (eds) *Foucault's New Domains*. London: Routledge.

Miriam, K. (1993) From rage to all the rage: Lesbian-feminism, sadomasochism and the politics of memory, in I. Reti (ed.) *Unleashing Feminism: Critiquing Lesbian Sadomasochism in the Gay Nineties*. Santa Cruz, CA: HerBooks.

Mitchell, T. (1991) The limits of the state: Beyond statist approaches and their critics, *American Political Science Review*, 85, 77.

Modleski, T. (1991) *Feminism Without Women: Culture and Criticism in a Post-feminist age*. London: Routledge.

Montgomery, J. (1991) Rights, restraints and pragmatism: The Human Fertilisation and Embryology Act 1990, *Modern Law Review*, 54, 224.

Mooers, C. and Sears, A. (1992) The 'new social movements' and the withering away of state theory, in W. Carroll (ed.) *Organizing Dissent: Contemporary Social Movements in Theory and Practice*. Toronto: Garamond.

Moraga, C. and Anzaldua, G. (1983) *This Bridge Called Me Back: Writings by Radical Women of Color*. Latham, NY: Kitchen Table, Women of Color Press.

Moran, L. (1991) The uses of homosexuality: Homosexuality for national security, *International Journal of the Sociology of Law*, 19, 149.

Morgan, P. (1981) From battered wife to programme client: The state's shaping of social problems, *Kapitalistate*, 9, 17.

Morgan, T. (1993) Butch-Femme and the politics of identity, in A. Stein (ed.) *Sisters, Sexperts, Queers: Beyond the Lesbian Nation*. New York: Penguin.

Mort, F. (1980) Sexuality: Regulation and contestation, in Gay Left Collective (eds) *Homosexuality: Power and Politics*. London: Allison and Busby.

Mort, F. (1985) Purity, feminism and the state: Sexuality and moral politics, 1880–1914, in M. Langan and B. Schwarz (eds) *Crisis in the British State*. London: Hutchinson.

Mosse, G. L. (1985) *Nationalism and Security*. Howard Fertig: London.

Mouffe, C. (1979) *Gramsci and Marxist Theory*. London: Routledge and Kegan Paul.

Mouffe, C. (1981) Hegemony and ideology in Gramsci, in T. Bennett *et al.* (eds) *Culture, Ideology and Social Process*. London: Batsford.

Mouffe, C. (1988) Hegemony and new political subjects: Toward a new concept of democracy, in C. Nelson and L. Grossberg (eds) *Marxism and the Interpretation of Culture*. Basingstoke: Macmillan.

Mouffe, C. (1992a) Preface: Democratic politics today, in C. Mouffe (ed.) *Dimensions of Radical Democracy*. London: Verso.

Mouffe, C. (1992b) Democratic citizenship and the political community, in C. Mouffe (ed.) *Dimensions of Radical Democracy*. London: Verso.

Mouffe, C. (1992c) Feminism, citizenship and radical democratic politics, in J. Butler and J. Scott (eds) *Feminists Theorize the Political*. London: Routledge.

Mouffe, C. (1993) Liberal socialism and pluralism: Which citizenship? in J. Squires (ed.) *Principled Positions: Postmodernism and the Rediscovery of Value*. London: Lawrence and Wishart.

Nelson, A. (1990) Equal opportunities: Dilemmas, contradictions, white men and class, *Critical Social Policy*, 28, 25.

Newburn, T. (1992) *Permission and Regulation: Law and Morals in Post-War Britain*. London: Routledge.

Ng, R. (1990) State funding to a community employment center: Implications for working with immigrant women, in R. Ng *et al.* (eds) *Community Organization and the Canadian State*. Toronto: Garamond.

O'Connor, P. (1993) When docile bodies dance, *Sinister Wisdom*, 49, 26.

Oddie, W. (1991) O brave new world, *The Spectator*, 267, 16.

O'Donovan, K. (1985) *Sexual Divisions in Law*. London: Weidenfeld and Nicolson.

Onlywomen Press (eds) (1981) *Love your enemy?* London: Onlywomen.

O'Rourke, S. (1985) Family law in a brave new world, *Berkeley Women's Law Journal*, 1, 140.

Otitoju, F. (1988) The should we, shouldn't we? debate, in B. Cant and S. Hemmings (eds) *Radical Records: Thirty Years of Lesbian and Gay History*. London: Routledge.

Ousley, H. (1984) Local authority race initiatives, in M. Boddy and C. Fudge (eds) *Local Socialism?* London: Macmillan.

Ousley, H. (1990) Resisting institutional change, in W. Ball and J. Solomos (eds) *Race and Local Politics*. Basingstoke: Macmillan.

Palumbo, D. *et al.* (1984) Measuring degrees of successful implementation, *Evaluation Review*, 8, 45.

Pateman, C. (1989) *The Disorder of Women*. Oxford: Polity.

Patton, C. (1990) *Inventing AIDS*. London: Routledge.

Patton, C. (1993) Tremble, hetero swine! in M. Warner (ed.) *Fears of a Queer Planet: Queer Politics and Social Theory*. Minneapolis, MN: University of Minnesota Press.

Penelope, J. (1990) The lesbian perspective, in J. Allen (ed.) *Lesbian Philosophies and Culture*. New York: SUNY Press.

Petersen, C. (1991) A queer response to bashing: Legislating against hate, *Queen's Law Journal*, 16, 237.

Phelan, S. (1989) *Identity Politics: Lesbian Feminism and the Limits of Community*. Philadelphia, PA: Temple University Press.

Phelan, S. (1990) Foucault and feminism, *American Journal of Political Science*, 34, 421.

Phelan, S. (1993) (Be)coming out: Lesbian identity and politics, *Signs*, 18, 765.

Phillips, A. (1994) Pluralism, solidarity and change, in J. Weeks (ed.) *The Lesser Evil and the Greater Good: The Theory and Politics of Social Diversity*. London: Rivers Oram.

Piven, F. F. (1984) Women and the state: Ideology, power and the welfare state, *Socialist Review*, 14, 12.

Poulantzas, N. (1973) *Political Power and Social Classes*. London: New Left Books.

Poulantzas, N. (1978) *State, Power, Socialism*. London: New Left Books.

Pringle, R. (1988) *Secretaries Talk: Sexuality, Power and Work*. London: Verso.

Pringle, R. and Watson, S. (1990) Fathers, brothers, mates: The fraternal state in Australia, in S. Watson (ed.) *Playing the State: Australian Feminist Interventions*. London: Verso.

Pringle, R. and Watson, S. (1992) Women's interests and the post-structuralist state, in M. Barrett and A. Phillips (eds) *Destabilising Theory: Contemporary Feminist Debates*. Cambridge: Polity.

Prottas, J. (1978) The power of the street-level bureaucrat in public sector bureaucracies, *Urban Affairs Quarterly*, 13, 285.

Quinby, L. (1994) *Anti-Apocalypse: Exercises in Genealogical Criticism*. Minneapolis, MN: University of Minnesota Press.

Radicalesbians (1973) The woman-identified woman, in A. Koedt *et al.* (eds) *Radical Feminism*. New York: New York Times Book Co.

Radway, J. (1987) *Reading the Romance*. London: Verso.

Ramazanoglu, C. (ed.) (1993) *Up Against Foucault*. Routledge: London.

Ramazanoglu, C. and Holland, J. (1994) Women's sexuality and men's appropriation of desire, in C. Ramazanoglu (ed.) *Up Against Foucault*. London: Routledge.

Randall, M. (1988) Feminism and the state: Questions for theory and practice, *Resources for Feminist Research*, 17, 10.

Rayside, D. (1992) Homophobia, class and party in England, *Canadian Journal of Political Science*, 25, 121.

Redner, H. (1990) Beyond Marx – Weber: A diversified and international approach to the state, *Political Studies*, 38, 638.

Reich, J. (1992) Genderfuck: The law of the dildo, *Discourse*, 15, 112.

Reti, I. (ed.) (1993a) *Unleashing Feminism: Critiquing Lesbian Sadomasochism in the Gay Nineties*. Santa Cruz, CA: HerBooks.

Reti, I. (1993b) Remember the fire: Lesbian sadomasochism in a post Nazi holocaust world, in I. Reti (ed.) *Unleashing Feminism: Critiquing Lesbian Sadomasochism in the Gay Nineties*. Santa Cruz, CA: HerBooks.

Rian, K. (1982) Sadomasochism and the social construction of desire, in R. Linden *et al.* (eds) *Against Sadomasochism*. San Francisco, CA: Frog in the Well.

Rich, A. (1981) *Compulsory Heterosexuality and Lesbian Existence*. London: Onlywomen.

Richardson, D. (1992) Constructing lesbian sexualities, in K. Plummer (ed.) *Modern Homosexualities*. London: Routledge.

Robson, R. (1992) Mother: The legal domestication of lesbian existence, *Hypatia*, 7, 172.

Ross, B. (1988) Heterosexuals only need apply: The Secretary of State's regulation of lesbian existence, *Resources for Feminist Research*, 17, 35.

Rubin, G. (1981) The leather menace: Comments on politics and s/m, in Samois (eds) *Coming to Power*. Boston, MA: Alyson.

Rubin, G. (1989) Thinking sex: Notes for a radical theory of the politics of sexuality, in C. Vance (ed.) *Pleasure and Danger: Exploring Female Sexuality*. London: Pandora.

Saffron, L. (1994) *Challenging Conceptions: Planning a Family by Self-Insemination*. London: Cassell.

St Clair Stephenson, P. and Wagner, M. (1991) Turkey baster babies: A view from Europe, *The Milbank Quarterly*, 69, 45.

Salaman, G. (1980) Organizations as constructors of social reality, in G. Salaman and K. Thompson (eds) *Control and Ideology in Organizations*. Milton Keynes: Open University Press.

Sargent, L. (ed.) (1986) *The Unhappy Marriage of Marxism and Feminism*. London: Pluto.

Savage, M. and Witz, A. (1992) *Gender and Bureaucracy*. Oxford: Basil Blackwell.

Sawicki, J. (1991) *Disciplining Foucault*. New York: Routledge.

Saxe, L. (1992) Sadomasochism and exclusion, *Hypatia*, 7, 59.

Schattschneider, E. (1960) *The Semi-sovereign People*. New York: Holt, Rinehart and Winston.

Schreader, A. (1990) The state funded women's movement: A case of two political agendas, in R. Ng *et al.* (eds) *Community Organizing and the State*. Toronto: Garamond.

Scott, J. (1988) Deconstructing equality-versus-difference: or the uses of post-structuralist theory for feminism, *Feminist Studies*, 14, 33.

Segal, L. and McIntosh, M. (1992) *Sex Exposed: Sexuality and the Pornography Debate*. London: Virago.

Seidman, S. (1992) *Embattled Eros*. New York: Routledge.

Seidman, S. (1993) Identity and politics in a 'postmodern' gay culture: Some histor-ical and conceptual notes, in M. Warner (ed.) *Fears of a Queer Planet: Queer Politics and Social Theory*. Minneapolis, MN: University of Minnesota Press.

Seyd, P. (1987) *The Rise and Fall of the Labour Left*. Basingstoke: Macmillan.

Shapiro, M. *et al.* (1988) A discursive practices approach to collective decision-making, *International Studies Quarterly*, 32, 397.

Sheridan, A. (1980) *Michel Foucault: The Will to Truth*. London: Tavistock.

Shiva, V. (1993a) The impoverishment of the environment: Women and children last, in M. Mies and V. Shiva (eds) *Ecofeminism*. London: Zed Books.

Shiva, V. (1993b) Decolonising the north, in M. Mies and V. Shiva (eds) *Ecofemi-nism*. London: Zed Books.

Showstack Sassoon, A. (1982) Hegemony, war of position and political intervention, in A. Showstack Sassoon (ed.) *Approaches to Gramsci*. London: Writers and Readers.

Showstack Sassoon, A. (ed.) (1987) *Women and the State*. London: Hutchinson.

Sims, K. *et al.* (1982) Racism and sadomasochism: A conversation with two black lesbians, in R. Linden *et al.* (eds) *Against Sadomasochism*. San Francisco, CA: Frog in the Well.

Smart, C. (1989) *Feminism and the Power of Law*. London: Routledge.

Smart, C. (1990) Law, the sexed body and feminist discourse, *Journal of Law and Society*, 17, 194.

Smart, C. (1991) Penetrating women's bodies: The problem of law and medical technology, in P. Abbott and C. Wallace (eds) *Gender, Power and Sexuality*. Basingstoke: Macmillan.

Smith, A. M. (1993) Outlaws as legislators: Feminist anti-censorship politics and queer activism, in V. Harwood *et al.* (eds) *Pleasure Principles: Politics, Sexuality and Ethics*. London: Lawrence and Wishart.

Smith, A. M. (1994) Hegemony trouble: The political theory of Judith Butler, Er-nesto Laclau and Chantel Mouffe, in J. Weeks (ed.) *The Lesser Evil and the Greater Good: The Theory and Politics of Social Diversity*. London: Rivers Oram.

Smyth, C. (1992) *Lesbians Talk Queer Notions*. London: Scarlet.

Snitow, A. (1983) Mass market romance, in A. Snitow *et al.* (eds) *Powers of Desire*. New York: Monthly Review.

Solomos, J. (1989) Equal opportunities policies and racial inequality: The role of public policy, *Public Administration*, 67, 79.

Solomos, J. and Ball, W. (1990) New initiatives and the possibilities of reform, in W. Ball and J. Solomos (eds) *Race and Local Politics*. Basingstoke: Macmillan.

Spallone, P. (1987) Reproductive technology and the state: The Warnock Report and its clones, in P. Spallone and D. Steinberg (eds) *Made to Order: The Myth of Reproductive and Genetic Progress*. Oxford: Pergamon.

Star, S. (1982) Swastikas: The street and the university, in R. Linden *et al.* (eds) *Against Sadomasochism*. San Francisco, CA: Frog in the Well.

Stein, A. (1993) The year of the lustful lesbian, in A. Stein (ed.) *Sisters, Sexperts, Queers*. London: Penguin.

Steinberg, D. (1987) Selective breeding and social engineering: Discriminatory policies of access to artificial insemination by donor in Great Britain, in P. Spallone and D. Steinberg (eds) *Made to Order: The Myth of Reproductive and Genetic Progress*. Oxford: Pergamon.

Stoker, G. (1988) *The Politics of Local Government*. Basingstoke: Macmillan.

Straayer, C. (1993) The seduction of boundaries: Feminist fluidity in Annie Sprinkle's art/education/sex, in P. Gibson and R. Gibson (eds) *Dirty Looks: Women, Pornography, Power*. London: BFI.

Stychin, C. (1992) Exploring the limits: Feminism and the legal regulation of gay male pornography, *Vermont Law Review*, 16, 857.

Sunstein, C. (1990) Paradoxes of the regulatory state, *University of Chicago Law Review*, 57, 407.

Terry, J. (1991) Theorizing deviant historiography, *Differences*, 3, 55.

Therborn, G. (1980) *The Ideology of Power and the Power of Ideology*. London: NLB.

Thomas, P. (1993) The nuclear family, ideology and AIDS in the Thatcher years, *Feminist Legal Studies*, 1, 23.

Thornton, M. (1986) Sex equality is not enough for feminism, in C. Pateman and E. Gross (eds) *Feminist Challenges*. Sydney: Allen and Unwin.

Tobin, A. (1990) Lesbianism and the Labour Party: The GLC experience, *Feminist Review*, 34, 56.

Tronto, J. (1993) *Moral Boundaries: A Political Argument for an Ethic of Care*. New York: Routledge.

Turkel, G. (1990) Michel Foucault: Law, power, and knowledge, *Journal of Law and Society*, 17, 170.

Tyler, G. (1991) Boys will be girls: The politics of gay drag, in D. Fuss (ed.) *Inside/Out: Lesbian Theories, Gay Theories*. New York: Routledge.

Valverde, M. (1989) Beyond gender dangers and private pleasures: Theory and ethics in the sex debates, *Feminist Studies*, 15, 237.

Vorst, J. *et al.* (ed.) (1991) *Race, Class and Gender: Bonds and Barriers*. Toronto: Garamond Press.

Wagner, S. (1982) Pornography and the sexual revolution: The backlash of sadomasochism, in R. Linden *et al.* (eds) *Against Sadomasochism*. San Francisco, CA: Frog in the Well.

Walkowitz, J. (1980) The politics of prostitution, *Signs*, 6, 123.

Walzer, M. (1986) The politics of Michel Foucault, in D. Hoy (ed.) *Foucault: A Critical Reader*. Oxford: Basil Blackwell.

Wartenberg, T. (1990) *The Forms of Power*. Philadelphia, PA: Temple University Press.

Watney, S. (1990) Practices of freedom: 'Citizenship' and the politics of identity in the age of AIDS, in J. Rutherford (ed.) *Identity: Community, Culture, Difference*. London: Lawrence and Wishart.

Watney, S. (1994) Queer epistemology: activism, 'outing', and the politics of sexual identities, *Critical Quarterly*, 36, 13.

Watson, S. (1990a) The state of play: An introduction, in S. Watson (ed.) *Playing the State: Australian Feminist Interventions*. London: Verso.

Watson, S. (ed.) (1990b) *Playing the State: Australian Feminist Interventions*. London: Verso.

Weber, M. (1946) *From Max Weber*. H. Gerth and C. Wright Mills (eds), Oxford: Oxford University Press.

Weedon, C. (1987) *Feminist Practice and Post-structuralist Theory*. Oxford: Blackwell.

Weeks, J. (1980) Capitalism and the organisation of sex, in Gay Left Collective (eds) *Homosexuality: Power and Politics*. London: Allison and Busby.

Weeks, J. (1985) *Sexuality and its Discontents*. London: Routledge and Kegan Paul.

Weeks, J. (1991) *Against Nature*. London: Rivers Oram.

Weeks, J. (1992) Values in an age of uncertainty, in D. Stanton (ed.) *Discourses of Sexuality*. Ann Arbor, MI: University of Michigan Press.

Weeks, J. (1993) Rediscovering values, in J. Squires (ed.) *Principled Positions*. London: Lawrence and Wishart.

Weinberg, M. *et al.* (1984) The social constituents of sadomasochism, *Social Problems*, 31, 379.

Weir, L. and Casey, L. (1984) Subverting power in sexuality, *Socialist Review*, 75–76, 139.

Weston, K. (1991) *Families We Choose*. New York: Columbia University Press.

Whisman, V. (1993) Identity crises: Who is a lesbian anyway? in A. Stein (ed.) *Sisters, Sexperts, Queers: Beyond the Lesbian Nation*. New York: Penguin.

Whitfield, R. (1991) Don't give in to pressure, *Community Care*, 24 January, 16.

Williams, L. (1993) A provoking agent: The pornography and performance art of Annie Sprinkle, in P. Gibson and R. Gibson (eds) *Dirty Looks: Women, Pornography, Power*. London: BFI.

Wilson, E. (1993) Is transgression transgressive? in J. Bristow and A. Wilson (eds) *Activating Theory: Lesbian, Gay, Bisexual Politics*. London: Lawrence and Wishart.

Witz, A. and Savage, M. (1992) The gender of organizations, in M. Savage and A. Witz (eds) *Gender and Bureaucracy*. Oxford: Basil Blackwell.

Wood, E. (1986) *The Retreat from Class: A New 'True' Socialism*. London: Verso.

Woodhull, W. (1988) Sexuality, power, and the question of rape, in I. Diamond and L. Quinby (eds) *Feminism and Foucault: Reflections on Resistance*. Boston, MA: Northeastern University Press.

Wrong, D. (1993) Problems in defining power, in M. Olsen and M. Marger (eds) *Power in Modern Societies*. Oxford: Westview.

Young, I. M. (1990) The ideal of community and the politics of difference, in L. Nicholson (ed.) *Feminism/Postmodernism*. London: Routledge.

Zita, J. (1992) Male lesbians and the postmodern body, *Hypatia*, 7, 106.

Index